中國菜 第二冊
Chinese Cuisine II

發　行　者：黃淑惠
編　著　者：葉澄惠
烹飪製作：葉澄惠
　　　　　李木村
翻　譯　者：席妮娜

Distributed by : Huang Su-Huei
Authored by　 : Yeh Cheng-Huei
Recipes by　　 : Yeh Cheng-Huei
　　　　　　　　 Lee Mu-Tsun
Translated by : Nina Simonds

ISBN: 0-941676-05-6

中國菜 第二冊
Chinese Cuisine II

■餐盤裝飾目錄　Vegetable Garnishes

■ 中國菜目錄　Chinese Cuisine

● 雞　類　Chicken

● 鴿　類　Pigeon

● 鴨　類　Duckling

● 魚　類　Fish

● 其他海產類　Sea Foods

● 蝦　類　Shrimp

● 蛋、豆腐、小菜　Bean Curd & Eggs & Appetizers

● 蔬　菜　Vegetables

● 湯　類　　Soups

中國菜的分佈

唐魯孫

　　古人說：「飲食男女人之大慾」這句話證明了飲食在我們日常生活裡，是佔有極重要地位的。歐美人士，一談到割烹之道，總認為飲食能達到藝術境界，必須有高度文化做背景，否則就不能算吃的藝術呢！世界上凡是講究飲饌，精於割烹的國家，溯諸已往必定是擁有高度文化背景的大國，不但國富民強，而且一般社會經濟繁華充裕，才有閒情逸致在飲食方面下功夫。

　　當此國步方艱，我們講求飲饌，有一個基本原則，就是要在最經濟實惠原則之下，變粗糲為珍餚，不但是色，香，味，三者具備，而且有充份均衡的營養，至於一飯數千金，一席數萬金的華筵盛饌窮奢極慾的揮霍浪費，那就不足為訓的了。

　　中國幅圓廣袤，山川險阻，風土，人物，口味，氣候，有極大不同，而省與省之間，甚至於縣市之間，足供飲膳的物產材料，也有很大的差異，因而形成了每一省份都有自己獨特口味，早年說，南甜，北鹹，東辣，西酸，時代嬗替，雖不盡然，總之大致是不離譜兒的。

　　中國菜到底分多少類呢？據早年一些美食專家分野，約可分為三大體系，就是「山東」，「江蘇」，「廣東」，按河流來說，又可分成「黃河」，「長江」，「珠江」，三大流域。

　　照以上劃分辦法，並不是隨便一說，也是淵源有自的，有清一代，最為重視治河，為了濬治黃河，特地設了一位一品大員「河道總督」，以專責成。治河經費不但異常龐大，遇到河水氾濫成災，可以儘先到撥，隨後霽實支銷，河督設在山東濟寧州，在當初算是一等一的肥缺，又是閒多忙少的差事，所以在飲食讌樂方面，就食不厭精，膾不厭細的講究起來，因此山東菜蔚成北方菜的主流了。

　　揚州在隋唐時代設治，隋煬帝玉輦清遊，廿四橋明月夜，吳歌鳳琯，早就成為詞人艷稱之地，乾隆皇帝駐蹕江南，鹽商們迷樓置酒，官家小宴，鄢中鹿尾，塞上駝蹄，瓊漿玉饔水陸雜呈，淮揚菜於是譽滿大江南北。

　　中國有句老話說：「吃在廣州」因為是通商口岸，華洋雜處，艫舳雲集，豪商巨賈，一個個囊囊充盈，自然都要一恣口腹之嗜，所出菜式，精緻細膩，力求花樣翻新，嗜之者爭誇異味，畏之者停箸搖頭，異品珍味，調羹之妙，易牙難傳，嶺南風味，簡直味壓江南了。

　　這種趨勢，連綿了數百年之久，七七事變，抗戰軍興，國都西遷重慶，於是川湘雲貴菜肴，成為天之驕子，由於西南霧重隔濕，嵐瘴侵人，調味多用麻辣葱薑，人的口味入鄉隨鄉也就為之大變。迨政府遷臺，悠悠歲月，漸惹鄉愁，每個人都想吃點自己家鄉口味，聊慰寂寥，不但各大都會的金薤玉膾紛紛登盤薦餐，就是村童野老愛吃的山蔬野味，也都應有盡有，真可以說集飲食之大成，彙南北為一爐，照目前臺灣飲食界來看，大致可分為：

　　「北平菜」名為北平菜，其實認真說來，北平以小吃著名，並沒有成桌的酒席，因為元，明，清都在北京建都，六七百年，人文薈萃，水陸珍異，五蘊七香，已經包羅萬有，用不着自己再來一套北平食譜啦，有人說：「燒燎白煮是地道的北平菜，追本溯源燒燎白煮是滿洲人在東北郊天祭神的胙肉演變而來的，說它是東北菜式則可，要說是北平菜，就未免有點勉強啦。」就淺見所知，祇有掛爐烤鴨才可以算是北平菜呢！現在臺灣北平、天津、山東的濟南、烟臺、甚至把河南、山陝一古腦兒統稱北方菜，因為這些省市都以炸、爆、溜、燴、扒、燉、鍋塌、拔絲最為拿手，尤其擅長用醬，五味調和，割烹層次，都是大同小異的，所以現在統稱為「北方菜」了。

　　「四川菜」，抗戰八年，大家都聚處南都，男女老幼，漸嗜麻辣，一旦成癮，非有辣味不能健飯，現在川菜風行，是時勢所造成的。

　　「湖南菜」，湘菜以腴滑肥潤是尚，一般菜肴辛辣尤勝川菜，不過成桌筵宴，照老規矩是不見絲毫辣味的。

「湖北菜」，湖北各式小吃種類不少，可是武漢三鎮没有一家自命湖北菜的飯館，一般古樸儼雅，氣格老成的飯館，大多挑着徽館牌號，上海有一家飯館名叫黃鶴樓，自稱是湖北館，可是曇花一現，即告消失，現在臺北僅僅有一家飯館以湖北菜號召，鳳毛麟角，算是一枝獨秀了。

　　「貴州菜」當年北平的長美軒，西黔陽都是貴州菜，濃郁帶辣，頗跟川湘菜味相近，可是有幾隻菜的火候比川湘菜另有獨到之處，尤其是菌類調製有十幾種之多，貴陽唐園主人能做菌類全席，跟淮城的全鱔席是可以互相媲美，可惜的是現在在臺灣想吃真正的貴州菜，還不太容易呢！

　　「上海菜」所謂上海菜，在臺灣已經跟寧紹菜混淆不清，其實真正的上海菜應當以浦東、南翔、真茹一帶菜式為主體，口味濃郁，大盆大碗，講究實惠，不重外貌，鄉土氣息濃重才算是地道上海菜。

　　「揚州菜」鎮江跟揚州雖然一在江南，一據江北，可是口味是不相左右的，所以鎮江菜肴，一般說來就包括在揚州菜裡了，揚州菜的特徵是不管如何烹調，都講究原湯原味，所以不同菜式，就滋味各異了。揚州點心花色繁多，加上廚師們肯下功夫去改良，揚州點心的聞名遐邇，也不是倖得的。不過油重厚膩，喜歡清淡的人，就不太歡迎了。

　　「蘇州菜」蘇州菜精緻細巧，是跟他文化水準有關係，況且自古有不少朝代在蘇州建都，古蹟名勝又多，飲食方面自然就精益求精了。至於有人把南京菜跟蘇州菜混在一起，統稱京蘇菜，若要認真品評，兩地口味是迴不相侔不能比併的。而且南京跟北平一樣，雖有不少菜式，可是要拿出成桌的南京菜，還不太容易呢！

　　「無錫菜」無錫靠近太湖，既多蝦蟹，後產菱藕，無錫船菜是聞名全國的，不過味尚甘甜，本地人習慣菜裡多糖，外地人偶嘗則可，吃久未免生厭，不過無錫菜刀工火候，都可列為菜裡上上之選。

　　「杭州菜」杭州古代既建過國都，西湖風景又馳名中外，所以杭州菜，博碩肥腯，濃淡具全，腴潤的有味醇質爛的東坡肉，清淡的有蒸香味永的西湖醋魚，推潭僕遠，堪稱上味。

　　「寧波菜」因為地近舟山群島海產特豐，就地取材，所以寧波菜以海鮮為主，漁客所獲，以鹽防腐保鮮，所以寧波菜比較味鹹，就是這個道理。

　　「安徽菜」典當在沒有錢莊票號之前，是民間互通有無的大生意，歙縣的朝奉是獨占的行業，徽省菜館的聲華，早就蜚名全國，不過自錢莊銀號代興，典當業一落千丈，提到徽館，已少人知，至於膾炙人口的鴨餛飩，就是徽館流傳下來的。

　　「江西菜」全國各大縣市，所有餐館酒肆，很難指出那家是江西飯館，可是贛州菜，割烹佳味，甘旨柔滑，也有其獨特之處，至於何以不能推拓及遠，就非所敢知了。請教了若干精於飲饌的朋友，也談不出所以然來。

　　「廣東菜」分廣州、潮州、東江三派，廣州菜因為開埠較早，各國人士雜沓紛來，有若干菜式是取法歐西烹飪方法，加上蛇、狸、鼠、蟲都能入饌，在中國菜裡是獨標一格的。潮州菜也重海鮮，煨燉皆精，每菜上桌，都有各式各樣的小碟小盅的調味料任客自調，甘洌香鮮，是別處所無為人艷稱的。東江菜也就是客家菜，用油較重，口味亦濃，大塊文章，充腸適口，烹調方法比較保守，所以最具鄉土風味。

　　「福州菜」福建也是精於飲食的省份，福州臨江近海水產特佳，雖然臨近廣東，可是兩者口味迴不相同，湯鮮口永，清淡宜人，擅用紅糟尤其所長。

　　味全叢書，將出餐點新編，編者囑介源流，謹就個人所知，舉其犖犖大者，舛誤自所難免，尚希邦人君子，進而教之。

Introduction

P. S. Tang.

To quote an ancient Chinese proverb, "The three basic human needs are eating, drinking and sex." This is a belief that has survived through the ages, compelling the Chinese to give food the priority that it so rightly deserves.

Europeans and Americans claim that cooking can be respected as an art form only when the culture elevates it to a sophisticated level. Consequently, the degree of refinement of a cuisine reflects the history and culture of a country.

China is a vast country with several mountain ranges and rivers, that tended to segregate the people to certain areas or provinces. Each province developed a cuisine and customs, often greatly differing from those of its neighbors.

In describing the various cuisines, the ancient people frequently said, "South is sweet, north is salty, east is hot, and west is sour." Today, these general characteristics still apply to the various regional flavors.

According to ancient historians, Chinese cuisine was divided into three main regions: Shantung, Kiangsu, and Kuangtung. The divisions could also be made according to the main regions of the Yellow River, the Yangtse River and the West River.

The Yellow River played a prominent role in distinguishing Shantung cuisine. In ancient China, the maintenance of rivers was of great importance. A viceroy was in charge of implementing the funds allocated for building dikes and dredging. Since the office of the viceroy was in Shantung, a sizable amount of money found its way into this area. The viceroy had very little to do outside of supervising the river funds. And being a true gastronome at heart, he took great pleasure in devoting his energy to the refinement of the preparation of food and drink. Hence, from that time on, Shantung became a noted center for eating.

Yangchou was a bustling city during the Sui and T'ang Dynasties. Emperor Chien-Lung, of the Chin Dynasty, and Emperor Yang, of the Sui Dynasty, were fond of visiting this ancient city. Wealthy merchants would attempt to surpass each other in offering sumptuous delicacies to the visiting monarch. The region conveniently abounded in animals and sea food, so that the cuisine soon became quite famous.

A frequently-quoted Chinese saying was, "If you want to eat, go to Canton." This was a common belief because the city was an ancient trading port, harboring Chinese and foreigners noted for its wealthy merchants whose tastes for delicacies and unusual foods were well-known throughout the country.

During the Sino-Japanese War, the central seat of government was moved from Nanking to Chungking. At that time, the spicy cooking of Szechuan, Hunan and Yunnan became very popular. The weather in this region was very humid so the ingredients frequently used included sesame oil, hot peppers, ginger and scallion. As people became accustomed to this type of spicy food, their appreciation of the fiery seasonings grew.

After the immigration of the Chinese to Taiwan, these people longed to taste the flavors of their native provinces. Fortunately, the restaurants of Taipei now offer a multitude of regional varieties which may be divided into the following categories:

"Peking dishes": Frequently, dishes are classified as originating in Peking, whereas in actuality, few banquet dishes were created here. This category of food is mainly composed of snacks or "small foods" ("hsiao ch'ih"). Since Peking was the capital for six to seven hundred years throughout the Yuan, Ming and Chin Dynasties, people from many provinces settled in this city and brought their native dishes with them; accordingly, the cuisine varied. An ancient Chinese cookbook claims that, boiling food is the true cooking method native to Peking. This technique originated in ancient times when the people in this area boiled meat to offer to the gods of Manchuria. I maintain that this is Manchurian cooking, not Peking cuisine. As far as I know, the only dish native to Peking is "Peking Duckling." In Taiwan, the provinces of Shantung, Honan, Shansi and the neighboring region are grouped together under the general classification of Peking cooking. All of these provincial cuisines excel in the techniques of Pan-frying, deep-frying, stewing and braising.

"Szechuan dishes": As mentioned earlier, this spicy food has become very popular since the Sino-Japanese War and its popularity exists today.

"Hunan dishes": Generally, this food is oilier and more pungent than Szechuan cooking, but the banquet dishes are often very delicately seasoned.

"Kweichow dishes": This type of cooking is even oilier and spicier than Szechuan and Hunan cooking; their flavors are very similar. There are dishes from this region however, that are even more refined than those of Szechuan and Hunan. Mushrooms are particularly a speciality of this region and may be prepared in more than ten different ways.

"Shanghai dishes": The dishes from this region tend to be oily and hearty, with a delicious flavor, but an undistinguishing appearance.

"Yangchou dishes": The food of this area was originally from the Yangtse River region. The distinguishing characteristic of this type of food is that seasonings are rarely used. Cooks of this area rely on the natural flavors of the ingredients. Lovers of pungent seasoning do not usually care for this type of food. The dishes are varied and due to its long history, the region has a reputation for fine food. The food, however, can be oily.

"Suchou dishes": Suchou was the capital of China during many dynasties. Its beauty and cultural refinement have been recognized through the ages. The habitants of this area placed great emphasis on eating and drinking. The dishes tend to be very delicate. Some combine the cuisines of Suchou and Nanking, labeling it Kiangsu food. I feel that these two varieties have very little in common; Nanking food is similar in flavor to that of Peking.

"Wuhsi dishes": Due to the close proximity of Lake Tai, these dishes contain much crab and shrimp, as well as water chestnuts. The natives of this region liked sugar and so, many of the dishes tend to be sweet. The cooks here are famous for their cooking and cutting skills.

"Hangchou dishes": Hangchou was also once an ancient capital and its beautiful scenery is very famous. The dishes vary greatly and may be very oily, subtley seasoned or spicy, depending on the food. "Tung-Po Pork" and "West Lake Fish" are two examples of the delicate dishes of this region.

"Ningpo dishes": Since Ningpo is situated near the Chou-san Islands, the dishes contain a tremendous amount of sea food. The fishermen of this region preserve fish with salt, consequently, many of the dishes tend to be salty.

"Kuangtung dishes": As mentioned earlier, Canton was an ancient port which attracted many foreigners. Many of the cooking methods used in this region were introduced by Westerners. The cooking of this region further distinguished itself as somewhat odd by using, snakes, cats, mice, and worms. Sea food is also an important ingredient. Included in this group are Hokka dishes, which tend to be somewhat oily, but very hearty and flavorful. This type of food often is called "country-style."

"Fuchou dishes": Fukien was another province where the importance of eating and drinking was stressed. Since Fuchou is close to the ocean and several rivers, sea food predominates in its cuisine. Despite Canton's close proximity, the food is distinctively different. The flavors are generally extremely fresh and unusual. This region is famous for its soups and red fermented wine rice, which is frequently used as a seasoning.

We firmly believe that it is possible to cook flavorful dishes at a minimum expense. Economical ingredients may be used to prepare dishes which may be judged sumptuous by our strict standards.

T'ang Lu Hsün
March 1979

Mr. T'ang Lu Hsün is one of Taiwan's foremost authorities on Chinese food and history.

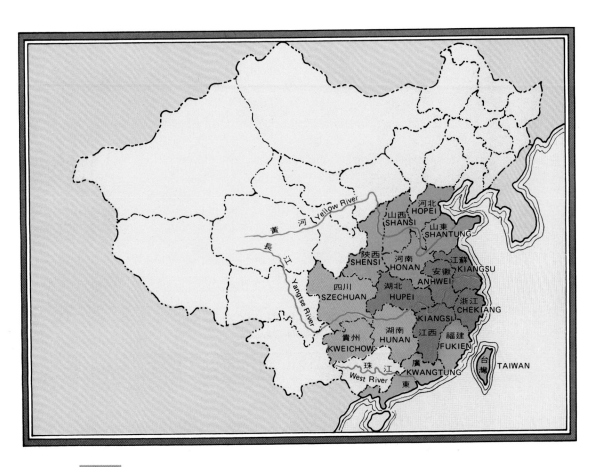

	北方菜	North Cuisine
東方菜	East Cuisine
西方菜	West Cuisine
南方菜	South Cuisine

容積換算表、重量比例表説明
Reference tables for Weights and Measures used in this book

容量換算表
EQUIVALENT MEASURES

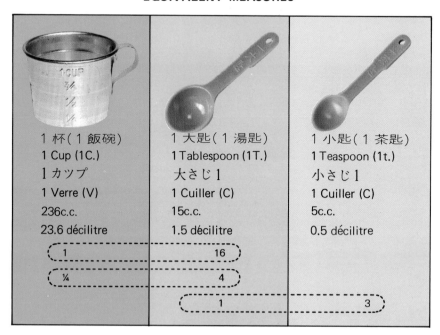

1 杯(1 飯碗)	1 大匙(1 湯匙)	1 小匙(1 茶匙)
1 Cup (1C.)	1 Tablespoon (1T.)	1 Teaspoon (1t.)
1 カップ	大さじ1	小さじ1
1 Verre (V)	1 Cuiller (C)	1 Cuiller (C)
236c.c.	15c.c.	5c.c.
23.6 décilitre	1.5 décilitre	0.5 décilitre
1	16	
¼	4	
	1	3

重量比例表
CONVERSION TABLE

中 制 Chinese Weight		英 制 Imperial Weight		公 制 Metric Weight	
兩	斤	盎斯 oz	磅 lb	公克 g	公斤 kg
		0.035		1	
1		1.33		37.5	
6		8		225	
12		16	1	450	
16	1		1 ⅓	600	
26 ⅔	1 ⅔			1000	1

Seasoning Used to Prepare Chinese Food

Five kinds of seasonings are frequently used to prepare Chinese food: salt, MSG, pepper, sugar, and sesame oil. Wine, vinegar, cornstarch, and oil for frying, etc., are also necessary.

做中國菜，點必備調味品

做菜時常用五味即鹽（或醬油）、味精、胡椒、麻油、糖，除此之外，酒、醋、太白粉、炸油，也是廚房不可缺少的必備品。

Soy sauce

Sesame oil

Vinegar

Cornstarch

Salt

MSG

Rice wine

Sugar

Black pepper

Oil for frying
(Fried Oil)

Utensils and Techniques Used to Cook Chinese Food

Cleavers, chopping block, spatulas, wok, and steamers are basic utensils used to prepare Chinese food. A rolling pin, for rolling dumplings, a sifter, and a hand-mixer are also used to prepare Chinese snacks. Roasting, frying, steaming, and stewing are techniques used to prepare a wide variety of delicious food.

做中國菜，點必備用具

僅刀、菜板、鍋鏟、漏杓、炒鍋、蒸籠等數樣用具，足夠多做炒、炸、蒸、燉、燴…等等多種美味菜餚，唯做點心得另備趕麵桿、篩子、打蛋器等。

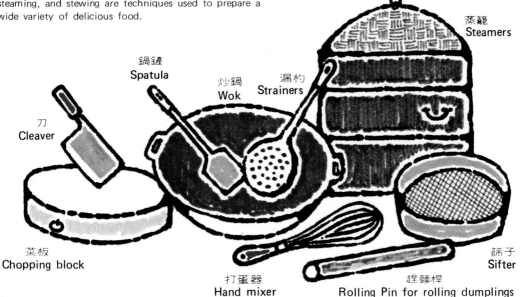

蒸籠
Steamers

鍋鏟
Spatula

炒鍋
Wok

漏杓
Strainers

刀
Cleaver

菜板
Chopping block

打蛋器
Hand mixer

趕麵桿
Rolling Pin for rolling dumplings

篩子
Sifter

烹飪慣用語說明

烹調在我國向無份量之規定，亦無一定之時間，全憑經驗由己去摸索所得。本書盡其所能的把材料、佐料之份量及所需時間簡要例出，為使能更進一步了解起見，茲將調理時之工作要點及慣用詞大略說明如次：

Culinary Idioms

In Chinese cuisine, cooking is a very subjective art; there are no definite quantities of any ingredient, nor any exact time limit for cooking any recipe. You are encouraged to develop and enhance the recipes through trial and error to suit individual taste. The basic information for the preparation of all dishes, as well as the ingredients needed are listed. Significant points and the explanation of some expressions which are used often in preparing Chinese food are also given.

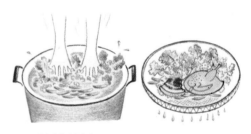

清洗材料
材料洗淨需漏乾水份。
CLEANING
Clean the ingredients before using, then drain and dry thoroughly.

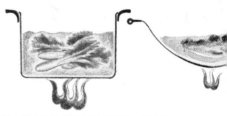

炒
把食物置炒菜鍋內，翻攪至熟了，即曰炒。
STIR-FRYING:
To put the material into a very hot pan, over high heat, and turn them over and over until done.

炒菜是速成之菜，故炒菜時宜將各項佐料調在碗內使用時，較方便。

Stir-frying is a very quick process. It is advisable to prepare all of the sauces in advance, including the cornstarch and water used to thicken the final sauce.

炒一盤菜，如遇使用多種材料，因其各材料性質不同，有些材料需經過泡油、煮熟或分開炒熟後再使用。

When several kinds of ingredients are used in cooking, the difference in tenderness of each ingredient will sometimes require that the material to be cooked in oil, boiled or fried before mixing. Whichever method is used, the ingredient must be precooked till tender.

炸
把食物投入多量沸油中炸熟謂炸。
DEEP-FRYING:
To immerse the food in deep, hot oil.

先將材料調上味，並視其種類，裹上麵糊。

To prepare the material for frying, first the food must be soaked in the prescribed sauce, then it must be covered with the proper flour or cornstarch mixture.

油的份量要多，注意，如果要炸出炒鍋之六分滿
There should be of oil in the pan; to cover the ma However if the m to be fried, is very

蒸
所謂蒸是把材料放蒸籠內，下放沸水，藉水蒸汽的熱力把食物蒸熟。

STEAMING:
To put the material in a "steaming cage," which is then put in a pan containing boiling water.

先將水放入外鍋燒開。

First, put water in the pan and allow it to come to a boil.

宜水燒開後才把食物放入蒸熟

Place the food in the cage and put it into boiling water.

切材料

配材料要切成同樣形狀，粗、細、
厚、薄要均一，則燒出來的菜肴嫩度
才會一致美觀。

CUTTING

All ingredients must be cut into the same size
and shape, so that the cooked food will look
uniform and have the same tenderness.

醃

鷄、肉、魚、蝦等要事先調
上味，必要時，如能拌入蛋
白及太白粉，則可增加其香
嫩。

PRE-CONDITIONING

Chicken, pork, fish and shrimp must
be soaked in the prescribed sauces
(soy sauce, wine or cornstarch) to
increase tenderness and taste of
food.

熱鍋

炒、煎、炸時，先空鍋燒熱，再倒進油，可
防材料黏鍋。

HEATING THE PAN

The pan must be thoroughly heated before adding oil
and then thoroughly lubricated with oil so that material
will not stick.

以上準備妥當，將鍋燒熱後放油再入葱、薑、蒜等
使其香味滲入油中，再把所要炒的材料及調在碗內
的調味料倒入鍋內炒拌，操作簡便迅速，且可防止
火候過久。

When the preliminary preparation is finished, heat the pan and pour
in the oil. Add the onion, ginger, or garlic so that they impart their
flavor. Add the ingredients with a few drops of wine, if desired,
to enhance the flavor of the food. Add the sauce and stir-fry until
all are mixed together. This entire process must be short and quick
so that the food will not overcook.

當臨起鍋時，淋下數滴油，可增加菜肴之光澤，並
有保溫之功效。

At this point, a few drops of fried oil may be sprinkled on the
food. This will help to increase the brilliancy of the food and keep
it warm.

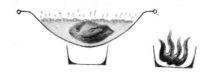

浸過食物爲準，但要
含水份多，則以不超
以免泡沫溢出危險。
contains much water, the
should not occupy more
60% of the pan, so
the oil will not splash

炸時先將油燒沸，如遇不容易炸熟者，將鍋暫時離
火，以中温或低温，但撈出時要大火，並視其材料
決定所需要的時間。

First boil the oil, remove the pan from the heat and when the oil
has cooled to medium temperature place the material in the pan.
Replace the pan over medium heat and cook until near-tender.
Turn heat to high and cook over high heat until done. This seals
the flavor and ensures that the material will be completely cooked
and crispy on the outside.

下鍋時如能同時下鍋，則撈出時宜一次
撈起，所炸出來的東西才會一致。

All material put into the oil, at the same time, must be
removed at the same time, to maintain uniformity.

燉

所謂燉與蒸略同，外鍋內放水，內鍋
放入食物及水或湯（注滿過食物）置
慢火經過長時間，至食物煮軟，做出
來的湯汁，非常澄清。

STEWING:

Stewing is similar to steaming; Put water in the
outer pan and the material to be heated with water
or stock to cover, in the inner pan. Cook over
moderate heat until food is tender. Soup prepared
this way is very clear and clean.

溜、燴：汁或湯注入鍋中燒開，隨即加入經過，炒、炸，或煮熟之食物勾成濃稠狀
　　　　其湯汁有，糖醋汁、茄汁、醬汁、白汁、奶汁等。
燒、燜：將水淹滿食物，燒開後，加入調味料用中火或小火，將食物煮軟。
煮　：將食物放入多量的水內，燒煮熟。
拌　：凡不必再加熱，涼着或生着切了，拌上佐料即可吃的均是涼拌。
燻　：用糖、木屑或茶葉上架鐵絲網盛放食物，四週罩蓋緊，加熱使煙與熱力慢慢
　　　把物烤熟或烤至上了茶煙之色與香味即曰燻。
烤　：加熱在食物炙熟即烤。

MIX-BOIL:
To put the sauce or soup into the pan by itself and allow it to boil; then add the food. The amount of cornstarch
in the sauce should be to individual taste. There should not be too much sauce.

MIXING:
If no cooking is required, to mix together ingredients after they are cut. If ingredients have been precooked, to allow
to cool, then mix together, add sauce and serve.

SMOKING:
To put food in an oven, or cover, on a grill over a fire, then throw sugar, wood powder, or tea into the
fire or oven so that the fumes will smoke the food and give it flavor.

ROASTING:
To cook or bake food in the oven with all of the ingredients, until done.

FRYING:
To cook food on each side until golden, in a little bit of oil.

特殊材料説明

1 辣豆瓣醬‥（辣椒醬）以紅辣椒及蠶豆爲原料加工製成，色紅、味辣。

2 甜麵醬‥饅頭醱酵製成（黑色）。

3 豆瓣醬‥黃豆醱酵製成（黑色）。

4 芝蔴醬‥芝蔴磨製而成（茶色）。

5 粟米粉‥即玉米粉。

6 澄　麵‥小麥之澱粉（無筋）。

7 魚　漿‥魚肉攪碎後加以調味，用機械甩打製成。

8 豆　豉‥即陰豉（烏豆）。

9 網　油‥猪肚外面一層油膜呈網狀。

10 豆　乳‥即豆腐乳（SOFU 或 CHINESE CHEESE）是以豆腐醱酵製成，浙江、江蘇兩省製造最有名，市售之豆腐乳，種類甚多，隨使用之調味香料不同而分紅、白、五香、酒槽腐乳等。

11 糯米紙‥利用馬鈴薯（POTATO），甘薯（蕃薯）（SWEET POTATO）之澱粉加工製造而成。

12 粉　絲‥即冬粉，細粉，原料爲綠豆。

13 蝦　子‥即蝦卵，深咖啡色，呈微小粒狀。

14 辣　油‥蔴油燒熱，葱、花椒粒炒香，隨即冲入辣椒粉，待冷即可。

15 蠔　油‥以生蠔爲原料，加工製成之調味料。

16 熟　油‥已經開滾或使用過之油，通常於炒菜後淋上少許熟油，可保持食物之光澤及保溫作用。

17 沙茶醬‥是以花生油、花生粉、油葱、香菜子、蒜頭粉、辣椒粉、花椒、八角、蝦米磨碎製成，在雜貨店購買。

18 五香粉‥是以八角、桂皮、小茴、花椒、三奈，炒香後磨成的粉。

19 花椒粉‥花椒粒炒香後磨成的粉。

20 花椒鹽‥是以乾鍋將鹽2大匙炒熱，呈微黃時，加1小匙花椒粉（或五香粉）拌勻而成，是供油炸食物沾食用的。

21 油　條‥參照中國餐點。

22 薑酒汁‥薑拍破，加酒所擠出的汁。

● 糖　粉‥將糖磨成粉狀，使用時易於溶化。

● 芥茉粉‥芥菜籽磨成的粉。

● 洋　菜‥即菜燕。

● 發泡粉（BAKING POWDER）‥發泡粉其成份隨種類而異，通常含有碳酸氫鈉、酒石酸氫鈉、酒石酸等，主要作用係此等物質加熱後會產生二氧化碳（CO_2）氣體，故將適當之發泡粉及水拌入麵粉內後再加熱，將會使麵塊發漲。

● 小蘇打（SODIUM BICARBONATE）：小蘇打即碳酸氫鈉（$NaHCO_3$）在水溶液中呈弱鹼性反應，可防止葉綠素之消失，故燒煮青綠色之蔬菜或豆類，可加入少許小蘇打粉；又因其爲鹼性之關係，使蛋白質保水性增加，亦可使肉之組織軟化。

● 嫩精（TENDERIZER）‥市售之嫩精包含蛋白質分解酵素、鹽、蔗糖等，由於蛋白分解酵素之作用，使肉之組織變軟，而達到嫩化效果。

● 碱塊（SODIUM CARBONATE）‥主要成份係碳酸鈉（$NaCO_3$），在水溶液中鹼性比小蘇打強，如本書36頁拌干絲內所用之碱塊係用來泡軟干絲用的。

● 洋　菇‥即毛菇。

● 麥芽糖（MALTOSE）‥甜味不如蔗糖，黏稠性大，多係由精白糯米製成。

● 炸　油‥備多量油，以供油炸用，沙拉油，花生油均可。

● 沙拉醬‥參照中國餐點。

● 太白粉‥是以樹薯或馬鈴薯做成的，可用玉米粉代替。

● 叉燒肉‥參照中國餐點。

● 麵包粉‥土司麵包烘乾，壓碎而成。

● 糖　色‥糖4大匙加水2大匙以小火煮5分鐘至呈褐色時，再加水半杯大火煮3分鐘，至糖有黏性時（約$\frac{1}{2}$杯）即成。

● 炸猪皮‥猪皮去毛並刮除垢穢洗淨，晒乾，「炸油」燒熱放入葱4枝及猪皮，以小火炸5分鐘至猪皮膨脹呈金黃色時撈起即成。

Description of some other special ingredients:

1. Hot bean paste ("la do ban jiang"):
   A thick, spicy paste made from ground hot red peppers and soy beans.
2. Sweet bean paste ("tien mien jiang"):
   A thick flavorful black paste made from ground, fermented steamed bread and spices.
3. Soy bean paste ("do ban jiang"):
   A thick black paste similar in taste to sweet bean paste, but made from fermented soybeans.
4. Sesame paste:
   A thick brown paste made from crushed sesame seeds.
5. Cornstarch:
   A white powder made from ground corn and primarily used to thicken sauces and soups and to coat foods before deep-frying.
6. "Cheng mien" (non-glutinous flour):
   A type of high-grade no-stick flour which has the gluten removed. It is used primarily in making Chinese pastries. Potato flour may be substituted.
7. Fish paste (fish timbale):
   A fine mixture of fish meat and spices chopped to a smooth paste. It is used to make fish balls and for coating various meats in soups and snacks.
8. Fermented black beans:
   Small black beans which have been marinated in soy sauce and salt and are used to flavor steamed fish and meat or in stir-fried dishes.
9. Pork net oil or caul fat:
   The lacy, outside layer of fat from a pig's stomach which is used to lend flavor to steamed fish and to wrap various foods before deep-frying.
10. Pickled bean curd or Chinese cheese ("do fu ru"):
    Bean curd cubes which are first dried and then mixed with wine, spices and salt and allowed to ferment. It is used to season braised pork and duckling.
11. Glutinous rice paper:
    A type of thin, edible paper-like sheet made from potato or sweet potato flour.
12. Bean threads:
    A type of thin, clear noodle made from the mung bean.
13. Shrimp eggs:
    The tiny, grainy eggs of the shrimp, which have been dried. They are used to add extra flavoring to chopped fillings. If it is unavailable, substitute dried brill fish.
14. Hot pepper oil ("la Yu"):
    A spicy, hot oil made from hot pepper powder, water and boiling oil.
15. Oyster sauce:
    A rich, brown sauce made from oysters and somewhat similar in flavor to soy sauce.
16. Fried oil:
    Oil that has already been used or boiled and usually used to sprinkle over dishes before serving to improve the appearance of the food and keep it hot.

17. "Sha chia jinag":
    A spicy sauce made from a mixture of peanut oil, peanuts, green onion oil, coriander seed, garlic powder, hot pepper powder, star of anise, Szechuan peppercorns and dried shrimp. If unavailable, substitute hoisin sauce.
18. Five-spice powder:
    A combination of anise, cinnamon, fennel, clove and Szechuan peppercorns which has first been stir-fried until fragrant and then ground to a fine powder.
19. Szechuan peppercorn powder:
    A powder made from the spicy Szechuan peppercorn, which has first been stir-fried until fragrant and then ground finely.
20. Szechuan Peppercorn Salt and Five-Spice Salt:
    A mixture of 2 tablespoons of salt, which has been stir-fried in an oil-less pan until it changes color and added to 1 teaspoon Szechuan peppercorn powder or five-spice powder. It is usually served with fried chicken, fish or shrimp balls for extra flavoring.
21. "Yu tiau":
    A deep-fried crispy Chinese cruller. Detailed directions may be found in "Chinese Snakes Wei-Chuan's Cook Book." It may be eaten plain or served shredded in hot soups. If unavailable, substitute toasted croutons.
22. Ginger wine:
    A mixture of rice wine and the juices of smashed ginger root.
* "dang guei":
  A type of dry, pungent herb used for flavoring in soups or braised dishes, which is very nutritionally beneficial to the body. It may be purchased at any Chinese herbal store.
* "Kau fu":
  A spongy type of vegetarian ingredient made from wheat gluten, primarily used in stir-fried dishes. It may be stored for a long period of time.
* Fried gluten ball ("mien jin pau"):
  A type of light, round, deep-fried ball made from wheat gluten and water. It may be stored indefinitely and is used primarily in stir-fried vegetarian dishes.
* "Su tsang":
  A type of long, thin roll made of wheat gluten and water. It may be stored indefinitely and is used primarily in stir-fried vegetarian dishes.
* Glutinous rice:
  A type of short-grained rice which becomes sticky after cooking and is used in stuffings, dumplings, puddings and as a coating for meat balls.
* "Mei gan tsai":
  The stalk of the mustard cabbage plant, which has been dried and salted. It is used for flavoring in braising pork and chicken and may be purchased at a Chinese grocery store.

Helpful Hints

If rice wine is unavailable, medium-dry or pale-dry sherry may be used.
All turnips used in recipes are Chinese turnips. If they are unavailable, substitute icicle radishes.
Straw mushrooms are available in cans; however, button mushrooms may be used.
If Chinese ham is unavailable, Smithfield or a high-quality smoked variety of ham may be used.
For recipes which call for green onion sections, use the white part of the stalk unless otherwise specified.
All stocks are made with chicken, beef, or pork bones.

To make a simple stock:
❶ Place bones in pan with water to cover.
❷ Boil briefly and remove scum from surface of water.
❸ Add 2 stalks green onion, 2 slices ginger root and 1T. rice wine.
❹ Simmer over low heat for 30 minutes and use as directed.

To prepare 1T. ginger wine, mix 2 slices smashed ginger root with 1T. rice wine; let soak brief, and remove ginger slices. Use as directed.

To precook pork tendons:
❶ Soak tendons for 1 hour in 5C. warm vegetable oil.
❷ Heat oil for deep-frying and drop tendons into hot oil.
❸ Sprinkle ½T. water into hot oil a few times until tendons have expanded. Remove tendons, drain and use as directed.

To precook vegetables:
❶ Cook in boiling water as directed or until tender.
❷ Remove vegetables from boiling water and plunge immediately into cold water until cool (This keeps colors bright and prevents further cooking).
❸ Drain and use as directed.

To pre-soak Chinese black mushrooms:
❶ Rinse black mushrooms lightly and place in warm water to cover until soft. (about 15 minutes)
❷ Remove stems (discard) and use caps as directed. (Soaking liquid may also be added to recipe to provided added flavor and to retain vitamins.)

To pre-soften shark's fin or fish skin:
❶ Place material in a pan with water to cover and heat until just below boiling point; turn heat to low and let simmer uncovered 1-2 hours.
❷ Remove pan from heat and let material cool to room temperature; rinse material lightly and place in fresh, cold water to cover. Let soak in refrigerator overnight.
❸ Repeat complete process 2—3 times until material is very soft and tender.

餐盤裝飾
Vegetable Garnish

本書"餐盤裝飾"承李木村先生、張水土先生、鄭阿福先生
（依姓氏筆劃爲序）、張琛惠小姐提供製作，謹此致謝！
THE EDITOR OF "VEGETABLE GARNISH" wishes to express the
heartiest APPRECIATION and extend to Messrs. Lee Mu-Tsun,
Chang Shui-Thu, and Cheng Ah-Fu together with Miss Chang Chen-
Huey for their kind efforts offered and contributed with valuable
materials used in this literature which made the publication possible.

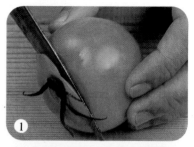

❶ 番茄去蒂頭，底朝上平放於檯面。

❷ 切爲六等份。

❸ 從尾端片切薄皮至⅓處。

❹ 輕輕用手撥成花瓣型，中間擺上綠葉及櫻桃點綴。

■ 可一片單獨使用或兩片相對擺飾。

❶ Slice off the tomato at the stem end so that it will lie flat on the plate.

❷ Cut the tomato into six wedges.

❸ Start to cut the skin (and the meat which is attached to the skin) away from the meat (center) of the tomato at the pointed end; stop about one-third of the length from the edge.

❹ Gently bend back the skin away from the rest of the wedge to form a petal shape.
Place on the side of the plate as illustrated. Further decorate with a maraschino cherry half and parsley, if desired.

■ One wedge may suffice as a simple garnish or arrange the two tomato wedges facing each other, as illustrated.

❶ 番茄去蒂頭，底朝上平放於檯面，再切成六等份。

❷ 每份中間切∧型（深約0.3～0.4公分）。

❸ 從尾端片切薄皮至⅓處。

❹ 輕輕用手撥成花瓣型。

■ 每份可單獨擺飾，亦可半個或整個使用。

❶ Slice off the tomato at the stem end and set it on the cut edge. Cut the tomato into six wedges.

❷ In the center of each wedge on the outside skin, make two deep cuts ⅛ - ⅙ -inch length to form a V-shape.

❸ Start to cut the skin (and the meat which is attached to the skin) away from the meat (center) of the tomato at the pointed end; stop about one-third of the length from the edge.

❹ Gently bend back the skin away from the rest of the wedge to form a petal shape. Repeat for the remaining tomato wedges. Regroup the sections to form the original tomato shape and arrange on lettuce leaves in the center of the serving plate.

■ A wedge may be set flat on the side of a plate to serve as a simple garnish; or a pair of wedges facing each other may be used.

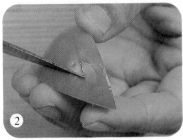

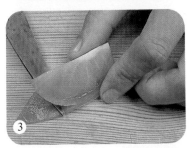

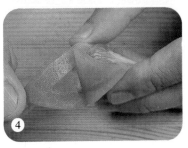

❶ 番茄去蒂頭，底朝上平放於檯面，從頂端劃十字刀痕於表皮上，劃至 $\frac{2}{3}$ 處。

❷ 把皮片開至 $\frac{1}{2}$ 處，輕輕用手撥成花瓣型。

❸ 中間用筷子穿洞。

❹ 插上葱枝，先將葱枝葉子修剪，根部斜切成尖狀，使其容易插入番茄內。

❶ Slice off the tomato at the stem end so that it will lie flat on the plate. Pierce the skin only and carve the outline of a cross with the cuts extending to within one-third of the stem end, on each side of the tomato.

❷ At the intersection of the cross, use a knife to peel the skin away from the meat about half of the length of the tomato. Repeat for the other three "flaps" and bend the skin back away from the tomato to form a petal shape.

❸ Slowly pierce the center of the tomato to make a hole.

❹ Vertically slice the green end of a scallion stalk so that it will "flower." Place in ice water for 10 minutes to "bloom" further. (See steps ❷,❸, and ❹. On page 10 for explicit directions.) Remove, drain, and diagonally cut the white tip of the scallion stalk to make a pointed end and slick into the tomato, as illustrated. Place in the center of the serving plate on several leaves of lettuce.

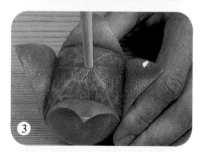

① 番茄去蒂頭，底朝上平放於檯面，在離中心點兩邊各約０.５公分處，切兩直刀至半中間。
② 由半腰向中央橫切兩刀至切口處。
③ 挖除多餘部份，使其呈花籃狀。
④ 在籃把上置一條冬菇絲，再以蔥絲環繞。
■ 可將籃中挖出少許呈╲╱狀，裝入番茄醬，供蘸食用，或擺上花朵。

① Slice off the tomato at the stem and set it on the cut edge. About ⅕ of an inch in each direction from the center of the tomato, make two cuts downward through about half of the tomato-length. (The strip of skin and attached meat will become a handle for this garnish.)
② On each side of the tomato, cut inward about halfway to meet the first vertical cuts.
③ Remove the inset, cut tomato pieces and hollow out the bottom portion of the tomato to form a basket with a handle.
④ Place a thin strip of softened Chinese black mushroom along the length of the handle and wind a green strip of scallion stalk to secure the mushroom. Arrange on a serving plate.
■ The tomato may be filled with a dipping sauce or garlic flower and parsley.

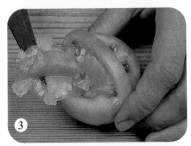

❶ 番茄去蒂頭，底朝上平放於檯面，離邊緣０.５公分直刀深切至⅘處。

❷ 連續切４片，第五刀即切斷。

❸ 將籽挖除，由第二片中心直切到底。

❹ 用刀輕輕拍扁，呈螃蟹狀。

❶ Slice off the tomato at the stem-end and set it on the cut-edge. Make a vertical slice about ⅛ -inch from the cut side of one side of the tomato, stopping about ⅕ of the length from the opposite edge.

❷ Make about 4 more equi-distant slices (in the same manner), cutting through one half of the tomato, and with the last slice cutting the tomato in half.

❸ Seed the cut tomato half and lay it flat on the counter with the cut-edge down. Do not cut the uppermost slice. Start at the second cut slice and make a vertical cut in the center of the slices.

❹ Lightly pound the tomato with the flat edge of a cleaver to flatten and spread the slices so that the tomato half resembles a crab.

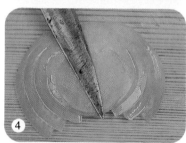

❶ 切 1 公分厚片，由中間切開成兩半。
❷ 從尾端片切薄皮至 $\frac{2}{3}$ 處。
❸ 兩片相對擺成蝴蝶狀，即可使用。
❹ 或將第五種覆蓋其上。

❶ Cut a ⅜ -inch slice out of the center of a tomato and cut into half.

❷ Begin at either end of tomato and cut the skin and the meat which is attached to skin away from the meat of the tomato. Stop about one-third of the length from the opposite edge. Repeat for the other half.

❸ Arrange the two slices, rounded edges together, to form a simple butterfly. (This may be used as a simple garnish.)

❹ Prepare "Tomato Garnish # 5" as directed on page 6 and place "Tomato Garnish #6" on top of "Tomato Garnish #5." Arrange on the side of the serving platter.

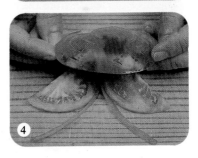

① 半個番茄，平放於檯面，在離中心點各〇.2公分處，以斜刀交切。

② 以同樣切法，每隔〇.5公分連續切數片，呈 ◠◠◠ 狀，最後一刀斜切之交叉點在中心，並切斷。

③ 將左右兩片取出，由尾端片切薄皮至 ⅔ 處，如 1—③，並放回原處。

④ 由第一片向前推出〇.5公分，以此類推向前，使呈桃型狀。

① Vertically cut the tomato in half. Place a tomato half on the counter with cut-edge down. About $\frac{1}{12}$-inch from the center of the tomato half in each direction, make a diagonal cut so that the two cuts form a V-shape and meet at the center.

② Continue to cut in the manner shown above at $\frac{1}{5}$-inch intervals. The final cuts should extend to the opposite cut edge of the tomato half.

③ Remove the two wedges at the bottom and cut their skin (and attached meat) away from the meat (center), stop about one-third of the length from the opposite edge. Bend back the skin away from the rest of the wedge to form a petal shape. Return the wedges to their original place.

④ Push away each tomato slice, as illustrated, so as to form a "step ladder" effect. Arrange on the side of the serving plate.

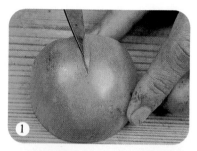

① 番茄由底端片切１．５公分寬之薄皮。
② 連續不斷將整個番茄皮片成一長條。
③ 由底部開始捲起。
④ 環繞成花朵狀。

① Use a very sharp paring knife, start to cut at the non-stem end of the tomato and peel away the skin (and meat which is attached) from the tomato in a ⅗ -inch strip.
② Continue to slice in a circular fashion and remove the entire skin in a long strip.
③ Place the strip end in the palm and wind the strip in a tight coil around itself. Place on the side of a serving plate.
■ An apple may be substituted for the tomato to make a similar garnish.

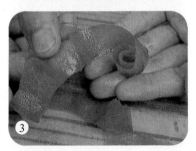

葱 類盤飾
Scallion Garnish

1

❶ 去根，切取5～7公分長段。

❷ 由中央剖切一刀，深約全長之一半。

❸ 再剖一刀成十字形，深度同上。

❹ 在十字形分成的4大瓣內，每瓣由上向下，以同樣大小的間隔用刀尖劃直條刀紋，經泡水後自然展成花朵。（亦可在花朵內插紅辣椒絲點綴）。

❶ Remove the leafy sections from a scallion and cut the stalk into 3-inch lengths.

❷ Cut lengthwise through the stalk to the center.

❸ Cut through the length again to the center, dividing each cut portion into quarters.

❹ Cut the stalk again to divide each cut section into eights. (Depending on the thickness of the stalk, cut into sixteenths.) Place the cut sections in ice water and let stand for 1 hour. The stalks will "bloom." A shred of red pepper may be placed in the center.

■ Leeks and fresh garlic stalks may also be used for this garnish.

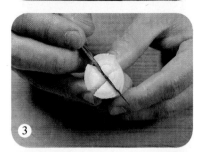

❶ 辣椒斜剪（或用刀斜切）。

❷ 亦可將辣椒平剪（或用刀平切）。

❸ 斜剪或平剪後，從切口處向上剪出同樣大小之花瓣。

❹ 經泡水數分鐘後，即自然捲成花朵。

❶ Use scissors or a sharp knife to diagonally cut off a piece about ⅔-inch from the tip of the red chili pepper;

❷ or cut straight across the pepper to remove a ⅔-inch piece from the tip.

❸ Make long, uniform cuts from the cut tip in toward the stem, continuing around the pepper.

❹ Place in ice water and soak for about 1 hour, or until the "petals" open.

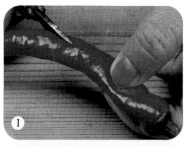

❶ 蒜修除老葉，用刀尖把蒜葉折疊著劃刀痕。

❷ 用大拇指及食指將蒜葉捏住向外打開使挺拔。

❸ 取白蘿蔔莖，修除葉後每隔０.５公分由底向上斜切，呈鱗片狀。

❹ 離底端１公分處，用刀尖由內向外剖開１～３朵（視莖大小），經泡水自然捲曲使用。

❶ Remove any old, wilted leaves from a scallion stalk. Fold the green leaves of the stalk in half and trim the ends to a crescent shape. Score the edges of the leaves at every $\frac{1}{6}$-inch.

❷ Use the index finger and thumb to open up the leaves and bend back. Place the stalks in ice water and let soak 1 hour. (Fresh garlic stalks and leeks may also be used for this garnish.)

❸ Remove the leaves from the stem of a carrot or radish. Trim to a thin stalk and diagonally score the length of the stalk.

❹ Start at a point ½-inch from the end of the stem and cut the piece lengthwise into two to four sections, depending on the length. Place in ice water and soak 20 minutes before using.

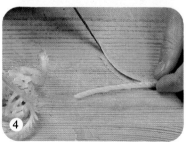

① 大蒜剝除外膜。

② 由尖端往下片約０.１公分薄皮，片至½處，底部留⅓不片斷，作為花瓣。

③ 視蒜之大小，在外層酌片４～５片，經泡水後，自然捲成花朵，則成單層花。

④ 亦可做雙層花，第二層以同樣方法片切。

① Peel several large cloves of garlic.

② Cut off the pointed end of the clove. Make a short, diagonal cut from the center of the clove, slice down to the stem end. (Do not cut through the stem.) This cut should resemble a petal.

③ Cut 4 or 5 more petals, depending on the size of the clove. Place in ice water and let stand for 1 hour. The petals will open to resemble a flower.

④ Or cut a second row of petals in the clove, slice in between the first cuts.

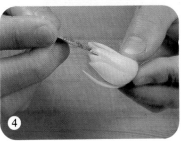

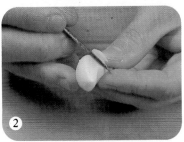

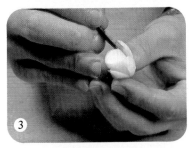

冬瓜類盤飾
Winter Melon Garnish

1

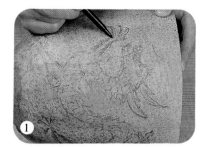

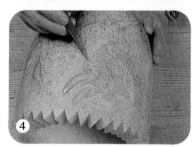

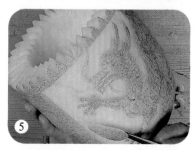

❶ 取冬瓜頭約２０公分長，先用筆在冬瓜皮上畫龍形素描。

❷ 挖除部份瓜肉，使空間較大，以備置放作料。

❸ 沿瓜邊週圍切鋸齒花紋。

❹ 從龍頭起，照素描順序將龍形刻好。

❺❻ 再把龍形四週之瓜皮刻除，使龍形現出。

❼❽ 除龍形外，可隨個人喜愛，刻成各種花紋，如萬字 ⊔⊓、竹子及福祿壽等等。

❶ Cut the winter melon to an 8-inch section. Cut off the tip at the end so that the melon will sit upright on a flat surface. Sketch the outline of a dragon on the side of the melon.

❷ Remove the seeds and some of the meat from the inside of the melon so that it will hold more soup.

❸ Carve V-shaped grooves along the upper edge of the melon.

❹ Use a sharp knife to carve the shape of a dragon; start at the head.

❺❻ Peel the skin away from the dragon, outward, to outline the design. Carve out the scales on the dragon;

❼❽ or use bamboo branches, the designs illustrated, or the Chinese characters signifying fortune, prosperity, and longevity on the melon. If winter melon is unavailable, a watermelon may be used; completely remove the seeds and meat. This garnish is usually used as a serving tureen for soup.

洋蔥類 盤飾
Onion Garnish

1

❶ 洋蔥去皮，在周圍中心處，劃分七等份，（可視洋蔥大小而定，每份距離須相等）然後左右各切斜刀，相交於每等份之中點使成鋸齒狀，將洋蔥分為上下兩半段。

❷ 上半段洋蔥去頭部，然後將上一片洋蔥沿鋸齒狀剝出。

❸ 下半段洋蔥去根部，然後將下一片洋蔥剝出，（剝洋蔥時須小心，不可弄破。）

❹ 洋蔥剝出後，再加以重疊，重疊時應放於間隔處，如此由外而內反覆剝出重疊，使成花狀，即可。

❶ Remove outer layers of skin. Around the middle of the onion, make deep V-shaped cuts down into the center; continue all the way around the outside edge. Cut the stem.

❷ Pull the onion apart into two halves or until the top layer separates from the onion, as illustrated.

❸ Continue to separate the layers from the onion until 3 or 4 layers are removed.

❹ Start with largest layer and place smaller layers inside each other as illustrated.

* For best results, use oval-shaped onion.

15

① 大黃瓜縱剖成兩半，再削去有籽的部份，斜切去除尾端後，
　 平行切〇.１公分之薄片，留底部１公分不切斷，連續切５或
　 ７片，切斷（切成奇數片）。
② 間隔內摺後，泡水使用。
③ 在表皮上刻直條花紋。
④ 切法與①相同，輕拍成扇型。

① Cut a cucumber lengthwise into half. Remove the seeds.
Diagonally cut away the end of the cucumber. Diagonally
cut into the cucumber, make a paper-thin slice and stop about
$2/5$-inch from the edge. Continue to cut 5 to 7 slices in the
same manner so that they are all joined. After the fifth or
seventh slice, cut completely through to separate the section.

② Fold inward every other slice and push the end securely in
towards the joining end of the cucumber section. Place in
ice water and let soak until you are ready to use.

③ To prepare a variation of the above pattern: Cut a cucumber
lengthwise into half. Remove the seeds and cut out V-shaped
grooves from the skin. Cut the slices as directed in Step ①.

④ Flatten the piece with the blade of a knife or cleaver and
"fan" out the slices. Place in ice water and soak for several
minutes.

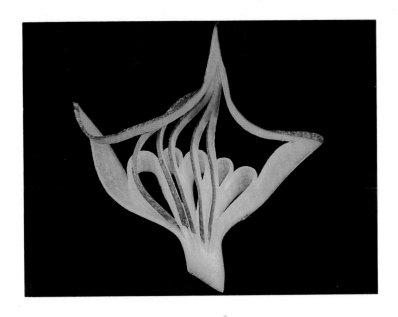

❶ 與黃瓜 1—❶相同，一端不切斷，連續切 9 片，切斷。

❷ 由相連接的一端片開至 3/4 處。

❸ 間隔內摺（或頭尾兩片不摺，餘均內摺）。

❹ 泡水數分鐘後使用。

❶ Cut a cucumber in half lengthwise and remove the seeds. Follow Step ❶ "Cucumber Garnish # 2" to cut 9 paper-thin slices. Cut completely through the cucumber to separate the section.

❷ Place the cucumber section on the counter, skinside down. Start at the joined end and cut the skin away from the meat, slice through three-quarters of the length.

❸ Fold in every other slice toward the joined end; or fold in every piece, but leave the two ends straight.

❹ Place the garnish in ice water and soak for 10 minutes before using.

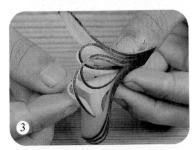

❶ 大黃瓜取尾段長約１５公分，由中間剖開成兩半，尾端中間刻∧形缺口，再把兩邊修成龍蝦尾 ⊲⊳，並在尾端切鋸齒形。

❷ 在尾端邊緣片開０.１公分薄皮。

❸ 尾端朝外，右邊用刀尖由外向內切成０.１公分寬之薄片共切４片最外一片保持原來長度，其餘３片各切短１公分，做為左邊的腳。

❹ 尾端朝內，右邊用刀頭翹起由內向外切成０.１公分寬之薄片共切４片最外一片保持原來長度，其餘３片各切短１公分做右邊的腳。

❺ 中間部份修成 形，作蝦頭。

❻ 在蝦頭尖、端兩邊切鋸齒花紋。

❼ 用刀在蝦頭尖端片０.１公分薄皮，並用大拇指及食指輕捏瓜皮使其往上翹起。

❽ 在蝦身橫刻眉形花紋，視頭部大小酌刻∧字後用刀尖片開並予挑起呈刺紋，用火柴棒黑頭做眼睛取火柴１公分長並斜切，使尾端成尖形，套上紅辣椒圓片後再插上。

把兩邊蝦腳，裡面３片往內摺為圈狀即成。

❶ Trim a cucumber to a section 7-8 inches long. Cut the section lengthwise into half and cut out a V-shaped groove at the very end. Trim the sides of the cucumber to curve in at the end. Cut out smaller V-shaped grooves on both sides of the first larger V-shape.

❷ On the underside, separate the cucumber meat and skin at the end (tail of the lobster). Carve all the way around the rounded edge.

❸ Turn the cucumber so that the "head" faces you and cut 4 thin slices 1½-inch long in the side. Trim ⅓-inch off the ends of the first 2 slices.

❹ Turn the cucumber section around (with the tail end closer) and cut 4 thin slices 1½-inch long in the side, using the end corner of the cleaver. Trim ⅓-inch off the ends of the first 3 slices.

❺ Cut two V-shaped wedges ¼-inch thick from the tip of the cucumber. Remove the wedges. (The end should curve to a point.)

❻ Carve small V-shaped grooves along the pointed edge.

❼ Cut the skin away from the meat and bend the skin upward.

❽ Carve small V-shaped grooves into the surface of the cucumber from the head back to the middle of the section. Bend the tips of the grooves upward. Carve straight lines on the remaining half of the section. Cut two small circles out of a red pepper for eyes. Secure the eyes to the body with two wooden matchsticks. Fold the first 3 slices on each side of the cucumber in toward the body.

■ A zucchini may also be used for this garnish.

19

❶ 大黃瓜切半，再切成梯形。

❷ 右邊用刀尖由外向內切成０.１公分寬之薄片，共切４片，做為蟹的左腳。

❸ 倒轉後，另一邊用刀頭翹起由內向外切成０.１公分寬之薄片，共切４片做為右腳。

❹ 在前端切除一塊梯形 ＼‾‾／ 。

❺ 並修成蟹螯。

❻ 把頭修圓，並切鋸齒花紋。

❼ 在蟹身刻Ｓ形花紋。

❽ 以火柴頭做眼睛，取１公分長段斜切尾端呈尖形再插上。兩端蟹腳把前３片往內摺成圈形。

❶ Cut a cucumber lengthwise into half. Cut one of the halves at different angles, into thirds.

❷ Turn the section so that the longest edge is closest and cut 4 thin slices, about 1½-inch long in the right side.

❸ Turn the piece around and cut 4 thin slices about 1½-inch long in the right side.

❹ Cut a trapezoid-shaped piece (＼‾‾／) out in the center of the longest side.

❺ Cut out a V-shaped wedge on each of the front edges (front claws).

❻ Trim the edge between the two front claws to a curve.

❼ Carve an "S" shape on the surface of the body and remove the skin.

❽ Push 2 wooden matchsticks into the end for eyes. Fold the first 3 slices on each side of the cucumber in toward the body.

■ A zucchini may also be used for this garnish.

❶ 芋頭去皮修成圓筒狀，先切 ⌣ ，再慢慢修成 ⌣ 。

❷ 在較高之一邊切波浪花紋 ⌣ 。

❸❹ 再由兩邊切０.２公分寬之兩刀，呈 ⌣ 。

❺ 以０.１公分寬爲準切薄片，第１刀切至距底部０.５公分處，留刀不切斷，再照同樣寬度切第２刀，切斷，成爲一組。

❻ 每組再由中間斜切１刀 ⌣ 。

❼❽ 用雙手，一手捏住底部，靠蝶頭之一手往上提起插入尾端，豎成蝴蝶形，經泡水數分鐘使用。

❶ Remove the skin from a medium-size taro root and carve to a round shape. Cut a section from the taro, cut in a 60° angle position. The cuts should extend just short of the center of the taro root. Carve out the angle to round out the shape.

❷ Carve out V-shaped grooves on the top edge of the taro section.

❸❹ Make two V-shaped cuts into the sides of the taro, as illustrated, and remove the wedges.

❺ Cut a slice about 1/8-inch thick, cut just short of the opposite edge. Cut a second cut 1/8-inch from the first and cut all the way through.

❻ On the connected section of the double-slice, make 2 cuts, (/ \ ) slanting inward, cutting past the center of the section.

❼❽ Hold the connected edge and push the head of the butterfly so that it rests on the "wings." Push the section in slightly to secure it. Place in ice water and soak 10 minutes.

■ A sweet potato may be used for this garnish.

❶ 切取茄頭（或小黃瓜頭），約5～7公分長段。

❷ 用刀尖以每隔０.３～０.５公分之等距離劃直條刀紋，深約 ０.３公分，將整條切好。

❸ 用刀尖片０.１公分薄皮，使成花瓣。

❹ 把中間茄肉切掉，在所留茄心處用刀尖劃成網狀花紋，做為 花心，經泡水後自然展成花朵。

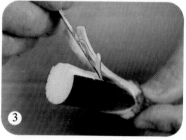

❶ Cut away a section measuring 3-inch from the stem of an eggplant.

❷ Score lines running from the cut edge to the stem end at every ¼-inch around the entire surface of the eggplant. (The scores should be ¼-inch deep.)

❸ With the tip of a sharp paring knife, peel the skin away from the meat to form petals.

❹ Cut the meat out of the eggplant section. Score the surface of the meat near the stem lengthwise and crosswise. Place the flower in ice water and let stand for 10 minutes.

■ Gherkin cucumbers and zucchini may be used for this garnish.

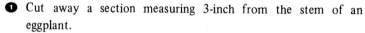

① 去頭部，切成7公分之長段。

② 用刀或筆在切面做記號，分成6等份。

③ 每等份內交叉斜切成V型，去除多餘部份，以此方法全部切好。

④ 將茄皮由尖端片開至⅓處。或切除中心，上置櫻桃點綴。

■ 茄子選直條（不彎曲），質硬挺為佳。

① Remove the stem from an eggplant and cut to a 3-inch length.

② Use the tip of a knife or a pen to divide the end into six sections.

③ Make six long V-shaped grooves in the surface of the eggplant, use the six divisions as a guide. (Center each V-shaped groove in the middle of each section. Remove the grooves.)

④ Start at the tip to separate the meat from the skin to form petals. Cut the meat out of the eggplant section and remove. Score the surface of the meat near the stem lengthwise and crosswise. Place the eggplant in ice water and let stand 20 minutes before using. Place a maraschino cherry in the center.

■ Zucchini may be used for this garnish.

① 茄子橫切成兩半。

② 斜切去除尾端，平行切〇.１公分之薄片，但留１公分不切斷，連續切５或７片，切斷（切成奇數片）。

③ 間隔內摺。

④ 摺處置入櫻桃片點綴。

① Cut an eggplant lengthwise into half. Diagonally cut away the stem.

② Diagonally cut into the eggplant, make a paper-thin slice and stop about ⅖-inch from the opposite edge. Continue to cut 5 to 7 slices in the same manner so that they are all joined. After the fifth or seventh slice, cut completely through to separate the section.

③ Leave the end slices on each section open, but fold the remaining slices inward and push the end securely in toward the center.

④ Place a maraschino cherry section in the middle of each folded slice.

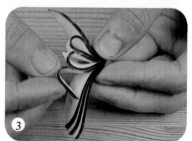

蘿蔔類盤飾
Carrot Garnish

1

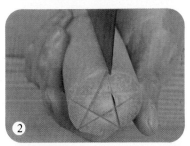

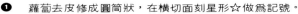

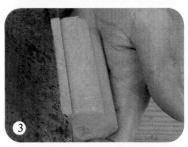

❶ 蘿蔔去皮修成圓筒狀，在橫切面刻星形☆做為記號。

❷ 順星型之尖端為準，垂直刻深1公分之直條刀紋，共切五條。

❸❺ 在每直條兩邊交叉斜切並修成梅花形 ✿ 。

❻ 在每朵花瓣中心交叉斜切V字切口成櫻花瓣狀 ♡ 。

❼ 由花瓣中央V字切口處順兩邊切0.3公分寬，1公分深之兩刀並稍切掉一點使其較為突出呈 ✋ 。

❽ 將前端修成圓錐形，順錐形切薄片1～3圈再捲成花朵，泡水後使用。

❶ Peel the carrot and trim the edges to a round shape. Sketch a star-shape in the center of the carrot.

❷ Cut a V-shaped groove out of the edge of the carrot at each of the points of the star. (The groove should be ½-inch deep.)

❸❺ Remove the V-shaped wedges and round out the tips of the star.

❻ Cut a V-shaped groove out of each tip of the star.

❼ On each side of the points of the star, cut out two, thin V-shaped grooves (petals).

❽ Trim the end of the carrot to a point and cut into the pointed end, and peel off a thin slice continue one to three times around the circumference. Gather the edges of the carrot slice together to form a cone-shape. Soak for 20 minutes in ice water.

蘿蔔類盤飾
Carrot Garnish

2

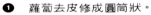

❶　蘿蔔去皮修成圓筒狀。
❷　以每隔〇.七公分之距離，切１公分深直條紋，將整條切完。
❸　在直刀兩邊交叉斜切成波浪形🤚。
❹　可單獨片切〇.三公分薄片做為花飾。
❺❻　或將前端修成圓錐形。
❼❽順錐形切薄片１～３圈，再捲成花朵狀，泡水後使用。

❶　Peel a carrot and form the edges to a round shape.
❷　Cut V-shaped grooves at every ⅓-inch around the surface of the carrot. (The grooves should be about ½-inch deep.)
❸　Remove the V-shaped wedges or grooves.
❹　Cut the carrot into slices ¼-inch thick;
❺❻ or prepare the carrot as directed above and then trim the end of the carrot to a point.
❼　Cut into the pointed end and peel off a thin slice, continue 1 to 3 times around the circumference of the carrot.
❽　Gather the edges of the carrot slice together to form a cone-shape. Soak for 20 minutes in ice water.

蘿蔔類盤飾
Carrot Garnish

3

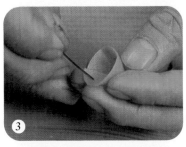

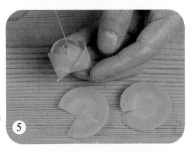

❶　蘿蔔去皮修圓，再片切極薄片。

❷　切成四種 ◗ ◔ ◕ ⬤ 每種３片一組。

❸❹依順序先將半圓片捲疊成弧形，用細竹籤在接合處插上３片做花心。

❺❻再將 ◔ 以同樣方法插上做為第二層，以此類推，把全部４組間隔插上即成一朵花。

❼❽把細竹籤往下拉出一些，用香菜莖（或巴西利）套上做花莖。

❶ Peel the carrot and trim the edges to a round shape. Cut 12 paper-thin slices off of the carrot section. (The slices must be as thin as possible.)

❷ In three of the circles, cut halfway through the circumference to the center. For another three circles, cut the circles into half. For the remaining six, cut out a section one-quarter of the area of the circle of three; cut a section one-third of the area of the circle of the other three sections.

❸❹Gather the edges of the half-circles together to form a cone-shape and pierce the seam of one with a toothpick. Gather the two other half-circle shapes, use a toothpick to pierce; seam side down. Arrange the cone-shape so that the three pointed tips form a triangle.

❺❻Wrap the circles, with a third removed, to a cone-shape and place over the first cones, pierce the seam with the toothpick and shape the tips to form a triangle.

❼❽Carefully, pull the toothpick down below the surface of the rose. Use a parsley or coriander stem to cover the exposed end of the toothpick. Place in ice water and soak for 10 minutes.

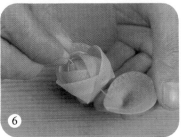

① 去頭修成圓形，底部稍小。

② 在中心先刻一條細紋圓圈，在圓圈外刻出４個鋸齒 做記號，在兩鋸齒間再刻上３個，共切成１６個鋸齒。

③ 在第一層的鋸齒與鋸齒間隔刻上第二層，交叉斜切剔出菱形塊。

④ 以同樣刻法，刻成多層花紋。

① Peel the carrot and cut to a section measuring about 3-inch from the stem end. Trim the section so that it is wide across the top and narrower towards the bottom. Round off the top edge.

② Remove a V-shaped circular groove around the stem to outline. Mark off four equi-distant points around the top of the carrot and carve out four V-shaped grooves in these points. Carve three more V-shaped grooves equi-distant, between the first four carvings. (There should be sixteen V-shaped grooves carved out of the top.)

③ Outline the V-shape from the first row and carve out a diamond-shape wedge in between the first carvings. Continue along this row, cut out diamond-shaped wedges between the first carvings.

④ Continue to carve out wedges, row after row, until the surface is completely carved.

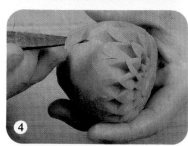

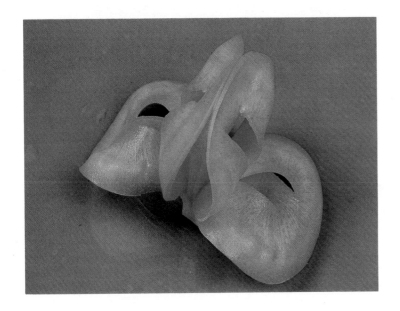

① 去皮修成圓筒狀，片切〇.1公分圓薄片，底端留少不切斷，共切4片，最後一刀切斷。

② 在接合處切兩刀呈八形。

③ 在每兩片間切斷，成二片一組共二組。

④ 用双手，一手捏住底部，另一手往上提起插在底中央。

① Peel the carrot and trim the edges to a circle. Cut three paper-thin slices, cut to within ½-inch of the opposite edge. (The slices should be connected.) On the fourth cut, slice through completely.

② On the connected section, make 2 cuts slanting inward, (/ \ ) cut past the center of the section.

③ Hold the section so that there are two slices on each side of your fingers and cut down through the section, stop just short of the cuts made in step ②. Repeat this procedure for the opposite edge.

④ Hold the connected edge, push up half of the section so that it will "fan" out and push in the bottom slightly so that the joined edge rests securely on itself. Repeat this procedure for the opposite edge. Turn the carrot section and repeat twice on the other side to form the shape which is illustrated.

❶ 蘿蔔修切成四方形。

❷ 筷子一端修尖,旋轉插入蘿蔔中央並穿透。

❸ 泡鹽水:按水2杯加鹽2大匙的比例,將蘿蔔上的筷子抽出,再泡鹽水約浸4小時,使蘿蔔泡軟,較容易切。

❹ 切法:循原洞插上筷子,按上下面,左右面相對稱的方式切刀,深切使觸及筷子,但上下面相對的兩刀與左右面相對的兩刀必須相隔0.3～0.5公分,按此距離把整條切好,距離越小,切出的網越細。

❺ 泡軟的蘿蔔容易出水,要擠拭水份。

❻ 用手夾緊蘿蔔,由四方形修成圓形。

❼ 旋轉片成厚薄一致的長條薄片。

❽ 取出筷子,順網紋切斷,攤開成魚網狀,覆蓋在菜肴上。

■ 快速製作法:先將第❹動作切妥後,抽出筷子再泡鹽水,約6分鐘蘿蔔即可變軟,其餘動作相同,惟蘿蔔未泡鹽水前水份多,較脆容易切裂,應格外小心。

1. Square off the four sides and ends of a thick carrot.
2. Plunge a wooden or steel skewer through the center of the carrot section.
3. Remove the skewer and place the carrot in 2 C. of cold water with 2 Tbsp. salt. Soak for 4 hours. (Soaking will soften the carrot and make it easier to cut.)
4. Reinsert the skewer into the carrot. Starting at ¼-inch from the end, cut the carrot down to the skewer. Turn the carrot to the opposite edge and cut ¼-inch from the end. Turn the carrot to the third side and cut down to the skewer at a point ½-inch from the edge. Turn the carrot to the fourth side and cut ½-inch from the edge. Turn the carrot to the first-cut edge and cut down ½-inch from the original cut. Continue to cut along each edge in the order specified, slicing ⅛-⅓inch from the previous cut on that side.
5. Remove the skewer and towel dry the carrot. Squeeze the carrot together to remove as much water as possible.
6. Reinsert the skewer through the carrot and squeeze together. Trim the sides of the carrot to a round shape.
7. Use a sharp knife, hold it parallel to the carrot, and slice into the carrot, cut around the outside edge.
8. Remove the skewer and continue to slice the carrot, cut one continuous piece. Cut the carrot between the first cuts made to separate and unfold the net.

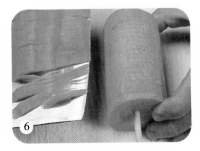

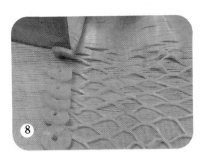

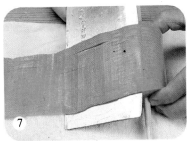

① 整條剖兩刀成４份，每份  修切後成 ⌂ 五角形（直徑約為２.５公分）。

② 順五角形修成錐形。

③ 由每角切薄片至頂端，順序片成五瓣，刀尖切至頂端使其搖動。

④ 用手輕輕拽動使其脫落，泡水後展開成花朵亦可染色使用。

① Peel the turnip and cut into quarters. Cut the quarters to a five-sided shape as illustrated. ⌂

② Trim the tip of each quarter to a point.

③ Make a cut down into the corner of each of the five sides. Stop just short of the bottom edge to form petals.

④ Twist the end of the flower stem and pull off. Place in water and soak for 10 minutes.

A thick carrot may also be used for this garnish.

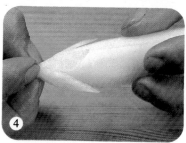

蘿蔔類盤飾
Carrot Garnish

8

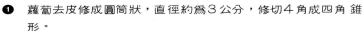

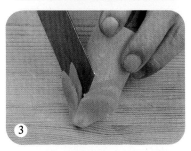

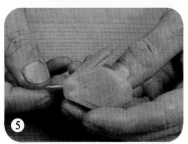

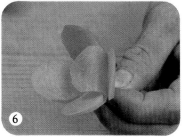

❶ 蘿蔔去皮修成圓筒狀，直徑約為３公分，修切４角成四角錐形。

❷❸ 順著四角錐形，切４薄片，以同樣方法切兩層，再用手輕輕捥掉。

❹ 兩花瓣間用剪刀修整齊。

❺❻ 由底部插上細竹籤，並把裡層４片花瓣插上在竹籤上，外層４片不用插，泡水展開成花朵。

❼ 將細竹籤往下拉，再套上香菜莖（或巴西利）做花莖。

❶ Peel the carrot and trim the edges to form a square. Make a cut down into each side, stop just short of the bottom edge to form petals. Cut a second layer of petals. Twist the end of the flower stem and pull it off.

❷❸ Make a cut down into each side, stop just short of the bottom edge to form petals. Cut a second layer of petals. Twist the end of the flower stem and pull it off. Round out the petals of the second layer and cut the tips of the petals from the first layer to points.

❹ Use scissors to cut out a V-shaped wedge between the petals.

❺❻ Insert a toothpick into the center of the flower. Gather the second layer of petals and pierce the tips through the toothpick. Place in ice water and soak for 20 minutes. (The inner petals will close to form the shape which is illustrated.

❼ Carefully, pull the toothpick down below the surface of the blossom. Use a parsley or coriander stem to cover the exposed end of the toothpick.

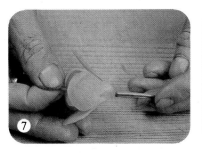

❶ 取紅蘿蔔一段（長度應超過模型），修成長方體。
❷ 用模型來壓出圖案。
❸ 片切薄片。
❹ 取出壓成的燕形，可用來做盤飾或菜餚內的作料。
■ 可用各種不同的模型和材料來製作各色各樣的盤飾。

❶ Cut a carrot into sections slightly longer than the mold. Trim the carrot sections to a rectangular shape.
❷ Place the mold over a carrot section and press.
❸ Remove the mold and cut the carrot section into thin slices.
❹ Remove the sparrow-shape from each slice. This shape may be used as a garnish or as a decorative slice in a stir-fried dish. If used as a garnish, soak for 10 minutes in ice water before using.
■ A variety of other shapes made from molds may be used, if available.

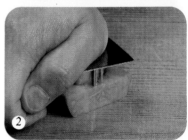

❶ 蘿蔔去皮修成圓筒狀，取一段約５公分長，由中央對半切開，在圓弧面上左右各留⅕做魚頭及魚尾，其餘中間⅗每隔０.５公分斜刀交叉切成鋸齒花紋。

❷ 翻轉底部朝上，修切成魚腹形。

❸ 修切成魚尾狀。

❹❺ 把魚頭修切成形，再刻除些許成嘴形。

❻❼ 在頭部用牙籤插洞，再穿進香菜莖（或巴西利）做眼睛。

❽ 片切薄片作花飾。

■ 紅白蘿蔔及筍均可刻製，如煮半熟後再刻比較容易。

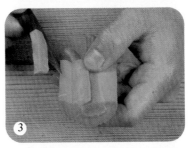

❶ Peel the carrot and trim the edges to a round shape. Cut the section to a piece three inches long. Cut into half. Cut out V-shaped grooves along the round edge, start at ⅕ of the length in from each edge.

❷ Cut out a V-shaped groove of the middle of the straight edge.

❸ To the left of the V-shaped wedge, cut out another, slightly more narrow, to form a tail.

❹❺ To the right of the V-shaped wedge (on the other side), carve out the shape of a head. Cut out a small V-shaped groove at the tip to form a mouth.

❻❼ Insert a steel or bamboo skewer through the head to form a hole for the eyes. Remove and insert a coriander or parsley stem through the hole.

❽ Cut the section into slices.

■ A radish, or bamboo shoot may be used for this garnish. The vegetables may be precooked slightly to facilitate cutting.

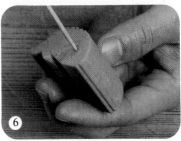

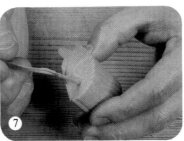

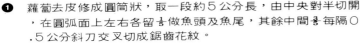

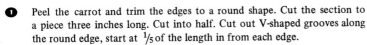

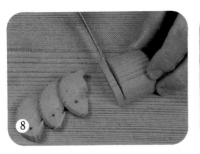

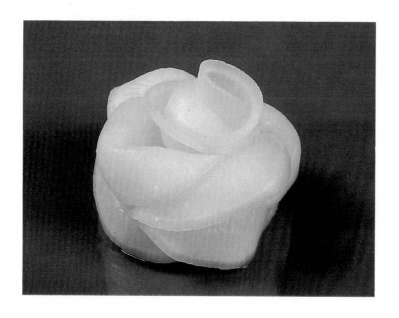

❶ 白蘿蔔切薄片，共切8片。

❷ 按水1杯加鹽1大匙的比例，製成鹽水，將蘿蔔片浸泡鹽水使軟，將每片用手指頭撕開至圓心，再交叉疊成圓錐形▽。

❸ 在疊合處，往外反摺成為花瓣，用3瓣做底。

❹ 第二層用4瓣相互疊好。

❺ 最上面以一片捲成螺旋狀做為花心，插於中央即可。

❶ Cut off 8 paper-thin round slices from a Chinese turnip. (The slices must be very thin.)

❷ Soak the slices in 1C. water with 1 Tbsp. salt for 20 minutes (The slices will become very soft.) Cut each slice halfway across to the center. Gather the edges of each slice and fold to a cone-shape. Set one slice aside.

❸ Fold back half of the edge of each slice to resemble a petal shape. Arrange 3 of the slices together, one on top of the other as illustrated. (First layer)

❹ Place 4 more slices on top of the first layer with the folded edge arranged on different sides of the flower.

❺ Wrap up the retained slice, fold it around itself and fold back the last layer slightly. Place this slice in the center. Place in ice water and soak for 5 minutes before using.

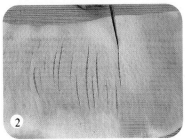

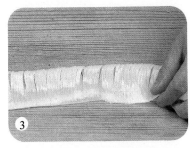

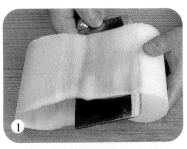

❶ 蘿蔔去頭尾，取１０公分長段，去皮修成圓筒狀，旋轉片成厚薄一致的長條薄片。

❷ 每隔０.３公分切直條刀紋，兩端各留２公分不切斷 ▦ 全部切好後平鋪菜板上，抹些鹽使軟。

❸ 蘿蔔軟後，對摺疊齊。

❹ 由一邊捲起成花朵狀，邊上插上兩枝牙籤成十字形固定，泡水後即展開成花朵。

❶ Cut off the stem and tip of a Chinese turnip and trim it to a section 5-6 inches long. Peel the turnip. Cut into the turnip, hold the knife parallel to the turnip and peel off a long, thin continuous slice about 12 inches long.

❷ Place the slice on a flat surface and cut long scores at every ¼-inch. (Slice to within 1 inch of each edge. Rub a little salt on the surface of the turnip.)

❸ Let stand for about 10 minutes until the turnip has become pliable and fold in half. Cut long scores in the turnip, begin ¼-inch from each side-end extending to within ½-inch from each edge.

❹ Roll up the turnip from one end to the other and secure with 2 toothpicks to form a cross. Place in ice water and soak for 20 minutes until it blooms. Remove and place a few shreds of red pepper in the center.

蘿蔔類盤飾
Turnip Garnish

13

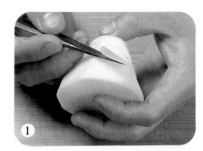

❶ 蘿蔔取頭部，約５～６公分長，在圓周的前後先片掉兩片做基準，在基準兩邊距離再各片掉兩薄片，共切成相等大小的六角形狀，以做記號。

❷ 順六角記號各片０.１公分薄片至⅔處，留⅓不切斷，共片成６個花瓣。

❸ 由上面直刀旋轉一圈挖除整圈多餘部份，使第一層花瓣更突出，第二層刻法，在第一層兩片花瓣間。

❹❺片切薄片至⅔處，共片成６花瓣，再按照❸的方法挖除第二圈多餘部份，使第二層花瓣突出分明。

❻ 照以上方法，連續刻成數層。

❼ 最外層一圈６花瓣修刻成鋸齒形。

❽ 也可隨個人喜愛修成圓形或任何形狀如 ◯◯ ………。

❶ Trim a Chinese turnip to a section 3-inch long to resemble a cone. Carve the edges to form a six-sided figure.

❷ Make a cut down into the corner of each of the six sides, stop just short of the bottom edge to form petals.

❸ Cut out a section from the center to round out the edge.

❹❺ Cut 6 petals, follow the procedure of cutting down the sides and stopping short of the bottom edge. The second row of petals should be cut in between the first row. Cut out a section from the center to round out the edge.

❻ Continue to cut out rows of petals until the center of the turnip is reached.

❼ Cut out small V-shaped grooves along the edge on the outside layer of petals, or;

❽ a design may be carved on the outside petals.

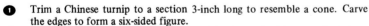

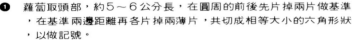

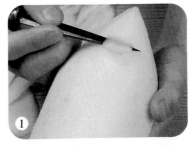

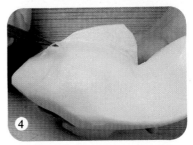

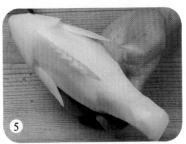

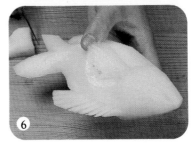

❶ 蘿蔔頭部修成圓錐形，做為魚頭。
❷ 修刻成魚背脊。
❸ 修切成魚尾。
❹ 鰓邊刻成眉形，再片切一片做鰭。
❺ 背脊刻成鋸齒花紋。
❻ 切出後鰭，並修出尾部。
❼ 切刻成嘴形。
❽ 魚身交叉斜切成菱形花紋呈魚鱗狀，鰭及尾修成直條紋。以火柴棒黑頭約1公分長，斜切底端成尖形，套上紅辣椒圓片後，插於兩旁做成眼睛。

❶ Rinse a Chinese turnip and carve the non-stem end to a point. (This will be the fish head.)
❷ On the top edge of the turnip, carve out the shape of the top fin.
❸ Trim the rear end of the turnip to conform to the back end of a fish.
❹ Sculpt the side gills and cheeks of the fish. Also carve the fins on both sides of the fish.
❺ Cut V-shaped grooves on the upper edge of the top fin.
❻ Sculpt the back end of the turnip to resemble a fish tail.
❼ Carve a mouth and eyes in the head of the fish.
❽ Score the surface of the fish to resemble scales. Cut V-shaped grooves in the tail and top skin. Cut two tiny dots out of red pepper for eyes and secure on the fish head with wooden matchsticks.

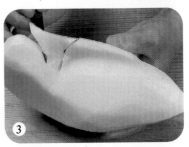

蘿蔔類盤飾
Carrot Garnish

15

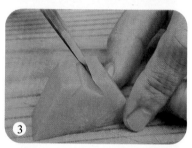

❶ 紅蘿蔔去皮，取一段，由中央對半切開。

❷ 將一個半塊，底朝下圓弧面朝上立於檯面，修平頂部，兩邊斜切兩刀，使呈梯形狀。

❸ 由頂部中央向兩邊斜切兩刀，再於切口處切除 1 小片。

❹ 於梯形兩腰中段各交叉斜切兩刀，切除一小三角形。

❺ 翻轉底面朝上，離中央０.２公分處切兩直刀（深０.５公分），兩邊再斜切兩刀去除小三角形。

❻ 離斜切面約０.３公分，再各斜切兩刀，並切除一片，使此斜片更形突出，切薄片後使用。

❶ Cook a carrot in boiling water for 2 minutes. Remove and refresh in cold water, drain. Cut the carrot into a 2-inch thick section and cut the section in half. Place the cut edge down toward the counter and trim the rounded edge of the carrot to a straight line.

❷ Make two diagonal cuts down on each side to form a trapezoidal-shape. (⬜)

❸ Make two V-shaped grooves in the top edge, facing in opposite directions. Space the grooves so that the center forms a point.

❹ Make a V-shaped groove in each of the two sides of the trapezoid and remove the wedge.

❺ On the last uncut edge, make four V-shaped grooves, carve so that each pair of wedges points toward the center.

❻ Cut the section into thin slices.

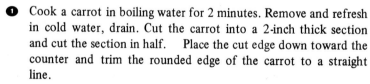

① 筍去硬殼後，取肉厚處修成三角形。

② 其中兩面對稱，每面分３等份，斜刀交叉切除兩條紋（切深約０.２公分）。

③ 另一面離中心各０.２公分處切兩直刀，並由兩邊斜刀切入與直刀口相交，切除多餘部份。

④ 刻好的筍再切薄片使用。

⑤ 紅蘿蔔去皮，取一段，由中央對半切開。將一個半塊，底朝下圓弧面朝上立於檯面，由弧面的¼處往前切除一片，使弧面前端較薄。

⑥ 由圓弧面的¼處往前，每隔０.５公分斜刀交叉切入，刻成鋸齒花紋。

⑦ 翻轉底面朝上，也是由¼處往前刻成鋸齒花紋。

⑧ 後端（剩餘¼未刻鋸齒的部份）兩面各垂直切兩直刀，使呈蒂狀，切薄片後使用。

■ 除紅蘿蔔外亦可用筍來刻但均煮半熟後再切。

① Blanch the bamboo shoot and refresh in cold water. Drain. (If using fresh bamboo shoot, remove the tough outer skin and boil the shoot 10-12 minutes until half-cooked. Remove, refresh in cold water and drain.) Trim the bamboo shoot to a triangular shape.

② Cut two V-shapes wedges in the two sides of the triangle. Remove the wedges.

③ Carve two V-shaped grooves on either side of the center of the long edge. Remove the grooves.

④ Cut the bamboo section into thin slices.

⑤ Cook a carrot in boiling water for 2 minutes. Remove, refresh in cold water and drain. Cut the carrot into sections 2-inch thick. Cut the section into half.
Trim the uncut edge to a half-circle.

⑥ Start at a point ¼ of the total length of the outside edge and cut V-shaped grooves in the surface. Remove the grooves.

⑦ Start at a point ¼ of the length of the cut, straight-edge, cut V-shaped grooves in the surface. Remove the grooves.

⑧ With the flat side down, cut out two right angle shapped-grooves from the uncut, quarter portion of the section.
Cut the carrot section into thin slices.

■ Bamboo shoot may be used for this garnish. If using canned, blanch quickly and refresh in cold water. If using fresh, see Step ① of "Garnish 42" for cooking directions.

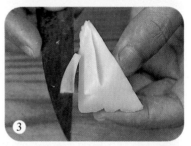

① 去除部份老葉。

② 分5等份，片薄小圓皮。

③④ 由根部片切0.1公分之薄皮以S型切至頂端，不切斷，以此法切4片泡水使薄片張開成花朵狀。

① Remove any leaves from the radish and trim the root.

② Cut off five circular pieces around the four sides of the radish and the top.

③ Remove any leaves from the radish and trim the root. Cut paper-thin slices in the four sides of the radish, slice down from the stem to the root, without cutting through completely. Twist the knife slightly as cut is made to make a petal shape.

④ Place the radish in ice water and soak for 20 minutes before using.

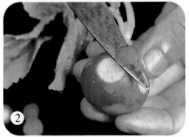

❶ 去除老葉，分五等份，先片薄小圓片（參照蘿蔔盤飾１６的做法❷），再往內切一刀，使此五片突出呈花瓣狀。

❷ 於兩片花瓣間切除約０.１公分寬之薄皮再往內切一刀。

❸ 去除根部多餘的部份。

❹ 將頂端修成尖型。

❶ Remove any leaves from the radish, if remaining. Cut off five thin circular pieces from the sides of the radish. Cut a paper-thin slice the five sides, slicing from the tip, four-fifths of the way through the length of the radish to the opposite edge.

❷ Remove a V-shaped wedge of skin in between each of the first five cuts. Cut a paper-thin slice in back of each of the V-shaped grooves, slice down to a point above the first row of petals.

❸ Cut into the root end and slice off a thin piece, trim the end to a cone-shape.

❹ Trim the root end to a point and place in ice water. Soak for 20 minutes before using.

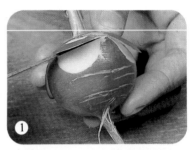

❶❷去頭，使能平放，根部中央斜刀交叉切入（深約０.２公分）
，刻成星形。

❸❹在半腰下，斜刀切成∧型，深０.３公分，依此法連續刻一圈
，全部刻好後，用手輕輕拉開。

❶❷ Remove any leaves from the radish if remaining. Cut off the
stem and the root. On the root surface, carve six V-shaped
intersecting grooves as illustrated, to form a star-shape.

❸❹ Along the bottom edge, cut V-shaped grooves completely
around the outside of the radish. Gently pull away each V-
shaped wedge from the radish. Place in ice water and soak for
20 minutes before using.

① 去葉部，分4等份，在表皮上片除０.１公分寬之薄皮（如眉月型）。

② 在其後，以直刀往下切至⅔處，成花瓣型。

③ 每花瓣內再斜切半片，並予去除，使花瓣更形突出。

④ 以根部為中心點，斜刀交叉切除，切成十字花型。

① Trim the stem end of the radish so that it will set flat. On four sides of the radish, make a slight cut through the skin as illustrated.

② Make four more cuts directly behind each of the first cuts, cut down through two-thirds of the radish to form petals.

③ Cut and remove a thin wedge from behind each of the four "petals" to make each petal stand out.

④ With the tip of a paring knife poised in the center of the radish, carve out two perpindicular V-shaped sections to make an X. Place in ice water and soak for 20 minutes before using.

❶　在中腰切鋸齒型，使刀深至中心。

❷　用手拉開成二朵花型。

❸❹去頭尾，在表皮上每隔０.３公分斜刀交叉切除０.２公分寬
之直條，呈灯籠狀。

❶❷Remove any leaves from the radish, if remaining. Cut off the stem and trim the root end. Around the middle of the radish, make deep V-shaped cuts down into the center, continue all the way around the outside edge. Pull the radish apart into two halves. Place the radish flowers in ice water and soak for 20 minutes before using.

❸❹Remove any leaves from the radish, if remaining. Cut off the stem and trim the root end. Carve V-shaped wedges around the sides of the radish, extending from one end to another. Place in ice water and soak for 20 minutes.

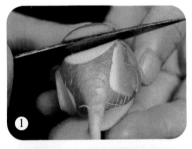

❶ 離根部〇.３公分各切一刀,厚約〇.１公分之薄片,片切至頂端(約全長⅘處)不切斷,共切四片。

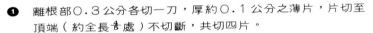

❷ 將根部修成尖型或圓錐型。

❸❹去頭尾,每隔〇.１公分切薄片深至⅘處,全部切好,泡鹽水使其軟,拉開成花朵狀。

❶ Remove any leaves from the radish, if remaining. Cut off the stem and the root end. Cut a thin slice on four sides of the radish, slice from the tip four-fifths of the way through the length to the opposite edge.

❷ Trim the root end to a circle or to a cone-shape. Place the radish in ice water and soak for 20 minutes before using.

❸❹ Remove any leaves from the radish, if remaining. Cut off the stem end. If the radish is round, trim the root end and cut thin slices in the radish, cut down almost to the opposite edge. (Do not cut through the end.) If the radish is oval or shaped, like a peach, cut the slices, start from both of the opposite sides and slice toward the center. Trim the root end. Place the radish in ice water and soak for 20 minutes before using.

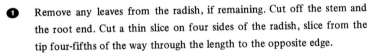

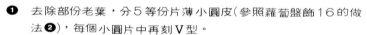

❶ 去除部份老葉，分5等份片薄小圓皮(參照蘿蔔盤飾16的做法❷)，每個小圓片中再刻V型。

❷ 離根部0.3公分各切一刀，厚約0.1公分之薄片，至頂端（約全長 $\frac{4}{5}$ 處）不切斷。

❸ 在每個小圓片後再斜切半片，去除。

❹ 以根部為中心點，向內斜刀交叉切成十字花型。

❶ Remove any leaves from the radish, if remaining. Cut off five thin small circular pieces from the sides of the radish. With the tip of a knife, carve a shallow V-shape into the center of each edge.

❷ Cut a paper-thin slice on five sides, slice from the tip, four-fifths of the way through the length of the radish to the opposite edge.

❸ Make another cut in each of the five sides, slice in at a slight angle so that this slice may be removed.

❹ Trim off the root end of the radish and carve an X-shape on the top. Place in ice water and let stand for 20 minutes before using.

❶ 蘋果切4等份。
❷ 將每一等份切除核心，修平，皮面朝上平放檯面。
❸ 每份在表皮上，離中心點各０.２公分處以斜刀交叉切成Ｖ型。
❹ 以同樣切法每隔０.５公分連續切４或５片，所切成之Ｖ型均可移動，照此方式切好三份（一份鳥身稍大，二份翅膀較小些）。
❺ 將每份切好的，由第一片向前推出０.５公分，以此類推向前。
❻ 另切一片１公分寬之蘋果片，切除核心部份。
❼ 在一端用牙籤穿洞，然後插入一小段葱葉做成眼睛，另一端切平，使易於站立。
❽ 拼排成鳥型。

❶ Cut the apple into quarters.
❷ Remove the core of each quarter section so that the edge is flat and even.
❸ On the skin-side of each apple section cut a thin V-shaped wedge from the center.
❹ Continue to cut V-shaped wedges at intervals until there are 4 to 5 moveable wedge sections. Repeat for 2 other apple quarters. If the quarters differ slightly in size, set a side the bigger section for the body of the bird and the two smaller sections for the wing sections.
❺ Push out the wedges in a "step-ladder" fashion as illustrated.
❻ Cut the remaining apple quarter to a slice 2/5-inch thick and cut out the core.
❼ Pierce a hole in the thin apple slice near one end and insert the green end of a scallion stalk in the hole to form eyes. Trim the scallion section to the thickness of the apple slice.
❽ Arrange the four sections as illustrated to form a bird-like shape.

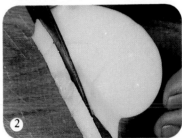

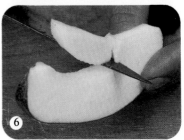

❶ 在皮上切直條紋。

❷ 切成薄片擺飾。

❸ 將橙子切半。

❹ 在平面上切出鋸齒狀，（ 此型亦可用檸檬來做 ）。

❶ Carve thin V-shaped wedges along the outside of an orange. Remove the grooves.

❷ Cut the orange into thin slices.

❸ Cut an orange in half.

❹ Carve V-shaped wedges out of the cut surface, cut completely around the edge.

❶　檸檬切０.２公分之薄片。

❷　切開至圓心點（為半徑長）。

❸❹用手扭轉成Ｓ型（綠皮或黃皮檸檬均可）。

■　此型亦可用橙來做。

❶　Cut a lemon into paper-thin slices.

❷　Make a cut from the edge to the center.

❸❹ Twist the slice into an S-shape.

■　Limes or oranges may also be used for this garnish.

❶ 將鳳梨片，每片切成四小片（ 新鮮或罐頭均可用 ）。

❷ 紅辣椒切小菱形片（ 櫻桃亦可 ）。

❸❹將辣椒片擺在鳳梨兩邊或中間點綴 。

❶ Cut a pineapple slice into quarters. (Canned or fresh pineapple may be used. If fresh, peel and core the pineapple.)

❷ Cut a hot red pepper or a maraschino cherry into diamond shapes.

❸❹Place two pineapple sections together and arrange the red pepper or maraschino cherry in the middle of the two slices. A red pepper or cherry section may be placed in the center of each double pineapple slice.

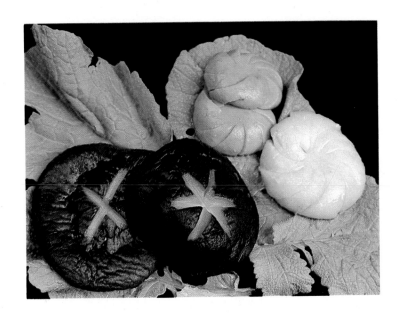

❶　毛菇（洋菇）去蒂頭，使能平放。

❷　在圓周切半徑長之直條，深切到底。然後用手輕壓，使花瓣
展開成菊花狀。

❸❹香菇去蒂頭，在表面中央交叉斜切，切深約０.２公分成十字
形或星形。

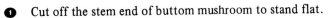

❶　Cut off the stem end of buttom mushroom to stand flat.

❷　Cut thin even slices all around the mushroom cap without
cutting through to the center. Gently press down at the center
to fan out into a flower shape.

❸❹Cut off stem end of Chinese black mushroom. Make three
intersecting cuts about $\frac{1}{12}$-inch long through the center of the
cap to form a star shape. Hold knife at a slant and make the
same cuts twice and remove the excess piece between the cuts.

Pictured on the next two pages are some of the many unusual and diverse vegetable sculptures possible with a little patience and creativity.

中 國 菜

Chinese Cuisine

魷魚、墨魚切花法
The Art of Cutting Squid ″Flowers″

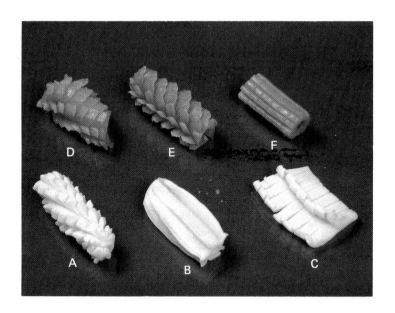

D E F

A B C

切花要領：

❶ 魚身內面(內臟面)之薄膜應先去除。

❷ 所切成的各種花紋，其間隔、深淺應求一致，如魚身肉較厚，
應切深些。

❸ 在魚身內面切花紋後，再經烹煮即捲成筒狀。

方法：

Ⅰ❶ 視魚身大小順直酌切１～３刀成２～４片(圖１)。

❷ 由一角用直刀方式切斜紋，全部切完(圖２)，再由另一角斜
刀切成菱形花紋，再切５公分×３公分的小塊(圖３)，烹煮
後即捲成 A 花形。

Ⅱ❶ 由上端起用斜刀酌切橫紋，再切５公分×３公分的小塊（圖
４），烹煮後即捲成 B 花形。

Ⅲ❶ 以每隔０.５～０.７公分的距離，由上至下切直條刀痕，深約
厚度之半，再斜切５公分×３公分的薄片（圖５）(刀與魚身
的角度越小，片出的面越大)，烹煮後即成 C 花形。請參照
本書第１７４頁「紅油魷花」。

Ⅳ❶ 將整條魷魚由一角開始切斜紋，全部切好。再由另一角以同
樣方法切斜紋成菱形花紋後，切成５公分寬之長片(圖６)每
片切成三角塊(圖７a)，烹煮後即捲成 D 花形。

Ⅴ❶ 以Ⅳ法切成菱形花紋後，再切５公分×３公分小塊(圖７b)
，烹煮後即捲成 E 花形。

Ⅵ❶ 以每隔０.３～０.５公分之距離，由上至下切直條刀痕，深約
厚度之½，再以直刀橫切成方格花紋(圖８)，切５公分×３
公分小塊，烹煮後即捲成 F 花形。

■ 另有用（壽字）花紋，請參照本書第１８２頁「鮮炸魷魚」。

■ 發乾魷魚的方法，請參照本書第１７６頁「爆雙花」。

Important points to remember:

❶ Remove the thin, skin-like membrane from the squid.

❷ Use uniformity in cutting the scores so that the design will be attractive. If the squid section is thick, score the surface deeply.

❸ Always score the squid on the inner surface (not the skin-side). After scoring the surface, blanch in boiling water.

Squid Flower I

❶ Cut the body of the squid into 2-4 sections, depending of the width (fig. 1).

❷ Start at the tail end of the body, score the squid sections lengthwise (fig. 2). The cleaver should be held at a 45° angle to the squid. Turn the squid sections and score crosswise, perpendicular to the first cuts (fig. 2). Cut the sections into 2-inch x 1-inch pieces (fig. 3). Blanch the pieces for 1 minute. Remove and drain. The resulting shape should resemble illustration "A".

Squid Flower II

Cut the squid lengthwise into 2-4 sections, depending on the width. Diagonally score the squid sections make cuts about ⅛ -inch apart. Cut the sections into pieces about ⅜ -inch wide (fig. 4). Blanch the pieces for 1 minute. Remove and drain. The resulting shape should resemble illustration "B".

Squid Flower III

Cut the squid lengthwise into 2-4 sections, depending on the width. Score the squid sections lengthwise, cut at every ¼-inch. Turn the sections and score crosswise perpindicular to the first scores. Cut through the section about ¼-inch from the last executed score (fig. 5). Blanch the pieces for 1 minute. Remove and drain. The resulting shape resemble illustration "C".

Squid Flower IV

Cut the squid lengthwise into half (fig. 1). Score the sections lengthwise and crosswise, perpindicular to the first scores (fig. 6). Diagonally cut the sections into 2-inch pieces with slanted sides (fig. 7-a). Blanch the pieces for 1 minute. Remove and drain. The resulting shape should resemble illustration "D".

Squid Flower V

Cut the squid lengthwise into half. Score the sections lengthwise and crosswise, perpendicular to the first scores. Cut the sections into 2-inch pieces with straight sides (fig. 7-b). Blanch the pieces for 1 minute. Remove and drain. The resulting shape should resemble illustration "E".

Squid Flower VI

Cut the squid lengthwise into half. Score the sections in straight lines at every ⅛ -inch. Turn the sections and score crosswise, perpindicular to the first cuts. Cut each section into 2-inch squares. Blanch the pieces for 1 minute. Remove and drain. The resulting shape should resemble illustration "F".

■ Squid may also be cut into the shape of the "longevity" symbol "卅". For cutting directions, see Step❶"Fried Squid" P. 182.

■ To pre-condition the dried squid, see directions in "Stir-Fried Squid Flowers," Page 176.

剝雞及排盤法

To Cut Whole Chicken for Serving

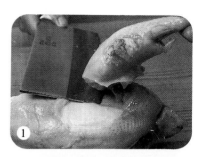

❶ 雞去頭頸，用手將雞翅掀起，由雞身與雞翅相連之關節處下刀
剁下雙翅，再剁雞腿(圖１)。

❷ 雞身橫刀剖切為背、胸(腹)兩半(圖２)。

❸ 雞背順大骨邊剁開成兩半，並切除中間大骨(圖３)。

❹ 雞背分切小塊，整齊排於盤底(圖４)。

❺ 雞胸(腹)用刀壓住肉，用手剔除大骨(圖５)。

❻ 淨肉斜刀切小塊(圖６)，整齊排於雞背上(圖７)。

❼ 雞腿切塊排於兩側，翅膀排於前端(圖８)，中間排上雞頭或雕
刻之蔬果來擺飾。 （完成圖參照第８４頁鹽焗雞）

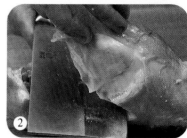

❶ With a sharp knife, cut off the wings from the carcass at the
shoulder joints. Cut off the wing tips and set aside. Remove the
legs from the chicken carcass at the joints. (fig. 1).

❷ Start to cut at the rear cavity of the chicken carcass and cut
lengthwise in half (fig. 2).

❸ To remove the central back bone from the chicken, cut the back
section into three, cut as closely as possible to the back bone
on each side (fig. 3). Discard the bony section and cut the two
side sections into serving pieces and arrange on the serving plate
(fig. 4).

❹ Lightly pound the breast section with the flat side of the cleaver
and remove the breast bone. (fig. 5).

❺ Cut the boned breast in half lengthwise and cut into serving
pieces. (fig. 6) Arrange the pieces on the serving plate as
illustrated. (fig. 7).

❻ Cut the legs through bones into serving pieces and arrange on
each side of the breast meat. Cut the chicken wings in half at
the elbow and place the first joint pieces of the chicken wings
on both sides of the breast meat (fig. 8). (The wings may also
be used instead of these pieces.) Place the chicken head or garnish
of choice (see garnish section in rear of book) at the front of
the plate next to the wings. See picture on Page 84.

剝鴨及排盤法
To Cut a Duckling for Serving

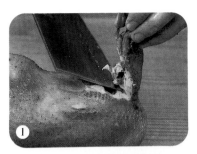

❶ 鴨切除頭尾，用手將翅拉起，由鴨身與翅相連之骨輪處切下鴨翅（圖1）。

❷ 切下鴨腿（圖2）。

❸ 由鴨身橫刀剖切為背、腹（胸）兩半（圖3）。

❹ 鴨背順中間大骨邊剁開，可先切除中間大骨，並分別剁小塊，整齊排於盤底（圖4）。

❺ 鴨胸（腹）除去大骨（圖5），淨肉由中間切開兩半，再分切小塊，排盤在鴨背上面（圖6）。

❻ 鴨腿分切小塊排於兩側（圖7）。

❼ 鴨翅排於前方（圖8），鴨頭可置正前方或用雕刻之蔬果來擺飾。
（完成圖參照第88頁醬鴨或92頁烤鴨）

❶ With a sharp knife, cut off the wings from the carcass at the shoulder joints. Cut off the wing tips and discard. Set aside the wings. (fig. 1).

❷ Remove the legs from the duckling carcass at the joints. (fig. 2).

❸ Start to cut at the rear cavity of the duckling and cut the carcass in half (fig. 3).

❹ To remove the central back bone, cut the back section into three, cut, as closely as possible to the back bone, on each side (fig. 4). Discard the central back section and cut the two side sections into serving pieces. Arrange the pieces on the bottom of the serving platter.

❺ Lightly smash the breast section with the flat side of the cleaver and remove the meat from the bone (fig. 5). Cut the boned breast section lengthwise in half and cut into serving pieces. Arrange on the serving plate (fig. 6).

❻ Cut the legs through bones into serving pieces and arrange on each side of the breast meat. (fig. 7).

❼ Cut the wings into serving pieces and arrange on both sides of the breast meat (fig. 8). Place the duckling head or garnish of choice (see garnish section in rear of book) at the front of the plate next to the wings.

全鴨取皮法
To Skin the Duckling

❶ 用一把鋒利的小刀，從鴨頸開始將皮與肉切開，慢慢的環繞着鴨身往下剝皮（圖１、２）。

❷ 在鴨翅與鴨身的相接關節處切一刀，並將鴨翅上的肉剔除（圖３）。

❸ 由關節處切斷翅膀的大骨，僅留下翅尖仍與皮相連（圖４）。

❹ 繼續環繞着鴨身往下剝皮，直到鴨腿（圖５、６）。

❺ 在腳脛骨的地方將骨頭切斷，保留下一小段的脛骨仍與皮相連（圖７）。

❻ 全部剝下後，皮上必須仍帶着翅尖，腳脛骨和尾部，如此才算是一張完整的皮（圖８）。

■ 取下的鴨皮，可用來做八寶鴨，或脆皮糯米鴨，做法請參照第６３頁。

❶ With a sharp paring knife, start at the neck and use short cuts to separate the skin from the carcass. Cut towards the meat and pull the skin away as you go along (fig. 1, 2).

❷ Make two cuts at the shoulder joints connecting the wings to the carcass, and scrape away the meat from the bones connected to the shoulders (fig. 3).

❸ Sever the wing joints at the elbow to remove the wing tips with the skin (fig. 4).

❹ Continue working slowly down along the body to the legs (fig. 5,6).

❺ Sever the leg bones just before the tips so that they are still attached to the skin (fig. 7).

❻ Remove the skin and turn inside out; the wings, leg tips, and tail should be attached with the skin (fig. 8).

■ Use the thoroughly whole duckling skin to prepare "Eight-Treasure Duckling" or "Crispy-Skin Eight-Treausre Duckling". See P. 63 recipe.

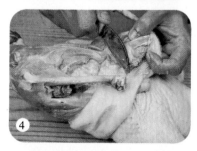

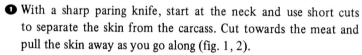

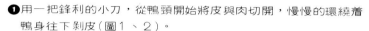

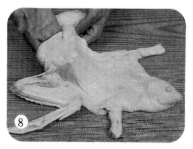

脆皮糯米鴨

鴨 1 隻	3 斤
① 鹽	1 大匙
酒	1 大匙
葱	2 枝
薑	2 片
八角	1 朶

② 蝦米（泡軟）	
冬菇丁	
紅蘿蔔丁	1 杯
筍丁	
青豆仁	
火腿丁（或洋火腿）	

糯米飯	2 杯
③ 鹽	$\frac{1}{2}$ 小匙
味精	$\frac{1}{4}$ 小匙
胡椒	$\frac{1}{4}$ 小匙

❶鴨整隻去骨，皮勿破（參照第62頁），以①料抹勻醃半小時。

❷油4大匙燒熱，將②料炒香，隨下糯米飯及③料拌炒均勻後，塞入鴨腹內約七分滿即可（以防蒸時鴨皮緊縮爆破），以牙籤封好或針線縫合鴨腹，再用針在鴨身四周打洞待蒸。

❸半鍋水燒開，將鴨大火蒸約1小時半以上至鴨肉熟軟（要時時加水），取出洒少許太白粉於鴨皮備炸。

❹「炸油」燒熱，即將鴨下鍋以中火炸約8分鐘，至鴨皮酥脆呈金黃色撈起，剁塊盛盤。

■ 糯米飯煮法：

1 杯糯米洗淨瀝乾水，再加 $\frac{3}{4}$ 杯水浸泡30分鐘（如煮出飯欲較乾可少加水），用大火燒開煮1分鐘，蓋鍋蓋改小火 續煮20分鐘，即熄火再燜10分鐘便可。亦可用電鍋煮成飯。

Crispy-Skin Eight-Treasure Duckling

	1	duckling (4 lbs.)	
①	2	stalks green onion	
	2	slices ginger root	
	1	star of anise	
	1	T. wine	
	1	T. salt	
	2	C. precooked glutinous rice	

	dried shrimp	
	pre-softened Chinese black mushrooms	combined
②	diced carrot	ingredients
	diced bamboo shoot	should
	green peas	equal
	diced Chinese ham (or ham)	1 cup

	½	t.	salt
③	¼	t.	MSG
	¼	t.	black pepper

❶ Rinse duckling and drain; debone duckling (see P. 62). Rub duckling insdie and outside with ① and marinate for 30 minutes.

❷ Heat pan and 4T. oil; stir-fry ② over medium heat until fragrant; add cooked rice and ③ and mix thoroughly (filling). Stuff filling into cavity of duckling (remain some spaces for shrink of duckling skin), sew up cavity openings with thread or secure closed with toothpicks. Make small holes on duckling skin with needle.

❸ Add 10 C. water to steamer and bring to a boil. Place duckling to a steamer and steam for 1½ hours (add water if necessary). Remove duckling, drain and coat outside with cornstarch.

❹ Heat oil for deep-frying; place duckling in oil and deep-fry 8 minutes over medium heat until golden brown; remove, drain; remove thread or toothpicks and cut into pieces; serve.

■ Method to cook glutinous rice: Place 1 cup rice in pan; wash until water is clear. Drain water. Add 1 cup water to pan. Let stand about 30 minutes. For drier rice, add less water. Bring to boil over high heat. Allow to boil one minute. Cover pan and turn to low flame for 20 minutes. Remove from heat and let stand for 10 minutes more. Do not open lid while cooking.

油淋去骨雞　　　江浙菜　　6人份

大雞腿2隻12兩

①
| 酒…………1大匙
| 醬油………2大匙
| 蔥(拍扁)……2枝
| 薑(拍扁)……2片
| 八角…………1朵

「炸油」………3杯

蔥粒………1大匙

②
| 麻油…………½大匙
| 油…………1大匙
| 糖…………½大匙

雞腿去骨法： 雞腿洗淨，拭乾水份，由內側劃一長條刀痕深觸大骨（圖1），在長骨邊輕刮，使骨與肉脫離，在關節處切一刀，並切斷周圍之筋（圖2），使骨輪突出，用刀壓住，另一手往反方向拉並剔除骨（圖3），在小腿末端用刀敲斷，並用圖3的方法，再剔除另一大骨（圖4）

❶ 把雞腿肉攤開，有筋部位用刀輕斬數下，使筋斷（參照第74頁「麻辣子雞」圖1），以防炸時縮捲，不易炸熟。

❷ 將①料與腿肉拌勻醃泡30分鐘以上。

❸ 鍋熱，「炸油」3杯燒熱（275℉），攤開雞腿，雞皮朝下，用中火炸2分鐘，翻面炸2分鐘，撈出，將油再燒熱（375℉），重炸雞腿約1分鐘，呈褐色時撈起，切塊（每隻切六塊），排盤內撒些蔥粒。

❹ 將醃雞所剩之醬油汁加②料燒沸，澆淋在蔥粒上趁熱供食。

■ 將雞腿改用雞半隻去骨，其他調味及做法同上。

■ 盤飾：參照第46頁，蘿蔔盤飾第20種。

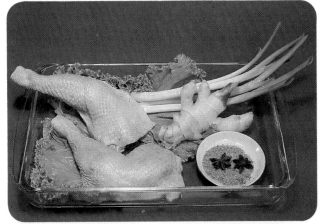

蛋白質···········７４克
脂質············６４克
醣質············６４克
熱量·········８９２仟卡

Protein 74g
Fat 64g
Carbohydrate. 64g
892 Kcal

Oil-Dripped Boneless Chicken

Chekiang-Kiangsu
6 servings

2 chicken legs (about 1 lb.)

① {
1 T. rice wine
2 T. soy sauce
2 stalks green onion, smashed
2 slices ginger, smashed
1 star anise
}

3 C. oil for frying

② {
1 T. chopped green onion
½ T. sesame oil
½ T. sugar
}

To bone chicken: Rinse the chicken leg and pat dry. Make two cuts on the underside of the leg, parallel to the two bones (fig. 1). Scrape gently along the two bones. At the joint, cut through the tendons and cartilage. Separate the joint from the meat (fig. 2). Bend the meat back so that the bone is exposed. Grasp the end of the bone and pull off the meat with the other hand (fig. 3). Break the joint bone connected to the foot, with the back of the cleaver and remove, following the method used in fig. 3 (fig. 4).

❶ Lay the boned leg on the counter and pound lightly with the blunt edge of the cleaver. (Pounding prevents the meat from curling during cooking and speeds the cooking.) Repeat for the other leg. (See "Spicy Fried Chicken," on P. 74. fig. 1).

❷ Place ① in a large bowl. Add the chicken and marinate for at least 30 minutes. Remove the chicken and strain the marinade. Reserve the strained marinade.

❸ Heat pan and add 3 cups oil, heat to 275°F. Add the chicken to the oil, skin-side down and spread out the pieces in the oil. Deep-fry about for two minutes over medium heat. Turn the chicken and fry two additional minutes. Remove the chicken and drain. Reheat oil to 375°F. Return the chicken to the oil and deep-fry until golden brown. Remove, drain and cut each leg into six pieces. Arrange on a platter and sprinkle with the chopped green onion.

❹ Heat pan and add mixture ② . Heat until smoking and sprinkle over the chicken pieces. Heat the pan and add the marinade and ½ tablespoon sugar. Heat until boiling and sprinkle over the chicken. Serve hot.

■ One half of a whole chicken may be substituted for the legs. Remove the bones and follow the procedure above.

■ Garnish: See "Vegetable Garnish," p. 46.

檸檬雞片

廣東菜　　6人份

雞胸肉⋯⋯⋯半斤

① 酒⋯⋯⋯⋯1小匙
醬油⋯⋯1½小匙
鹽⋯⋯⋯⋯¼小匙
胡椒粉⋯⋯⅛小匙
蛋黃⋯⋯⋯1個
太白粉⋯⋯1大匙

② 太白粉⋯⋯4大匙
麵粉⋯⋯⋯2大匙

「炸油」⋯⋯3杯

③ 鹽⋯⋯⋯⋯¼小匙
糖⋯⋯⋯⋯3大匙
鮮檸檬汁⋯2大匙
太白粉⋯⋯½小匙
水⋯⋯⋯⋯3大匙

❶ 將雞胸肉去皮（圖1），切成6公分×4公分×0.3公分之大薄片（圖2），調入①料拌勻醃10分鐘（圖3），炸前再沾預先拌勻的②料（圖4）。

❷ 鍋熱，加「炸油」3杯燒熱（375°F），放進雞片，用中火炸15秒，用鍋鏟拌開，續炸15秒撈出，將油再燒熱（400°F），重炸雞肉10秒，撈起盛盤。

❸ 鍋熱，加油1大匙，倒入③料燒滾，再淋下油1大匙，即可澆淋在雞片上，趁熱供食。

■ 盤飾：參照第51頁，橙、檸檬類盤飾第2種做法。

糖醋雞片

將③料內的檸檬汁改用白醋，其做法同上。

蛋白質‥‥‥‥‥‥‥‥７２克
脂質‥‥‥‥‥‥‥‥‥４６克
醣質‥‥‥‥‥‥‥‥‥６４克
熱量‥‥‥‥‥９７２仟卡

Protein. 72g
Fat 46g
Carbohydrate. 64g
972 Kcal

1

2

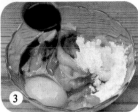
3

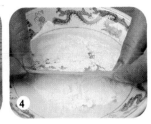
4

Lemon Chicken

Cantonese 6 servings

¾ lb. boneless chicken breast
    meat

① {
1 t. rice wine
1½t. soy sauce
¼ t. salt
⅛ t. black pepper
1 egg yolk
1 T. cornstarch
}

② {
4 T. cornstarch
2 T. flour
}

3 C. oil for frying

③ {
¼ t. salt
3 T. sugar
2 T. lemon juice
3 T. water
½ t. cornstarch
}

❶ Remove the skin from the chicken meat (fig. 1). Lay the breast flat on counter and diagonally cut into thin slices 2½-inch x 1½-inch x ⅛-inch (fig. 2). Place the chicken meat in a bowl and add mixture ① . Marinate for 10 minutes (fig. 3). Remove the slices and dredge in mixture ② (fig. 4).

❷ Heat pan and add oil, heat to 375°F. Deep-fry the chicken slices over medium heat for 15 seconds. Stir to separate. Continue frying for 15 seconds, then remove. Increase the heat to 400°F. Deep-fry the chicken again for 10 seconds. Remove, drain, and arrange on a serving platter.

❸ Heat pan and add 1 tablespoon oil. Add mixture ③ and heat until boiling. Add 1 tablespoon oil to give the sauce a sheen. Pour over the chicken and serve immediately.

■ Garnish: See "Vegetable Garnish," P. 51.

Sweet and Sour Chicken

Substitute rice vinegar for lemon juice in mixture ③ . Prepare the recipe as directed above.

香酥雞腿

四川菜　　6 人份

雞腿(約１斤)６隻
① 鹽…………½ 大匙
　花椒粒……１ 小匙
② 酒…………１ 大匙
　蔥…………２ 枝
　薑…………２ 片
醬油………½ 大匙
麵粉………３ 大匙
(或太白粉)
「炸油」………４ 杯
椒鹽………１ 大匙

❶ 雞腿洗淨，拭乾水份，把①料炒成金黃色迸發出香味時取出（圖１），加入雞腿拌勻醃約１小時。

❷ 將醃好的雞腿放蒸盤，上擺②料，水燒開大火蒸４０分鐘，雞肉熟透取出，拭乾雞腿所溢油漬，抹上醬油（圖２），待涼沾麵粉備炸（圖３）。

❸ 鍋熱，加「炸油」４杯燒熱（３７５°F），放進雞腿炸１５秒，用鍋鏟拌動，改中火炸約３分鐘呈金黃色，視皮酥脆撈出（圖４），整隻排盤，或剁塊亦可，食時沾椒鹽。

■ 椒鹽製法：參照第１５４頁「鹽酥魚」。

■ 此菜可日常、餐宴食用，若供自助餐、野餐或便當菜亦相宜。

■ 盤飾：參照第３８頁，蘿蔔類盤飾第１３種。

蛋白質·············１０３克
脂質···············４９克
醣質···············１５克
熱量············９４０仟卡
Protein. 103g
Fat 49g
Carbohydrate. 15g
940 Kcal

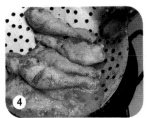

Crispy Chicken Legs

Szechuan 6 servings

6 chicken legs (about 1⅓ lbs.)

① ½ T. salt
1 t. Szechuan peppercorns

② 1 T. rice wine
2 stalks green onion
2 slices ginger root (about 3″ long)

½ T. soy sauce
3 T. flour (or cornstarch)
4 C. oil for frying
1 T. Szechuan peppercorn salt*

❶ Rinse the chicken legs and pat dry. Heat pan and add mixture ① Stir-fry until golden and fragrant (fig. 1). Mix with the chicken legs and marinate one hour.

❷ Arrange the chicken legs in a steamer tray and sprinkle mixture ② over the top. Cover and steam for 40 minutes over high heat, or until the chicken is tender. Remove and pat dry. Rub the chicken skin with soy sauce (fig. 2). Dredge the chicken legs in flour when cool (fig. 3).

❸ Heat pan and add oil, heat to 375°F. Add the chicken legs and deep-fry for 15 seconds, stir with a spatula. Continue deep-fry until golden (for about 3 minutes), over medium heat, until the skin is crisp (fig. 4). Remove and arrange the legs on a platter. Place the Szechuan peppercorn salt on a plate for dipping.

* To prepare the Szechuan peppercorn salt, see "Savory Fried Fish" on P. 154.

■ This dish is equally ideal for family dinners, banquets, buffets, picnics and lunch boxes.

■ Garnish: See "Vegetable Garnish," P. 38.

塩酥雞翼　　　　　臺灣菜　　6人份

雞翼……1斤2兩
（整隻6隻）

①┌酒…………½大匙
　│鹽…………1小匙
　└胡椒粉……¼小匙
太白粉………⅓杯
「炸油」………3杯
椒鹽………1大匙

❶ 雞翼洗淨，每隻剁3節（圖1），共剁成18塊，拭乾水份，調①料拌勻醃20分鐘，炸前沾太白粉（圖2）。

❷ 鍋熱，加「炸油」3杯燒熱（375°F），放進雞翼（圖3），炸15秒，用鍋鏟拌動，續以中火炸約2分鐘，呈金黃色皮酥脆撈起瀝淨油（圖4），盛盤上灑少許椒鹽，或將椒鹽置放盤邊，以供沾食。

■ 椒鹽製法：參照154頁「鹽酥魚」。
■ 盤飾：參照第26頁，蘿蔔類盤飾第2種。

塩酥雞腿

雞腿………12兩
①料
太白粉………⅓杯
「炸油」………3杯
椒鹽………1大匙

❶ 將雞翼改用雞腿，先把雞腿剁塊，調①料拌勻醃20分鐘，炸前沾太白粉。

❷ 參照本頁「鹽酥雞翼」做法❷。

蛋白質 ･････････１０２克
脂質 ･･･････････５０克
醣質 ･････････････５６克
熱量 ･･･････１１２８仟卡
Portein. 102g
Fat 50g
Carbohydrate 56g
1,128 Kcal

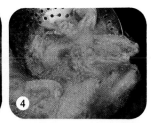

Crispy Savory Chicken Wings

Taiwanese
6 servings

6 chicken wings (about 1¾ lbs.)

① ½ T. rice wine
1 t. salt
¼ t. black pepper

⅓ C. cornstarch

3 C. oil for frying

1 T. Szechuan peppercorn
salt*

❶ Rinse the chicken wings, and cut each, through bones, into thirds. (fig. 1). Place in a bowl with mixture ① . Marinate for 20 minutes, remove and dredge the wings in cornstarch (fig. 2).

❷ Heat pan and add oil, heat to 375°F. Deep-fry the chicken wings for 15 seconds (fig. 3), stir with a spatula. Reduce heat and continue to fry for 3 minutes, or until the wings are golden and the skin is crisp (fig. 4). Remove the wings, drain and arrange on a serving platter. Sprinkle the chicken wings with the Szechuan peppercorn salt or arrange the salt in a pile on the edge of the plate for dipping.

* To prepare Szechuan peppercorn salt, see "Savory Fried Fish" on P. 154.

■ Garnish: See "Vegetable Garnish," P. 26.

Crispy Savory Chicken Legs

3-4 chicken legs (about lb.)

① same as above

⅓ C. cornstarch

3 C. oil for frying

1 T. black pepper

❶ Cut the chicken legs, through bones, into bite-size pieces. Mix with mixture ① . Marinate for 20 minutes. Before frying, coat the chicken pieces with cornstarch.

❷ Follow the procedure as outlined in Step ❷ of the recipe above.

貴妃雞　　　　　江浙菜　　6人份

雞腿２隻⋯⋯１２兩
洋葱⋯⋯⋯⋯⋯半個
紅蘿蔔⋯⋯⋯⋯半條
「炸油」⋯⋯⋯⋯３杯
① ┌ 醬油⋯⋯⋯⋯１大匙
　│ 番茄醬⋯⋯⋯３大匙
　│ 鹽⋯⋯⋯⋯⋯$\frac{1}{2}$小匙
　│ 糖⋯⋯⋯⋯⋯１大匙
　└ 水⋯⋯⋯⋯⋯１杯
② ┌ 太白粉⋯⋯⋯$\frac{1}{2}$大匙
　└ 水⋯⋯⋯⋯⋯１大匙

❶ 雞腿剁塊（圖１），調醬油１大匙拌勻備炸。洋葱切半再切片（圖２）。紅蘿蔔切滾刀塊（圖３）。
❷ 鍋熱，加「炸油」３杯燒熱（３７５℉），將雞塊順鍋邊放入，用大火炸約３０秒，呈金黃色撈出。
❸ 鍋熱，加油２大匙炒香洋葱約１分鐘，入紅蘿蔔略炒３０秒（圖４），下酒１大匙及雞塊和①料先用大火燒沸，改中火續煮１５分鐘，至汁剩一半時，以②料勾芡再淋麻油半小匙即可盛盤，趁熱佐餐。

乾烹雞

雞腿２隻⋯１２兩
① ┌ 酒⋯⋯⋯⋯⋯１大匙
　│ 醬油⋯⋯⋯１$\frac{1}{2}$大匙
　└ 「炸油」⋯⋯⋯３杯
葱・薑・蒜末(各)
⋯⋯⋯⋯⋯$\frac{1}{2}$大匙
② ┌ 醬油⋯⋯⋯⋯１大匙
　│ 鹽⋯⋯⋯⋯⋯$\frac{1}{4}$小匙
　│ 糖⋯⋯⋯⋯⋯１大匙
　│ 黑醋⋯⋯⋯⋯１大匙
　└ 水⋯⋯⋯⋯⋯３大匙

❶ 雞塊加①料攪拌，醃２０分鐘以上，炸前加太白粉１大匙半拌勻。
❷ 鍋熱，加「炸油」３杯燒熱（３７５℉），隨入雞塊，以大火炸約３分鐘呈金黃色撈出，瀝淨油。
❸ 油２大匙燒熱，炒香葱、薑、蒜末後，下酒１小匙及雞塊和②料，用大火爆炒約１分鐘至汁收乾，淋下麻油半小匙拌一下即可盛盤。
■「貴妃雞」及「乾烹雞」除用雞腿外，可用雞半隻或雞翼，其調味及做法同上。

蛋白質‥‥‥‥‥‥‥‥７６克
脂質‥‥‥‥‥‥‥‥‥４５克
醣質‥‥‥‥‥‥‥‥‥３１克
熱量‥‥‥‥‥‥‥８４３仟卡
Protein 76g
Fat 45g
Carbohydrate. 31g
843 Kcal

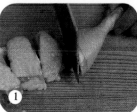

Saucy Chicken

Chekiang-Kiangsu 6 servings

4 chicken legs (about 1 lb.)
1 T. soy sauce
½ onion carrot
½ large carrot
3 C. oil for frying
1 T. rice wine

① { 1 T. soy sauce, ½ tsp. salt
3 T. catsup. 1 T. sugar
1 C. water

② { ½ T. cornstarch
1 T. water

❶ Cut the chicken, through bones, into bite-size serving pieces (fig. 1), mix the chicken pieces with soy sauce. Cut the onion into bite-size pieces (fig. 2) and roll-cut the carrot into bite-size pieces (fig. 3).

❷ Heat pan and add oil heat to 375°F. Slide the chicken pieces down the sides of the pan into the hot oil. Deep-fry for one minute or until golden over high heat. Remove the chicken and drain.

❸ Heat pan and add 2 tablespoons oil, heat until hot. Add the shredded onion and stir-fry until fragrant. Add the carrot and continue to mix for about 30 seconds (fig. 4). Sprinkle about 1 tablespoon rice wine over the chicken and add mixture ① . Bring to a boil over high heat. Reduce the heat to medium and cook for about 15 minutes, or until the liquid is reduced to half of the original amount. Add mixture ② to thicken. Sprinkle the sesame oil over the top. Toss briefly to mix and serve.

Dry-Cooked Chicken

4 chicken drumsticks
(about 1 lb.)
2 chicken thighs (about ½ lb.)

① { 1 T. rice wine.
1½T. soy sauce.
1 T. cornstarch
3 C. oil for frying

② { ½ T. minced green onion
½ T. minced ginger
½ T. minced garlic
1 t. rice wine

③ { 1 T. soy sauce
¼ t. salt
1 T. sugar
1 T. rice vinegar
3 T. water
½ t. sesame oil

❶ Cut the chicken legs and thighs, through the bones, into 6 to 8 pieces. Marinate in mixture ① for at least 20 minutes. Dredge the pieces in the cornstarch.

❷ Heat pan and add the oil. Heat the oil to 375°F. Add the chicken pieces and deep-fry over high heat for about 3 minutes, or until golden brown. Remove the chicken and drain the oil from the pan.

❸ Reheat pan and add 2 tablespoons oil, heat until hot. Add mixture ② and stir-fry until fragrant. Add the rice wine, chicken pieces and mixture ③ . Stir-fry over high heat for about 1 minute, until the liquid is almost dry and sprinkle the sesame oil over the top. Toss lightly to mix and remove to a serving platter. Serve immediately.

■ For "Saucy Chicken" and "Dry-Cooked Chicken," half a chicken or chicken wings 1 lb. may be substituted for the chicken. Prepare the recipe as directed above.

麻辣子雞

四川菜　　6人份

雞腿２隻…１２兩

① 醬油………½大匙
蛋白…………½個
（或水……１大匙）
太白粉……１大匙

青椒…………１個
紅辣椒………３條
大蒜……１½大匙
（切薄片）．
酒…………½大匙

② 醬油……１½大匙
鹽…………¼小匙
糖…………½大匙
黑醋………２小匙
太白粉……１小匙
水………１½大匙
麻油………１小匙

❶ 雞腿去骨(參照第６４頁「油淋去骨雞」圖１、２、３、４)。
將雞腿肉攤開，有筋部位用刀輕斬數下，使筋斷（圖１）
，切１.５公分寬之長條（圖２），再切成１.５公分四方小
丁（圖３），調①料拌勻，醃２０分鐘以上。

❷ 青、紅椒切開去籽，洗淨，切成與雞丁同大小之塊狀（圖４）。

❸ 鍋熱，加「油」半杯燒熱（３００℉），放進雞丁，馬上用鍋
鏟拌開，以防沾鍋，用中火泡炒約３０秒，見雞肉色變撈
出，留油３大匙炒香蒜片，再入青、紅椒略炒至剛熟約３
０秒，下酒半大匙及雞丁和②料用大火爆炒，並淋麻油１
小匙後盛盤。

■ 除雞腿肉外，改雞胸肉亦可，淨重約半斤。

蛋白質 ⋯⋯⋯⋯⋯⋯77克
脂質 ⋯⋯⋯⋯⋯⋯⋯64克
醣質 ⋯⋯⋯⋯⋯⋯⋯16克
熱量 ⋯⋯⋯⋯⋯967仟卡
Protein 77g
Fat 64g
Carbohydrate 16g
967 Kcal

Spicy Fried Chicken

Szechuan 6 servings

3-4 chicken legs (about 1 lb.)

① { ½ T. soy sauce
½ egg white (or 1 Tbsp. water)
1 T. cornstarch

1 green pepper
3 red chili peppers
1½T. minced garlic
1 C. oil for frying
½ T. rice wine

② { 1½T. soy sauce
¼ t. salt
½ T. sugar
2 t. rice vinegar
1 t. cornstarch
1½T. water

1 t. sesame oil

❶ Bone the chicken legs (as directed in "Oil-Dripped Boneless Chicken," P. 64, fig. 1, 2, 3, 4). Spread the boned meat flat on the counter and pound lightly to tenderize (fig. 1). Cut the meat, with skin, into serving pieces, ½" square and ½" thick (fig. 2, 3). Toss with mixture ① and marinate for at least 20 minutes.

❷ Remove the seeds from the green and red peppers. Rinse the peppers and cut into serving pieces (the size should be equal to the chicken). (fig. 4).

❸ Heat pan and add the oil. Heat the oil to 300°F. Add the chicken pieces and stir with a spatula to prevent sticking. Fry over medium heat for about 30 seconds, or until the chicken changes color and is almost cooked; remove. Drain all but 3 tablespoons of oil from the pan and reheat until very hot. Add the garlic and stir-fry until fragrant. Add the red and green peppers and stir-fry for 30 seconds. Add the rice wine, chicken and mixture ② . Toss lightly to mix and sprinkle with sesame oil. Toss again and remove. Serve.

■ Two-thirds pound of boneless chicken breast meat may be substituted for the chicken legs. Prepare the recipe as directed above.

三杯雞 北方菜 6人份

雞半隻‥‥‥‥1斤
冬菇‥‥‥‥‥5朵
薑片‥‥‥‥‥2片
大蒜(拍破)‥‥2粒
① 酒‥‥‥‥‥¼杯
醬油‥‥‥‥¼杯
麻油‥‥‥‥¼杯
糖‥‥‥‥‥2小匙

❶ 生雞（半隻）剁法：雞洗淨，在關節處先剁下翅膀(圖1)，雞身順直切成兩半（圖2），再將兩半分別剁成小塊（圖3）。冬菇用水泡軟，去蒂，分切成兩半（小朵勿切）。
❷ 鍋熱，加油2大匙燒熱，薑、大蒜炒香，放入雞塊用大火爆炒至雞皮呈金黃色（圖4），加入冬菇及①料，蓋上鍋蓋，中火燒開改小火燜煮20分鐘，翻轉後再燜至雞肉軟，湯汁快收乾時起鍋盛盤。或可用砂鍋燜煮至熟透時，連砂鍋一齊上桌供食。
■ 三杯雞由來：本菜原用雞一隻（約三斤重），以其①料為酒、醬油、麻油各一杯燒煮而取名。倘雞之重量如有變更，其①料得酌量增減。

三元蒸雞

雞半隻‥‥‥‥1斤
乾桂圓‥‥‥‥10粒
（或荔枝肉）
① 紅棗‥‥‥‥‥10粒
枸杞‥‥‥‥‥1大匙
鹽‥‥‥‥‥½小匙
水‥‥‥‥‥3杯

❶ 雞剁法參照本頁「三杯雞」做法❶。
❷ 將雞塊放入滾水內川燙30秒撈出，入燉盅加①料蓋燉盅蓋，擺進蒸籠（鍋）內，水燒開大火蒸約40分鐘。（宜於秋冬進補食用。）

蛋白質・・・・・・・・・・・７５克
脂質・・・・・・・・・・・・・・・・４４克
醣質・・・・・・・・・・・・・・・・・５克
熱量・・・・・・・・・・・７２３仟卡
Protein. 75g
Fat 44g
Carbohydrate. 5g
723 Kcal

1

2

3

4

"Three-Cup" Red-Cooked Chicken

Peking
6 servings

½ whole frying chicken
 (about 1⅓ lbs.)
5 Chinese black mushrooms
2 slices ginger, smashed
2 Cloves garlic, smashed

① ⎧ ¼ C. rice wine
 ⎪ ¼ C. soy sauce
 ⎨ ¼ C. sesame oil
 ⎩ 2 t. sugar

❶ To cut the chicken: Rinse the chicken-half and pat dry. Cut away the wings (fig. 1). Cut the chicken in half, through the bones, (fig. 2), and cut into bite-size serving pieces (fig. 3). Soak the black mushrooms in warm water to cover until soft and spongy. Drain, discard the stems and cut the mushroom caps in half.

❷ Heat pan and add 2 tablespoons oil until very hot. Add the ginger, garlic and stir-fry until fragrant. Add the chicken pieces and stir-fry over high heat until the pieces are golden (fig. 4). Add the black mushrooms, mixture ① , and cover the pan; or, the mixture may be placed in a casserole. Heat until boiling over medium heat. Reduce the heat to low and simmer for 20 minutes, or, until the chicken is tender. Remove the lid, turn over the chicken and continue to cook until the liquid is almost evaporated. Remove to a serving plate. When using a casserole, serve directly from the pot.

■ Traditionally, a whole chicken is used in this recipe, with one cup each of wine, soy sauce, and sesame oil. It is from these 3 cups of ingredients that the name is derived. Since this recipe uses only half a chicken, the rest of the ingredients have been reduced proportionately.

Steamed Flavorful Chicken

½ whole chicken
 (about 1⅓ lbs.)

① ⎧ 10 longans or dragon eyes
 ⎪ 10 Chinese dried red dates
 ⎪ softened in warm water
 ⎨ about 30 minutes
 ⎪ ½ t. salt
 ⎩ 3 C. water

❶ Prepare the chicken as directed in Step ❶ of the recipe above.

❷ Blanch the chicken pieces to cover for 30 seconds. Remove, drain, and place in a heatproof bowl with mixture ① . Cover, place in a covered steamer tray and steam for 40 minutes over high heat. Remove and serve. (This dish is especially fine during winter).

醉雞

四川菜　6人份

雞半隻………1斤
（或雞腿）
① | 葱…………2枝
　 | 薑…………2片
　 | 鹽…………2小匙
② | 紹興酒………1杯
　 | （或米酒）
　 | 雞湯汁………1杯

❶ 雞洗淨拭乾水份，將①料抹勻雞身內外，醃1小時以上。

❷ 蒸法：將醃過的雞擺在蒸盤內，雞胸朝上，水燒開大火蒸
　　　　15分鐘，熄火待涼取出（圖1）。

　煮法：鍋內加水5杯，將醃過的雞放入，水需淹蓋雞身，
　　　　蓋上鍋蓋，大火燒開改小火燜煮約10分鐘，熄火
　　　　再燜約5分鐘，取出待涼。

❸ 蒸（或煮）好的雞剁成小塊（圖2），備中型湯碗，將有
　肉的雞塊雞皮朝碗底整齊排列（圖3），中間添滿較有骨
　的雞塊，排滿後倒入②料（圖4），擺進冰箱浸泡約1天
　取出用小盤或鍋鏟壓住雞塊，傾斜倒出酒汁，再反扣菜盤
　內，淋進泡雞酒汁即成。

❹ 另一方法：將蒸（或煮）好的雞，待涼分切成兩大塊，放
　進大碗或其他容器內，調入②料，擺進冰箱浸泡約1天，
　食時取出再剁成小塊置盤，再澆淋泡雞酒汁少許便可。

■ 如不喜愛酒味太濃，可將②料之酒酌量減少。

醉蛤蜊

大蛤蜊………1斤
紹興酒………½杯
① | 高湯…………½杯
　 | 鹽…………½小匙
　 | 味精………¼小匙
　 | 大蒜(拍破)…6粒
　 | 葱段(2公分)6枝
　 | 薑片………6片

❶ 水6杯燒沸，放入蛤蜊川燙約1分鐘，至蛤殼微開撈起。

❷ 將①料盛大碗內，放進燙好之蛤蜊，擺進冰箱浸泡1小時
　以上即可食用。

■ 蛤蜊吐沙法：參照第204頁「蛤蜊蒸蛋」。

蛋白質・・・・・・・・・・・・９０克
脂質・・・・・・・・・・・・・・・１７克
醣質・・・・・・・・・・・・・・・１７克
熱量・・・・・・・・・・・５３６仟卡

Protein. 90g
Fat 17g
Carbohydrate 17g
536 Kcal

Drunken Chicken

Szechuan 6 servings

½ whole frying chicken or chicken legs (about 1⅓ lbs.)

① {
2 stalks green onion, smashed
2 slices ginger root, smashed
2 t. salt
}

② {
1 C. Shaohsing wine (or rice wine)
1 C. chicken broth
}

❶ Rinse the chicken and pat dry. Prepare mixture ① and rub into the cavity of the chicken and along the exterior. Marinate for at least 1 hour.

❷ Steam or boil the chicken:
To steam: Place the chicken in a steamer and cover. Place the steamer over boiling water and steam for 15 minutes over high heat. Remove the chicken and reserve the broth from steaming for mixture ② . (If necessary, add water to equal 1 cup.) (fig. 1).
To boil: Place the 5 cups water in a pot and heat until boiling. Add the chicken and additional water to cover the chicken. Cover and heat over high heat. When the water boils, turn the heat to low and simmer for 10 minutes. Remove from heat and let stand, covered, for 5 minutes. Remove the chicken and reserve 1 cup of chicken broth for mixture ②

❸ Cut the chicken, through bones, into bite-size serving pieces (fig. 2). Arrange the meatier pieces of the chicken to cover the bottom of a heatproof medium-size soup bowl (fig. 3). Place the pieces so that the skin-side of the chicken pieces face the bowl. Layer the rest of the chicken on top and pour ② over all (fig. 4). Place the bowl in the refrigerator for one day. To serve, use a small plate or the flat part of a spatula to hold the meat in the bowl and drain off the marinade. Hold a serving plate over the top of the bowl and invert the chicken onto the plate.

❹ Alternate method: Allow the steamed chicken to cool, cut in half, and place in a large bowl with mixture ② . Refrigerate for 1 day; remove and cut into bite-size serving pieces. Arrange the cut pieces on a serving platter, spoon some of the wine marinade on top and serve.

■ The quantity of wine in mixture ② may be reduced if the flavor is too strong.

Drunken Clams

1⅓ lbs. steamer clams

[1] {
½ C. rice wine
½ C. chicken broth
½ t. salt
¼ t. MSG
6 cloves garlic
6 1-inch sections green onion
6 slices ginger
}

❶ To clean the clams, place the clams in water as directed in step ❶ "Steamed Eggs with Clams," P. 204.

❷ Place 6 cups water in a pot with the clams and heat until boiling. Cook briefly, until the clam shells being to open. Remove quickly, and drain. (These clams should not cook too long or they will lose their flavor.)

❸ Place mixture [1] and the clams in a bowl and mix. (The marinade should cover the clams, if it doesn't increase the quantity.) Refrigerate for at least 2 hours before serving.

腰果雞丁

廣東菜　　6人份

雞胸‥‥‥‥１２兩
（淨重約‥８兩）

① {
酒‥‥‥‥‥‥１小匙
鹽‥‥‥‥‥½小匙
蛋白‥‥‥‥½個
（或水１大匙）
太白粉‥‥‥２小匙
}

青椒‥‥‥‥‥１個
葱段‥‥‥‥‥６枝
薑‥‥‥‥１２小片
腰果‥‥‥‥‥３兩

② {
水‥‥‥‥‥‥１杯
鹽‥‥‥‥‥½小匙
}

「炸油」‥‥‥‥３杯
酒‥‥‥‥‥‥２小匙

③ {
鹽‥‥‥‥‥½小匙
味精‥‥‥‥¼小匙
糖‥‥‥‥‥½小匙
胡椒粉‥‥‥⅛小匙
麻油‥‥‥‥½小匙
太白粉‥‥‥１小匙
水‥‥‥‥‥２大匙
}

腰果‥‥‥‥‥３兩
（或核桃、松子）

1 {
水‥‥‥‥‥‥１杯
糖‥‥‥‥‥４大匙
蜂蜜‥‥‥‥２大匙
「炸油」‥‥‥３杯
}

雞胸去骨法：由翅膀關節處切開，骨輪周圍之筋切斷（圖１），順鎖骨兩邊各劃一刀，使骨與肉脫離（圖２），一手抓住兩翅，另一手抓緊骨架，互拉取出肉（圖３），再將兩條雞柳先以刀劃開再取出（圖４）。

❶ 將胸肉攤開，用刀背搥鬆，先切１.５公分寬之長條，再切成１.５公分之四方小丁，調①料拌勻，醃３０分鐘以上。青椒去籽切１公分小塊。

❷ 腰果洗淨，放入②料內，用中火煮約５分鐘撈起，瀝乾。「炸油」３杯燒熱（２７５℉），放進煮過的腰果，需時時用鍋鏟攪動，小火炸約６分鐘呈金黃色，撈出，攤開在鋪有紙之盤上，便於吸油，待涼即脆。

❸ 鍋熱，加「炸油」３杯燒熱（２７５℉）放入雞丁泡炒約４０秒見雞丁色轉白撈出；留油２大匙先炒香葱、薑入青椒略炒，再下雞丁、酒及③料用大火爆炒數下熄火，再加入腰果拌勻，速以盛盤，趁熱供食。

■ 除雞肉外，可用豬里肌或嫩牛肉，牛肉切片，處理參照第128頁「芥蘭牛肉」做法❶，其他做法及調味同上。腰果可改用核桃、松子或花生代替。

糖酥腰果

❶ 參照本頁「腰果雞丁」做法❷，祇把②料改用1料，其他做法相同。

■ 除蜂蜜外，可用麥牙糖或冰糖，如無可全部用糖，祇是炸出後較無光澤。

蛋白質·············９８克
脂質··············９９克
醣質··············３３克
熱量········１３８５仟卡

Protein 98g
Fat 99g
Carbohydrate. 33g
1,385 Kcal

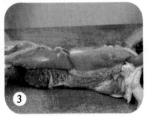
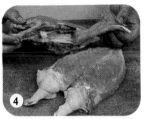

Stir-Fried Chicken with Cashews

Cantonese 6 servings

1 lb.	whole chicken breast (or ¾ lb. boneless chicken meat)

① {
- 1 t. rice wine
- ½ t. salt
- ½ eggwhite (or 1 Tbsp. water)
- 2 t. cornstarch

- 3 C. oil for frying
  stalks green onions
  (½-inch lengths)
- 12 slices ginger (⅜-inch square)
- ½ t. rice wine
- 1 green pepper
- ¼ lb. raw cashews*

② {
- 1 C. water
- ½ t. salt

③ {
- ½ t. salt
- ¼ t. MSG
- ½ t. sugar
- ⅛ t. black pepper
- ½ t. sesame oil
- 2 T. water
- 1 t. cornstarch

To bone the chicken breast: Rinse the chicken breast and past dry. To remove the breast bones, first cut away the wings. Cut through the tendons (fig. 1). Make a cut in each shoulder joint to serve the shoulder muscles. Start to cut away the meat from the bones (fig. 2). Hold the carcass in one hand and pull away the meat from the carcass with the other hand (fig. 3). Remove the wishbone and run the knife between the filet mignon pieces and the carcass. Pull away the filet mignon pieces from the carcass (fig. 4).

❶ Cut the meat into ½-inch squares. Toss the chicken with mixture ① and marinate for at least 30 minutes. Remove the seeds from the green pepper and cut into ⅜-inch pieces.

❷ Wash the raw cashews. Place in a pan with mixture ② and boil over medium heat for 5 minutes. Remove the cashews and drain. Heat pan and add the oil. Heat the oil to 275°F and deep-fry the cashews, stir occasionally. Reduce the heat to low and continue to fry for about 6 minutes, or until golden. Remove the cashews and drain on brown paper to absorb the excess oil.

❸ Reheat pan and add oil, heat to 275°F. Add the chicken and deep-fry for about 40 seconds, or until the color of meat changes, and the chicken is almost cooked. Remove and drain. Remove all but 2 Tbsp. oil from the pan and reheat until very hot. Add the green onions, ginger slices, and stir-fry until fragrant. Add the green pepper and stir-fry for several seconds. Add the rice wine, chicken and mixture ③ . Toss lightly to combine the ingredients and remove from the heat. Add the cashews and toss quickly. Serve immediately.

* If dry-roasted cashews are used, omit Step ❷ .

■ Boneless pork loin or flank steak may be substituted for the chicken. To prepare, thinly slice flank steak or pork loin and marinate in mixture ① (see "Stir-fried Saucy Beef") Prepare the recipe as directed above. Walnuts, pine nuts or peanuts may also be substituted for the cashews.

Crunchy Cashews

❶ Prepare the recipe as directed above, substitute mixture ⬜1 for mixture ②
■ Malt sugar or rock sugar may be substituted for the honey.

- ¼ lb. raw cashews
  (walnuts or pine nuts)

⬜1 {
- 1 C. water
- 4 T. sugar
- 2 T. honey
- 3 C. oil for frying

松子雞米

江浙菜　　6人份

雞胸 1 個…12 兩

①
酒…………½ 大匙
鹽…………½ 小匙
蛋白…………½ 個
（或水…1 大匙）
太白粉……½ 大匙

「炸油」……3 杯
松子…………1 兩
葱花……1 大匙

②
鹽…………½ 小匙
味精………¼ 小匙
太白粉……1 小匙
水…………2 小匙

❶ 雞胸去骨、皮後淨肉 6 兩，片切薄片（圖 1），再切細絲（圖 2），然後切小丁成粒狀（圖 3），調①料拌勻醃 20 分鐘。

❷ 鍋熱，加「炸油」3 杯，冷油放進松子，用鍋鏟不停攪動，以中火炸約 4 分鐘呈金黃色撈出，瀝淨油備用。
將油擱置片刻，使油溫降熱（275℉），放入雞肉粒，迅速以筷子或鍋鏟撥散，至肉色轉白且熟撈出。

❸ 鍋熱，加油 1 大匙，將葱花炒香，隨入雞米及②料，以中火拌炒即可盛盤，上灑炸好的松子（圖 4），食時拌勻。

■ 雞胸去骨法：參照第 80 頁「腰果雞丁」。

蛋白質⋯⋯⋯⋯⋯６２克
脂質⋯⋯⋯⋯⋯⋯７２克
醣質⋯⋯⋯⋯⋯⋯１１克
熱量⋯⋯⋯⋯⋯９４１仟卡
Protein. 62g
Fat 72g
Carbohydrate. 11g
941 Kcal

1

2

3

4

Stir-Fried Chicken Shreds with Pine Nuts
Chekiang-Kiangsu 6 servings

1 lb. boneless chicken
breast meat

①
½ T. rice wine
½ t. salt
½ t. egg white (or 1 Tbsp. water)
½ T. cornstarch

②
1 T. chopped green onion
½ t. salt
¼ t. MSG
1 t. cornstarch
2 t. water
1½ oz. pine nuts
3 C. oil for frying

❶ Cut the chicken into paper-thin slices (fig. 1) and shred the meat to pieces about the size of rice grains (fig. 2, 3). Place in a bowl with mixture ① and marinate for 20 minutes.

❷ Heat pan and add oil, heat to about 200°F. Add the pine nuts and fry for about 4 minutes, or until golden. Remove and drain. Reduce heat so that the oil temperature is about 275°F. Add the chicken and stir-fry until the color changes, stir constantly with a spatula. Remove and drain.

❸ Reheat pan and add 1 Tbsp. oil until very hot. Add the green onions and stir-fry until fragrant. Add the chicken shreds and mixture ② . Toss lightly to mix the ingredients. Remove to a serving platter and sprinkle the top with the pine nuts (fig. 4). Toss lightly, before eating.

塩焗雞 (改良)　　　　　　　　　　廣東菜　　12人份

雞1隻………2斤

① {
酒…………2大匙
鹽…………1大匙
葱…………2枝
薑…………2片
八角………1朵
花椒粒……$\frac{1}{2}$大匙
}

沾料 {
鹽…………2小匙
味精………$\frac{1}{4}$小匙
葱末………1大匙
薑末………2大匙
雞湯………$\frac{1}{4}$杯
葱…………2枝
}

❶將①料抹勻雞身內外，醃1小時以上，最後將葱、薑、八角、花椒粒塞入腹內（圖1）。

❷煮法：鍋內加水約10杯，將醃過的雞擺進，水需淹至雞身一半以上為宜（圖2），蓋鍋大火燒開改小火燜煮約10分鐘，把雞翻轉續煮10分鐘，熄火再燜約10分鐘，取出待涼。

　蒸法：將醃過的雞擺在蒸盤內，雞胸朝上，水開大火蒸約25分鐘，熄火待涼取出。

❸備乾淨炒鍋，置爐上燒至極熱，手持雞腿，將雞身在極熱的鍋面觸炙，使雞身遍呈焦黃色（圖3、4），即可剁塊置盤，食時蘸沾料。（剁雞及排盤法：參照第60頁。）

❹沾料製法：將油2大匙燒滾，沖入沾料內再加煮（或蒸）雞湯汁$\frac{1}{4}$杯拌勻即可沾食。

塩焗雞 (古法)

雞1隻………2斤
①料
宣紙…………1張
（或玻璃紙）
粗鹽…………6斤
八角（拍碎）…2朵
花椒粒……1小匙
沾料

❶參照「改良塩焗雞」做法❶，將醃好的雞用宣紙包裹備用。

❷粗鹽放進炒鍋內，加八角、花椒粒炒極熱至鹽發出爆音（試鹽的熱度，可用一張紙捲成筒狀，插入熱鹽中，立即冒出烟，且紙呈焦黃色時即可），將鹽先倒$\frac{1}{3}$入深底鍋內，把雞放進，再將餘鹽倒入，把雞全埋入鹽內，蓋上鍋蓋，以小火用鹽焗15分鐘後，熄火再燜5分鐘，至雞熟取出，把紙撕開，剁塊擺盤，即可與盛沾料之小碟一齊上桌，以供沾食。

84

蛋白質‧‧‧‧‧‧‧‧‧‧‧１９４克
脂質‧‧‧‧‧‧‧‧‧‧‧‧‧‧‧３６克
醣質‧‧‧‧‧‧‧‧‧‧‧‧‧‧‧３６克
熱量‧‧‧‧‧‧‧‧‧１１５８仟卡

Protein. 194g
Fat 36g
Carbohydrate. 36g
1,158 Kcal

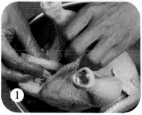

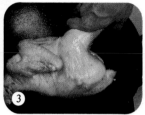
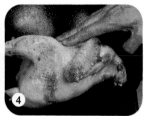

Seared Chicken — Cantonese 12 servings

1 whole frying chicken
  (about 2½ lbs.)

①
2 T. rice wine
1 T. salt
2 stalks green onion, smashed
2 sices ginger, smashed
1 star anise
½ T. Szechuan peppercorns

Dipping sauce:

②
2 t. salt
¼ t. MSG
1 T. minced green onion
2 T. minced ginger
¼ C. chicken broth

❶ Prepare mixture ① and rub it in the cavity and over the exterior of the chicken. Stuff the green onion stalks, ginger slices, star anise and Szechuan peppercorns into the cavity of the chicken and marinate for 1 hour (fig. 1).

❷ **To boil:** Add 10 cups of water to a pot and heat until boiling. Place the chicken in the water (add, more water if necessary, so that the chicken is half-covered, (fig. 2). Cook over high heat until boiling. Lower the heat to medium and cook for 10 minutes. Turn over the chicken and cook for an additional 10 minutes. Turn off the heat and let the chicken stand for 10 minutes. Remove the chicken and let cool.
To steam: Place the chicken in a steamer and cover. Place the steamer over boiling water and steam for 25 minutes over high heat. Remove the chicken and let cool.

❸ Rub the inside of a no-stick pan with a paper towel dipped on oil. Heat the pan until very hot. Grasp the chicken by the legs, place it against the side of the pan for about 10 seconds, until that section of skin becomes scorched. Repeat this procedure until most of the body is covered with dark brown patches (fig. 3, 4). Cut the chicken into bite-size pieces and arrange on a serving platter (see P. 60). Before eating, dip the chicken in the dipping sauce.

❹ To prepare the dipping sauce, heat 2 tablespoons oil in a pan until very hot, add mixture ② and stir-fry until fragrant. Add the chicken broth and mix. Remove and pour into a small bowl.

Traditional Seared Chicken

1 frying chicken (about 2½ lbs.)
① same as above
30-inch square rice paper or
  parchment paper
8 lbs. coarse salt
2 chopped stars anise
1 t. Szechuan peppercorns

Dipping sauce:
  same as above

❶ Prepare mixture ① and marinate with the chicken as directed above in step ❶ . Wrap the chicken in the rice paper or the parchment paper.

❷ Heat pan and add the salt, star anise and Szechuan peppercorns. Stir-fry over high heat until the salt begins to pop. To test the temperature, insert a rolled-up piece of white paper in the salt. If the paper turns brown or begins to smoke, turn off the heat and transfer one-third of the salt to a deep pot. Place the wrapped chicken on top of the salt and cover the chicken completely with the remaining heated soft. Cover the pot and cook over low heat for 15 minutes. Turn off the heat and let the pot stand for 5 minutes. Remove the chicken from the pot and tear off the paper. Cut the chicken, through bones, into bite-size serving pieces. Arrange the chicken on a serving platter and serve with the dipping sauce (see recipe shown above).

滷水乳鴿

廣東菜　　6人份

乳鴿…………2隻
水…………2½杯
紹興酒……2大匙
① （或酒）
鹽…………½大匙
冰糖（或糖）3大匙
醬油…………1杯
花椒
八角
② 陳皮
香 桂皮 ┐共半兩
料 丁香 ┘
草菓
甘草
麻油………½大匙

❶ 乳鴿去除內臟及鴿脚，再用熱水燙洗乾淨。

❷ 將①料，②料盛鍋燒開，隨加醬油，用小火續煮１０分鐘後，放進乳鴿小火燜煮５分鐘，即把乳鴿翻轉，再燒５分鐘，熄火，蓋鍋蓋浸泡１０分鐘後，取出抹上麻油（以增光澤）待剁。

❸ 剁法：先切斷鴿頸（圖１），再由鴿背切開成兩半（圖２）。每半部剁成３大塊，１隻共剁６塊（圖３）整齊排盤（圖４）。

滷雞：將鴿子改用雞半隻約１斤，把①料加倍，燒煮時間延長至１５分鐘，其他烹調方式同上。

滷鴨：鴨半隻，做法，調味料與滷雞同；煮的時間延至２５分鐘。

簡易滷法：又稱醬油滷，香料不易購得或不喜歡香料味，可免用②料，僅以①料燜煮。

■②料可在中藥店購買，並用小布袋裝妥。

■冰糖裝進塑膠袋內，用刀背拍碎使用。

■滷汁使用次數愈多愈香，如滷汁漸減少，可按原比例酌量加入，爲避免滷汁變質，可放進冰箱。滷汁亦可用來滷豬肝、豬舌、豬肚、蛋、豆腐干……等。

■盤飾：參照第４４頁，蘿蔔類盤飾第１８種。

蛋白質‥‥‥‥‥‥‥74克
脂質‥‥‥‥‥‥‥‥49克
醣質‥‥‥‥‥‥‥‥49克
熱量‥‥‥‥‥‥754仟卡
Protein. 74g
Fat 49g
Carbohydrate 49g
754 Kcal

Red-Cooked Squab

Cantonese 4 servings

2 squab (about 1 lb.)

① {
2½ C. water
2 T. rice wine
½ T. salt
3 T. rock sugar or granulated sugar
1 C. soy sauce
}

*② pices {
Szechuan peppercorns
star anise
dried tangerine peel
stick of cinnamon
whole cloves
fennel
liquorice powder
½ T. sesame oil
} weight equal to total ¾ oz.

❶ Rinse the squab inside and out and remove the feet. Pour boiling water over each squab to clean.

❷ Heat ① and ② until boiling, then add the soy sauce. Simmer for 10 minutes and add the squab. Simmer 5 minutes; turn the squab over. Cook for 5 minutes more. Turn off the heat, cover, and let stand for 10 minutes. Remove the squab and rub the skin of each with sesame oil.

❸ Cutting method: First cut off the neck (fig. 1). Cut the body in half lengthwise along the backbone (fig. 2). Divide each half into 3 pieces, for a total of 6 pieces per bird (fig. 3). Arrange the pieces on a plate to resemble the whole bird (fig. 4).

Red-Cooked Chicken

Substitute half of a whole chicken (1⅓ lbs.) for the squab. Double the amount of mixture ① . Increase the initial cooking time to 15 minutes. The remaining steps are the same as directed above.

Red-Cooked Duckling

Use half of a whole duckling. The ingredients and cooking procedures are the same as for "Red-Cooked Chicken," but the initial cooking time should be increased to 25 minutes. Simple Red-Cooked Method: If the spices are unavailable or the combination does not suit your taste, they may be omitted. Use only ① to cook the food.

* The ingredients of ② may be purchased at a Chinese food store. Wrap up in a piece of cheese cloth to cook as a "bouuet garni." Place the rock sugar in a plastic bag and mash into smaller pieces with the back of a cleaver.

■ The red-cooked liquid becomes tastier, the more it is used. As the amount of liquid decreases, add ingredients ① and soy sauce proportionately. Refrigerate to prevent spoilage.

■ Garnish: See "Vegetable Garnish," P. 44.

醬鴨

北方菜　　12人份

鴨１隻………３斤
　酒…………３大匙
　甜麵醬……４大匙
　醬油………４大匙
①　糖…………１大匙
　五香粉……１小匙
　葱…………２枝
　薑…………２片
　滾水………５杯

❶ 鴨洗淨拭乾水份（圖１）， 把①料預先調拌（圖２）， 抹匀鴨身内外（圖３），醃約２小時。

❷ 將醃好的鴨連醃汁及滾水５杯置鍋内（圖４），蓋上鍋蓋，燒沸後改小火燜煮約１小時半，燜煮時須常常翻轉鴨身，以防黏鍋，俟鴨身熟透（用筷子或叉子可輕易插入），湯汁約剩１杯時即熄火再燜２０分鐘後取出，待涼剁塊，再澆淋醬鴨汁於其上便成。（剁鴨法請參照第６１頁）

■ 可用快鍋燒煮，醃好的鴨連汁及滾水４杯置鍋内，蓋鍋，燒沸後用中火煮約３０分鐘至鴨肉熟透，待涼打開快鍋蓋，如鴨未熟透時，仍用原鍋繼續燒煮至湯汁剩約１杯，其他做法同上。

■ 可用烘烤方法：將烤箱燒至３５０℉，把醃好的鴨置烤盤放進烤箱底層，以３５０℉烘烤約１小時半後，試以筷子或刀叉，若易於插入鴨身則已熟透。

■ 除鴨外，雞、豬前腿肉均可，做法同上。

蛋白質‥‥‥‥‥１９８克
脂質‥‥‥‥‥‥１６１克
醣質‥‥‥‥‥‥１５８克
熱量‥‥‥‥１７５９仟卡
Protein. 198g
Fat 161g
Carbohydrate. 158g
1,759 Kcal

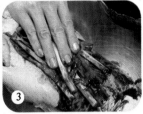
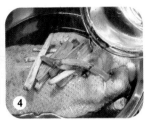

Saucy Stewed Duckling Peking 12 servings

1 whole duckling (about 4 lbs.)
3 T. rice wine
4 T. sweet bean paste
4 T. soy sauce
① 1 T. sugar
1 t. five-spice powder
2 stalks green onion
2 slices ginger root
5 C. boiling water

❶ Rinse the duckling and pat dry (fig. 1). Prepare mixture ① (fig. 2) and rub evenly into the cavity and over the entire exterior of the duckling (fig. 3). Marinate for about 2 hours.

❷ Place the duckling and marinade in a pot with 5 C. of boiling water (fig. 4). Cover and heat until boiling. Turn the heat to low and cook about 1½ hours until the duckling is done. Turn frequently to prevent the duckling from sticking to the pan. To test for doneness, stick the breast with of fork or chopstick. The sauce should be reduced to about 1 cup. Turn off the heat and let stand sit covered for 20 minutes. Remove the duckling and allow to cool. Cut through the bones into bite-size serving pieces (see P. 61 for cutting method). Arrange the pieces on a serving platter and spoon the reduced sauce over the duckling. Serve.

■ Pressure cooker method: Place the marinated duckling and 4 C. boiling water in a pressure cooker and cook over medium heat about 30 minutes on until the duckling is cooked. When the duckling is cool, open the pressure cooker. If the duckling is not done, cook again until 1 cup of liquid remains. Cut and serve as above.

■ Roasting method: Preheat the oven to 350°F. Place the duckling (omit water) in a roasting pan on the lowest shelf and roast for about 1½ hours. Test with a chopstick or fork for doneness.

■ A whole chicken or a fresh ham may be substituted for the duckling. The seasoning should be adjusted in relation to the weight of the meat. Other steps of the procedure are the same as stated above.

鳳梨炒鴨片

廣東菜　　6人份

鴨肉…………4兩

薑酒汁……1大匙

① 鹽…………¼小匙
胡椒粉……⅛小匙
太白粉……1大匙

鳳梨…………適量
（罐頭或新鮮）

青椒…………1個

嫩薑………1大匙
（切小片）

② 鳳梨汁……3大匙
（或水）
鹽…………¼小匙
味精………¼小匙
太白粉……¼小匙

麻油………½大匙

❶ 鴨肉去皮斜切薄片（圖１），調①料拌勻。鳳梨每片切４小塊（圖２）。青椒切塊（圖３、４）。

❷ 熱鍋，加「油」半杯燒熱（３５０℉），將鴨肉下鍋馬上用鍋鏟拌開，以大火泡炒見肉色轉白，約３０秒鏟出，餘油略炒嫩薑片，隨入鳳梨片，青椒拌炒約３０秒，再倒進已泡過油之鴨肉及②料用大火爆炒，最後淋油拌勻（以增光澤），便可盛盤。

■ 薑酒汁：薑片拍碎加酒所擠出的汁。

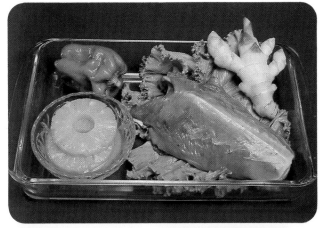

蛋白質‧‧‧‧‧‧‧‧‧‧‧‧‧‧３６克
脂質‧‧‧‧‧‧‧‧‧‧‧‧‧‧‧‧７７克
醣質‧‧‧‧‧‧‧‧‧‧‧‧‧‧‧３７克
熱量‧‧‧‧‧‧‧‧‧‧‧９６９仟卡
Protein 36g
Fat 77g
Carbohydrate 37g
969 Kcal

Stir-Fried Duckling and Pineapple

Cantonese 6 servings

6 oz. duckling meat

① {
1 T. ginger-wine*
¼ t. salt
⅛ t. black pepper
1 T. cornstarch
}

3 slices pineapple
  (canned or fresh)

1 green pepper

1 T. diced fresh ginger

② {
3 T. pineapple juice
  (or water)
¼ t. salt
¼ t. MSG
¼ t. cornstarch
}

½ T. oil

❶ Remove the skin from the duckling meat. Cut the meat into thin slices (fig. 1). Mix the duckling slices with ① ; marinate 20 minutes. Cut each pineapple slice into 4 pieces (fig. 2). Remove the stem and seeds from the green pepper and cut into bite-size pieces (fig. 3, 4).

❷ Heat pan and add ½C. oil heat to about 350°F. Add the duckling slices, stir immediately to separate. After 30 seconds, or when the meat changes color, remove. Reheat oil and stir-fry ginger until fragrant. Add the pineapple and green peppers and stir-fry for about 30 seconds. Add the cooked duckling slices, mixture ② and heat until boiling. Toss lightly to combine the ingredients. Add ½ Tbsp. oil to make the dish shiny. Remove to a serving plate. Serve.

* To prepare ginger-wine, mash 1 slice ginger root and mix with 1 Tbsp. rice wine. Pinch the ginger slice to imbibe the wine with the ginger flavor. Remove the ginger slice and use the liquid as directed.

烤鴨　　　　　　　　　　廣東菜　　12人份

鴨1隻‥‥‥‥3斤
①{
五香粉‥‥‥1小匙
鹽‥‥‥‥‥1大匙

繩子‥‥‥‥‥1條

②{
麥芽糖‥‥‥2大匙
（或蜂蜜）
滾開水‥‥‥1杯
白醋‥‥‥‥½大匙
酒‥‥‥‥‥2大匙

❶鴨洗淨拭乾水份，把①料放入鴨肚內抹勻（圖1），開口處以牙籤封好或針線縫合（圖2）。將繩打結由鴨頸或雙翅處套上吊起（圖3），用滾開水燙淋鴨身多次，使鴨皮燙熱易於吸收②料的糖汁。

❷將②料依序放入碗內調勻後，把糖汁澆淋在鴨身上盡量淋勻鴨皮（圖4），澆淋後不要碰觸鴨皮，以防糖汁脫落使烤出的鴨皮色澤（醬紅色）不勻，然後吊在通風處風乾（約需6小時）。

❸用烤箱以350°F烘烤45分鐘即可取出，待涼剁塊。（剁法：請參照第61頁）

■做此菜時宜天氣晴朗，晾在通風處風乾，如時間不夠可在陽光下曝曬至鴨皮上的糖汁曬乾（約2小時），遇天氣不好可用烤箱200°F烘烤約1小時至鴨皮乾，或電扇吹乾。

烤雞

❶將鴨改用雞（2～2½斤），參照烤鴨做法❶❷。

❷用烤箱以350°F烘烤約30分鐘即成。

❸或用油炸法：「炸油」6杯燒熱（275°F），將雞胸朝下放入鍋裏（預先弄破眼球以免油爆），用小火炸10分鐘後，翻面再炸5分鐘，試以筷子、鐵針或刀叉插入腿或胸肉厚處，若無血水流出即熟，臨起鍋改用大火炸1分鐘炸至皮脆肉嫩時，撈出剁塊。（剁法：參照第60頁）。

蛋白質 ··········· ２０５克
脂質 ················ ９７克
醣質 ··············· １６克
熱量 ········ １８０５仟卡

Protein 205g
Fat 97g
Carbohydrate 16g
1,805 Kcal

 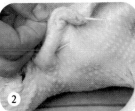 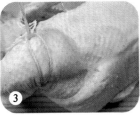 

Roasted Duckling

Cantonese 12 servings

1 whole duckling (about 4 lbs).

① { 1 t. five-spice powder
    1 T. salt

1 piece of trussing string

② { 2 T. brown sugar or honey
    1 C. boiling water
    ½ T. rice vinegar
    2 T. rice wine

❶ Rinse the duckling and pat dry. Rub mixture ① in the cavity of the duckling (fig. 1). Sew up the opening or secure with toothpicks (fig. 2). Tie the trussing string around the neck of the duckling or across both wings and hold suspended (fig. 3). Rinse the duckling several times by repeatedly pouring boiling water over the skin to open the pores. (The duckling skin will then absorb liquid easier).

❷ Mix together the ingredients of ② , in descending order, in a wok or bowl. Spread the mixture repeatedly and evenly over the entire duckling until well-coated (fig. 4). Avoid touching the skin after coating so that the marinade will coat evenly and the color of the roasted duckling will also be even. Hang up the duckling in a well-ventilated area and let dry about 6 hours.

❸ Preheat the oven to 350°F. Roast the duckling for 45 minutes. Allow to cool for a moment, then cut into bite-size serving pieces and arrange on a serving plate. (See P. 61 for cutting method.)

■ A cool, breezy day is ideal for making this dish. Hang the duckling in a windy, well-ventilated place to dry out. To hasten the drying process, hang the duckling in a sunny place about two hours, until the marinade on the skin appears dry. If the weather conditions are not favorable, preheat the oven to 200°F and roast the duckling suspended for about an hour or until the skin appears dry. A fan may also be used to dry the skin. If the duckling is not to be roasted immediately after drying, refrigerate until roasting.

Roasted Chicken

❶ Use a 2½ to a 3-lb frying or roasting chicken instead of a duckling. Follow steps ❶ and ❷ of the recipe shown above.

❷ Preheat the oven to 350°F and roast for about 30 minutes. Remove and serve as directed above.

■ Alternate deep-frying method: Slice the chicken's eyes before frying so that they won't explode in the hot oil. Heat 6 C. oil until medium hot (275°F). Place the chicken, breast-side down in the oil. Reduce the heat to low and deep-fry for 10 minutes. Turn the chicken over and for 5 minutes. To test the chicken for doneness, prick a thick section of the leg or breast with a fork or chopstick. If the resulting liquid is clear, the chicken is done. Turn the heat to high and deep-fry 1 minute until the skin is crisp. The meat should be moist and tender. Remove and drain. Allow the chicken to cool for a moment, then cut into bite-size pieces and serve. (See P. 60 cutting method.)

薰鴨

湖南菜　　12人份

鴨１隻………３斤
酒…………２大匙
鹽…………１大匙
①葱(拍扁)……３枝
薑(拍扁)……２片
花椒粒………½大匙
②茶葉………４大匙
糖…………２大匙
麻油………½大匙

❶鴨洗淨拭乾水份，把①料抹勻鴨身並塞入鴨肚（圖１），醃３０分鐘以上，置蒸鍋，水燒開大火蒸４０分鐘至熟，待薰。

❷烤箱薰法：烤箱燒至４５０℉，把錫紙或紙放烤盤內，上置②料（圖２）擺進烤箱底層，將鴨擺在烤架上，入烤箱中層（圖３），薰約８分鐘至鴨皮呈金黃（薰時鴨身需翻轉），取出抹麻油（圖４），便可剁塊排盤。

❸鐵鍋薰法：在鍋底鋪錫紙或紙，上置②料（以免糖液粘鍋），再擺鐵絲網或筷子，以備將鴨擱在上面，蓋好鍋蓋，用小火薰約５分鐘至鴨皮呈金黃取出抹麻油，剁塊置盤。（剁鴨法參照第６１頁）

■盤飾：參照第４６頁，蘿蔔類盤飾第２０種。

薰雞

❶將鴨改用雞約２斤重，祇使用⅔的①料，大火蒸２０分鐘，薰法與上同。

■鴨、雞薰前除蒸的方法外，可用煮的方式，將鴨、雞加水約１０杯，水需淹蓋鴨或雞身，鴨燒煮約３０分鐘，雞約２０分鐘，熄火再燜１０分鐘，取出待薰。

蛋白質・・・・・・・・・・２０５克
脂質・・・・・・・・・・・・・１０４克
醣質・・・・・・・・・・・・・１０４克
熱量・・・・・・・・１８０９仟卡

Protein 205g
Fat 104g
Carbohydrate 104g
1,809 Kcal

Smoked Duckling   Hunan 12 servings

1 whole duckling (about 4 lbs.)

①
- 2 T. rice wine
- 1 T. salt
- 3 stalks green onions, mashed
- 2 slices ginger, mashed
- ½ T. Szechuan peppercorns

②
- 4 T. black tea leaves
- 2 T. sugar
- ½ T. sesame oil

❶ Rinse the duckling and pat dry. Rub ① evenly over the duckling exterior and in the cavity (fig. 1). Marinate for at least 30 minutes, then place in steamer. Cover and cook 40 minutes over high heat, or until cooked. Set aside.

❷ Oven-smoking-method: Preheat the oven to 450°F. Cover a baking pan with heavy-duty aluminum foil or paper, and sprinkle ② over the oil (fig. 2). Set the pan on the lowest shelf in the oven. Place the duckling on the middle shelf (fig. 3). Close the oven and bake 8 minutes. Turn the duckling over once during smoking. When the skin becomes golden, remove. Rub the skin with sesame oil; cut into serving pieces and serve (fig. 4).

❸ Wok-smoking-method: Cover the bottom of an iron wok with heavy-duty aluminum foil or paper. Sprinkle ② on the foil. Place a wire grill or several criss-crossed chop-sticks in the wok. Set the duckling on the grill so that it does not touch the tea leaves. Cover the wok and smoke over low heat for 5 minutes or until the skin turns golden. Remove and rub the duckling skin with sesame oil. Cut into bite-size serving pieces. (See P. 61 for cutting method.)

■ Garnish: See "Vegetable Garnish", p. 46.

Smoked Chicken

Substitute a 2⅔ lb. chicken for the duckling. Reduce the ingredients in ① as listed above by two-thirds. Steam over high heat for 20 minutes. Prepare the remaining steps as directed above.

■ Boiling method: The chicken and the duckling may be boiled in 10 cups water in place of steaming. The duckling should be boiled for 1 hour; the chicken, 40 minutes. Turn off the heat and let rest for 20 minutes. Remove and cut into bite-size serving pieces. Arrange the pieces on a platter and serve.

■ Adjust the ingredients proportionately to the size of the duckling.

捲筒肉排

廣東菜　　6人份

里肌肉……１２兩

①
酒…………½大匙
鹽…………１小匙
味精………¼小匙
糖…………１小匙
胡椒粉……⅛小匙
蛋…………１個
麵粉………２大匙
（或太白粉）

小黃瓜………１條
熟筍…………１枝
熟紅蘿蔔……１條
大多菇………２朵
麵包粉………１杯
「炸油」………５杯

❶ 里肌肉切法有兩種：

　⬜1 選較寬長塊之里肌肉約１４公分×１２公分，切除白筋，再橫切１公分厚大片，約切５片（圖１）。

　⬜2 切除白筋後，直切１公分厚片，第一刀離底部１公分不切斷，再切第二刀之１公分厚片後切斷，攤開成一大片。將肉片用刀背搥兩面各數下，使肉質鬆軟，調入①料拌勻。

❷ 筍、多菇（加水泡軟）各切０.５公分寬粗條（０.５公分×０.５公分×５公分）約１０條，紅蘿蔔、小黃瓜切長條各５條，小黃瓜削去籽（圖２），加少許鹽醃１０分鐘。

❸ 將肉片攤開，邊上橫放筍、多菇各２條，紅蘿蔔、小黃瓜各１條（圖３），然後捲成筒狀（圖４），全部捲好後再沾麵包粉，並用手輕輕握緊，使麵包粉黏住肉排，備炸。

❹ 鍋熱，加「炸油」５杯燒熱（２７５℉），將肉捲放入油鍋內，以小火炸約３分鐘後，先取出一條切開，若肉色轉白且熟時，改大火炸１分鐘，呈金黃酥脆撈出。

　每條肉捲切４～５小塊，排放盤內，蘸番茄醬，趁熱供食。

■里肌肉可先放入冰箱中冷凍稍硬，比較好切。

■盤飾：參照第２１頁，芋頭類盤飾。

蛋白質‥‥‥‥‥‥‥‥‥９０克
脂質‥‥‥‥‥‥‥‥‥‥１４９克
醣質‥‥‥‥‥‥‥‥‥‥‥７８克
熱量‥‥‥‥‥‥２０２２仟卡
Portein. 90g
Fat 149g
Carbohydrate. 78g
2,022 Kcal

1

2

3

4

Stuffed Pork Rolls

Cantonese 6 servings

1 lb. boneless pork loin
½ T. rice wine
¾ t. salt
¼ t. MSG
① 1 t. sugar
⅛ t. black pepper
1 egg
2 T. flour or cornstarch
1 gherkin cucumber
1 bamboo shoot, precooked
1 carrot, precooked
2 large Chinese black mushrooms, presoftened
1 C. bread crumbs
5 C. oil for frying

❶ Remove any fat or muscle from the pork loin and cut, use one of the following methods below:
a. Hold the cleaver parallel to the meat and cut the loin lengthwise into 5 slices (fig. 1).
b. Cut a ⅜-inch slice across the grain, slice just short of the opposite edge. Make another cut ⅜-inch from the first and cut completely through the loin. Continue to cut double-slices in this manner to the end of the loin. Pound the meat lightly with the blunt edge of the cleaver to tenderize.
Mix the meat slices with ① and marinate for 20 minutes.

❷ Cut the bamboo shoot and black mushrooms into julienne strips. Cut the cucumber and carrot into 5 strips each. Remove the seeds from the cucumber (fig. 2) add a little salt and let stand for 10 minutes. Drain off any excess water.

❸ Spread the slices of pork out flat on a counter and place 2 strips each of bamboo shoot and black mushrooms across the meat. Add a strip of cucumber and carrot (fig. 3). Start at one end of the meat and roll it up to enclose the vegetable strips and form a cylinder (fig. 4). Roll each pork roll in the bread crumbs, make sure that the surface is completely coated. Squeeze the rolls to adhere the bread crumbs to the meat surface.

❹ Heat pan and add 3 C. oil, heat to 300°F. Add the rolls and deep-fry 3 minutes over low heat. Turn the heat to medium and cook for another 3 minutes, until the rolls are golden. Remove one roll and cut it open to see if the rolls are cooked. If the meat has changed color, it is done. Remove and drain. Cut each pork roll into bite-size serving pieces. Arrange on a serving platter and serve with catsup.

■ To facilitate cutting partially freeze the pork loin.
■ Garnish: See "Vegetable Garnish" P. 21.

97

家鄉排骨

江浙菜　　6 人份

排骨…………半斤
① 酒…………1 大匙
　 鹽…………$\frac{1}{2}$ 大匙
　 葱…………2 枝
　 薑…………2 片
「炸油」………3 杯
葱…………2 枝
薑…………2 片
酒…………1 大匙
② 鹽…………$\frac{1}{2}$ 小匙
　 糖…………$\frac{1}{2}$ 大匙
　 桂皮………1 小片
　 八角…………$\frac{1}{2}$ 朵
　 高湯…………1 杯
錫紙…………6 張
（15 公分×15 公分）

❶ 排骨順肋骨條分切開（圖１），加①料拌勻（圖２）醃隔夜，炸前洗過瀝乾。

❷ 鍋熱，加「炸油」３杯燒九分熱（３７５℉），入排骨以中火炸約３分鐘呈金黃色撈出，油再燒沸重炸排骨以大火炸３０秒撈出瀝淨油，留油１大匙爆香葱薑，加排骨，淋酒及②料，蓋上鍋蓋以小火燜煮３０分鐘，至排骨軟熟透湯汁將收乾熄火（圖３）。

❸ 每張錫紙１５公分見方，將排骨一塊擺上包裹（圖４），全部包好錫紙，烤箱燒至４５０℉放進排骨烤約８分鐘即成。

■ 排骨煮好再烤過，味道更香醇，如無烤箱可免烤。

■ 餐館做法①料內加硝$\frac{1}{2}$小匙醃泡，肉色紅較美觀，家庭自製可免加硝。

■ 盤飾：參照第２５頁，蘿蔔類盤飾第１種。

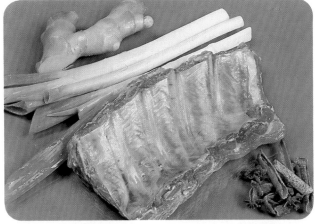

蛋白質⋯⋯⋯⋯⋯２克
脂質⋯⋯⋯⋯⋯３５克
醣質⋯⋯⋯⋯⋯３５克
熱量⋯⋯⋯⋯３２２仟卡
Protein. 2g
Fat 35g
Carbohydrate. 35g
322 Kcal

  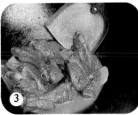 

① ② ③ ④

Home-Style Spareribs   Chekiang-Kiangsu 6 servings

¾ lb. spareribs

① {
1 T. rice wine

½ T. salt

2 stalks green onion, smashed

2 slices ginger, smashed
}

3 C. oil for frying

2 stalks green onion

2 slices ginger root

1 T. rice wine

② {
½ t. salt

½ T. sugar

1 stick cinnamon peel

½ star anise

1 C. stock
}

1 length aluminum foil

❶ Rinse the spareribs and pat dry. Separate the ribs, then add mixture ① (fig. 2). Marinate for one night. Rinse before frying and pat dry.

❷ Heat pan and add oil, heat to 375°F. Add the spareribs and fry 3 minutes, until golden brown. Remove and drain. Reheat oil until very hot and add the spareribs and fry for 30 seconds. Remove and drain. Drain all but 1 Tbsp. oil from the pan and reheat. Stir-fry the green onion and ginger until fragrant. Add the spareribs, rice wine and mixture ② . Cover and simmer for 30 minutes over low heat, or until the spareribs are tender and the liquid has almost evaporated. Turn off the heat.

❸ Cut a 6-inch square of aluminum foil for each sparerib. Wrap each sparerib to completely enclose. Preheat the oven to 450°F. Arrange the spareribs on a pan and cook for 8 minutes. Remove and serve.

■ Baking gives the spareribs a succulent flavor. If no oven is available, serve after Step ❷ .

■ Garnish: See "Vegetable Garnish" P. 25.

無錫排骨

江浙菜　　6 人份

中排骨‥‥‥‥半斤
（或小排骨）

① 酒‥‥‥‥‥1 小匙
　醬油‥‥‥‥$\frac{1}{2}$ 大匙
　「炸油」‥‥‥‥3 杯

② 酒‥‥‥‥‥1 大匙
　醬油‥‥‥‥2 大匙
　糖‥‥‥‥‥2 大匙
　水‥‥‥‥‥1 杯

　青菜‥‥‥‥‥6 兩

③ 鹽‥‥‥‥‥$\frac{1}{3}$ 小匙
　味精‥‥‥‥$\frac{1}{3}$ 小匙
　水‥‥‥‥‥2 大匙

❶ 排骨洗淨，順肋骨條切開（圖1），再剁成3公分之長塊約16塊（圖2），調上①料拌勻，醃約30分鐘。

❷ 鍋熱，加「炸油」3杯燒熱（350℉），將排骨下鍋，馬上用鍋鏟拌開以免黏鍋，中火炸約4分鐘呈深金黃色撈出（圖3）。

❸ 將②料燒開，即刻倒入炸酥之排骨，以中火燒煮5分鐘至汁剩$\frac{1}{3}$杯時，盛於湯碗內，水燒開用中火蒸40分鐘取出倒入盤（圖4）。亦可採燒煮的方法，請參照本頁「翡翠子排」做法❷。

❹ 油2大匙燒熱，入青菜加③料用大火爆炒熟擺於兩旁。

翡翠子排

小排骨‥‥‥‥半斤
葱段‥‥‥‥‥6 枝
（3公分長）

　酒‥‥‥‥‥1 小匙

① 醬油‥‥‥2$\frac{1}{2}$ 大匙
　糖‥‥‥‥‥2 小匙
　白醋‥‥‥‥$\frac{1}{2}$ 小匙
　水‥‥‥‥‥2 杯

② 太白粉‥‥‥$\frac{1}{2}$ 小匙
　水‥‥‥‥‥$\frac{1}{2}$ 大匙

　麻油‥‥‥‥$\frac{1}{2}$ 小匙
　青菜‥‥‥‥‥6 兩

❶ 排骨處理：參照本頁「無錫排骨」做法❶，但免醃①料。

❷ 鍋熱，加油2大匙燒熱，葱段炒香，再下排骨爆炒約2分鐘呈金黃色，下酒及①料，蓋好鍋蓋，以中火燒煮25分鐘，至湯汁剩$\frac{1}{3}$時，再以②料勾芡，並淋麻油即可盛盤，兩邊擺上炒好的青菜。

蛋白質‥‥‥‥‥３７克
脂質‥‥‥‥‥１００克
醣質‥‥‥‥‥‥３３克
熱量‥‥‥‥１１７７仟卡
Protein. 37g
Fat 100g
Carbohydrate. 33g
1,177 Kcal

1

2

3

4

Saucy "Wuhsi" Spareribs

Chekiang-Kiangsu
6 servings

	¼	1b.	spareribs
①	1	t.	rice wine
	½	T.	soy sauce
	3	C.*	oil for frying
②	1	T.	rice wine
	2	T.	soy sauce
	2	T.	sugar
	1	C.	water
	½	1b.	heart of green vegetable*
③	⅓	t.	salt
	⅓	t.	MSG
	2	T.	water

❶ Rinse the spareribs and drain. Cut to separate each rib (fig. 1), then cut each crosswise to 1¼-inch lengths. There should be about 16 pieces (fig. 2). Mix with ① and marinate about 30 minutes.

❷ Heat pan and add oil, heat to 350°F. Add the spareribs to the oil and immediately mix to separate the spareribs. Deep-fry over medium heat for about 4 minutes until golden brown. Remove and drain (fig. 3).

❸ Heat mixture ② until boiling, then add the fried spareribs. Cook over medium heat for 5 minutes or until the liquid is reduced to ⅓ cup. Transfer the mixture to a heatproof bowl, and place in steamer. Cover and steam for 40 minutes over medium heat. Remove and arrange the spareribs on a serving platter (fig. 4). Pour the sauce over the meat; or this dish may be stir-fried rather than steamed. See Step ❷ of the recipe shown below for directions.

❹ Heat pan and add 2 Tbsp. oil, heat until very hot. Add the green vegetable and ③ . Stir-fry over high heat until slightly wilted. Remove and arrange around the spareribs. Serve.

* If unavailable, substitute spinach or watercress.

Stewed Spareribs and Heart of Green vegetable

	¾	1b.	spareribs
	6		1¼-inch sections green onion
	1	t.	rice wine
1	2½	T.	soy sauce
	2	t.	sugar
	½	t.	rice vinegar
	2	C.	water
2	½	t.	cornstarch
	½	T.	water
	½	1b.	heart of green vegetable*
	½	t.	sesame oil

❶ Rinse the spareribs, drain and cut as directed in step ❶ of the recipe above. Do not mix with ① .

❷ Heat pan and add 2 Tbsp. oil, heat until hot. Add the green onion sections and stir-fry until fragrant. Add the spareribs and fry for 2 minutes on both sides until golden brown. Add the rice wine and mixture 1 . Cover and heat until boiling. Reduce the heat to medium and cook for 25 minutes, until the liquid is reduced to about ⅓ cup. Add mixture 2 to thicken. Add ½ tsp. sesame oil, toss lightly and remove to serving plate. See Step ❹ of the recipe shown above for directions on stir-frying the green vegetable. Arrange the vegetables around the spareribs and serve.

* If unavailable, substitute spinach or watercress.

吉利肉排

廣東菜　　6人份

里肌肉………6兩

①{
酒…………1小匙
鹽…………⅓小匙
味精………¼小匙
糖…………1小匙
胡椒粉……⅛小匙
}

②{
太白粉………¼杯
雞蛋(打散)…1個
麵包粉………1杯
}

「炸油」………3杯
椒鹽………½大匙

❶ 里肌肉切除白筋(參照第１０４頁「滑溜里肌」圖１)，每隔１公分直切１片約切８片，用搥肉器（或刀背）搥鬆（圖１），使肉質嫩，調①料拌勻醃２０分鐘。

❷ 把②料分別備在盤內，將醃好的肉片按太白粉、雞蛋、麵包粉等順序兩面沾勻備炸（圖２、３、４）。
另簡易法：將醃好肉片加②料之太白粉１大匙，雞蛋半個拌勻後，再遍沾麵包粉待炸亦可。

❸ 鍋熱，加「炸油」３杯燒熱（３５０℉），放進肉排，炸３０秒，再翻面炸３０秒，呈金黃色肉熟撈出，切塊置盤，食時蘸椒鹽、番茄醬或辣醬油等任選。

■ 椒鹽製法：參照第１５４頁「鹽酥魚」。
■ 盤飾：參照第２７頁，蘿蔔類盤飾第３種。

吉利魚排

將里肌肉改用魚肉，其調味及做法同上。

吉利雞排

將里肌肉改用雞胸肉，其調味及做法同上。

吉利明蝦

將里肌肉改用明蝦６隻，蝦摘除蝦頭去殼，留尾端不剝，洗淨拭乾，每條由蝦背順直剖切一刀，深至蝦厚度之一半，抽出沙腸，使腹部連着成一大片，其他調味及做法同上。

蛋白質‥‥‥‥‥‥‥５４克
脂質‥‥‥‥‥‥‥‥１０９克
醣質‥‥‥‥‥‥‥‥１００克
熱量‥‥‥‥‥１５９８仟卡
Protein 54g
Fat 109g
Carbohydrate 100g
1,598 Kcal

  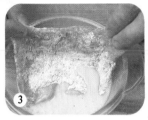 

Deep-Fried Pork Cutlets — Cantonese 6 servings

½ 1b. boneless pork loin

① 1 t. rice wine
⅓ t. salt
¼ t. MSG
1 t. sugar
⅛ t. black pepper

② ¼ C. cornstarch
1 egg, lightly beaten
1 C. bread crumbs

3 C. oil for frying
½ T. Szechuan peppercorn salt

❶ Remove any fat or muscle from the pork loin (see P.104 fig. 1 of "Stir-fried Pork with Cucumber Slices"). Cut into 8 slices ⅜-inch thick. Use the blunt edge of the cleaver to pound the meat lightly to tenderize (fig. 1). Add ① and marinate for 20 minutes. Arrange each ingredients of mixture ② in separate bowls.

❷ Dip the pork slices in the cornstarch, then the egg and then coat with the bread crumbs. Make sure that the slices are well-coated. Press lightly to adhere the breadcrumbs to the pork slices; or the pork slices may be mixed with the cornstarch and egg. Then dip each slice into the breadcrumbs.

❸ Heat pan and add oil, heat to 350°F. Add the coated pork cutlets and deep-fry for 30 seconds, turn with a spatula to separate the slices. Continue to fry over medium heat for 30 seconds until the meat is golden and cooked. Remove, drain and cut into bite-size serving pieces. Before eating, dip the slices in the Szechuan peppercorn salt, catsup or Worcestershire sauce.

■ To prepare Szechuan peppercorn salt, see "Savory Fried Fish," P. 154.

■ Garnish: See "Vegetable Garnish," P. 27.

Deep-Fried Fish Cutlets

Substitute ½ 1b. fish meat* for the pork loin. Follow the recipe as directed above.
* Haddock, sea bass or pickerel fillets may be used.

Deep-Fried Prawns

Substitute 6 prawns or scampi for the pork loin. Remove the head and shell, leave the tail intact. Devein, rinse lightly and drain. Along the back of each prawn slice halfway through the thickness. Spread open each prawn and flatten to one piece. Prepare the recipe as directed above in "Deep-Fried Pork Cutlets."

滑溜里肌　　　北方菜　　4人份

里肌肉‥‥‥‥4兩
①{
酒‥‥‥‥‥1小匙
鹽‥‥‥‥‥$\frac{1}{6}$小匙
蛋白（或水）1大匙
太白粉‥‥‥1小匙
}
小黃瓜‥‥‥‥1條
木耳（泡軟）‥‥6朵
「油」‥‥‥$\frac{1}{2}$杯
蒜末‥‥‥‥2小匙
酒‥‥‥‥‥1小匙
②{
鹽‥‥‥‥‥$\frac{1}{3}$小匙
味精‥‥‥‥$\frac{1}{4}$小匙
糖‥‥‥‥‥$\frac{1}{2}$大匙
高湯（或水）‥‥$\frac{3}{4}$杯
}
③{
太白粉‥‥‥1小匙
水‥‥‥‥‥$\frac{1}{2}$大匙
}

❶里肌肉切除白筋（圖1），先切大薄片（圖2），再橫紋斜切成2～3小片約2公分×3公分，調①料拌勻。小黃瓜切薄片（圖3、4）。木耳切小塊。
❷鍋熱，加「油」半杯燒熱（275℉），放進肉片馬上用鍋鏟拌開，以防黏鍋，用小火翻炒約20秒至肉色轉白剛熟即刻撈出，留油2大匙，先炒香蒜末，入木耳及②料煮沸加小黃瓜、肉片並由鍋邊淋下酒略炒後，以③料勾芡盛盤。
■無木耳可免用，酌加筍片或豌豆角（雪豆）亦可。
■將肉先放在冰箱中冷凍20分鐘，比較好切。

生溜魚片

草魚（中段）‥‥1斤
①{
蛋白‥‥‥‥$\frac{1}{2}$個
太白粉‥‥‥4大匙
}
洋葱‥‥‥‥‥$\frac{1}{4}$個
青椒‥‥‥‥‥2個
「炸油」‥‥‥3杯
酒‥‥‥‥‥‥1大匙
②{
鹽‥‥‥‥‥$\frac{1}{2}$小匙
味精‥‥‥‥$\frac{1}{4}$小匙
糖‥‥‥‥‥1小匙
水‥‥‥‥‥2大匙
太白粉‥‥‥1小匙
}
麻油‥‥‥‥‥1小匙

❶草魚由背鰭順大骨邊剖切成兩半，去除中間大骨及皮（淨肉約4兩），橫切成0.2公分薄片加①料拌勻。洋葱、青椒（去籽）切片備用。
❷鍋熱，加「炸油」3杯燒熱（275℉），將魚片放入待15秒才用鍋鏟輕輕拌動，魚肉色轉白且熟即撈起，留油2大匙炒香洋葱，再加青椒及②料燒沸，下酒隨入魚片輕輕拌，淋上麻油即可盛盤。

蛋白質‥‥‥‥‥‥３４克
脂質‥‥‥‥‥‥‥７８克
醣質‥‥‥‥‥‥‥１３克
熱量‥‥‥‥‥８３５仟卡
Portein. 34g
Fat 78g
Carbohydrate. 13g
835 Kcal

  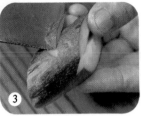 

Stir-Fried Pork with Cucumber Slices

Peking 4 servings

	6 oz. boneless pork loin
①	1 t. rice wine
	⅙ t. salt
	1 T. egg white (or water)
	1 t. cornstarch
	1 gherkin cucumber or ½ gourmet, seedless cucumber
	1½ oz. pre-softened wood ears
	2 t. minced garlic
	1 t. rice wine
②	⅓ t. salt
	¼ t. MSG
	½ T. sugar
	¾ C. stock or water
③	1 t. cornstarch
	½ T. water

6 oz. fish fillets

| ☐1 | ½ egg white |
| | 4 T. cornstarch |

¼ onion
2 green peppers
3 C. oil for frying
1 T. rice wine

☐2	½ t. salt
	¼ t. MSG
	1 t. sugar
	2 T. water
	1 t. cornstarch
	1 t. sesame oil

❶ Remove any fat or muscle from the pork loin (fig. 1). Cut into 3-4 slices, about ¾-inch thick (fig. 2). Mix with ① and marinate for 20 minutes. Cut the cucumber into thin decorative slices (fig. 3 and 4). Remove any hard ends from the wood ears and cut into small pieces.

❷ Heat pan and add ½C.oil, heat to 275°F. Add the pork slices and mix constantly to separate. Cook for about 20 seconds over low heat until the meat changes color. Remove and drain. Drain all but 2 Tbsp. oil from the pan and reheat. Add the garlic, wood ears and stir-fry briefly, then and mixture ② . Heat until boiling, and add the cucumber slices, pork and rice wine. Stir-fry briefly and remove to serving plate. Serve.

■ To facilitate slicing the pork loin, place in freezer until partially frozen, then slice.

Stir-Fried Fish Fillets

❶ Skin the fillets and cut diagonally into paper-thin slices. Mix with ☐1 . Marinate for 20 minutes. Remove the seeds and core from the green peppers. Slice and dice the onion.

❷ Heat pan and add 3 C. oil, heat to 275°F. Add the fish and deep-fry for about 15 seconds until the color changes. Remove and drain. Remove all but 2 Tbsp. oil from the pan and reheat until very hot. Add the onion and stir-fry until fragrant. Add the green pepper, ☐2 and heat until boiling. Sprinkle rice wine over the mixture, add the fish slices and mix carefully. Add 1 tsp. sesame oil and toss lightly. Remove and serve.

肉絲拉皮
Spicy Pork and Green Bean Salad

凉拌三絲
Three-Havor Tossed Salad

凉拌三絲　　　　北方菜　　6人份

里肌肉‧‧‧‧‧‧‧‧4兩
①
醬油‧‧‧‧‧‧‧‧1大匙
水‧‧‧‧‧‧‧‧‧‧‧1大匙
太白粉‧‧‧‧‧‧½大匙
「油」‧‧‧‧‧‧‧‧½杯
小黃瓜‧‧‧‧‧‧‧2條
粉皮‧‧‧‧‧‧‧‧‧5張
醬油‧‧‧‧‧1½大匙
糖‧‧‧‧‧‧‧‧‧1小匙
白醋‧‧‧‧‧‧‧½大匙
②
味精‧‧‧‧‧‧‧¼小匙
麻油‧‧‧‧‧‧‧½大匙
高湯(或水)‧‧‧¼杯

❶里肌肉切片後再切絲，加①料拌勻醃２０分鐘以上。把②料先煮沸備用。

❷小黃瓜切片後再切絲或刨絲（圖２），加少許鹽醃軟，用冷開水沖洗擠乾備用。粉皮切寬條（圖３），在熱水中川燙１０秒撈起（圖４），用冷開水沖涼，上撒少許鹽盛盤，再擺上小黃瓜絲。

❸熱鍋，加「油」半杯燒熱（２７５℉）倒下醃過之肉絲，馬上用鍋鏟拌開，以大火泡炒見肉色轉白且熟，約２分鐘撈起，置小黃瓜上，再澆上已煮好的②料，食時拌勻。

■如喜食辣味者，可澆適量辣椒油。除上述調味汁外，可將②料改用芥末汁或芝麻汁。

　芥末汁：芥末醬、醋、醬油各１大匙、鹽½小匙、糖１小匙、胡椒粉⅛小匙、麻油½大匙溫開水２大匙調勻即可。芥末醬做法參照第１８６頁「鹽蒸蝦」。

　芝麻汁：芝麻醬、醋、醬油各１大匙，鹽½小匙，糖１小匙、麻油½大匙、溫開水２大匙調勻使用。

■除里肌肉、小黃瓜、粉皮外，可用洋火腿、紅蘿蔔、西洋包生菜、綠豆芽（摘除頭尾為宜）在沸水內川燙２０秒。或蛋皮絲，做法是蛋２個打散煎成薄皮切絲。

里肌肉‧‧‧‧‧‧‧‧4兩
①料
葱段‧‧‧‧‧‧‧‧‧‧6枝
（２公分長）
「油」‧‧‧‧‧‧‧‧½杯
四季豆‧‧‧‧‧‧‧4兩
粉皮‧‧‧‧‧‧‧‧‧5張
紅辣椒‧‧‧‧‧‧‧1條
②料

肉絲拉皮

❶里肌肉處理，參照本頁「凉拌三絲」做法❶。紅辣椒切半去籽切碎。

❷四季豆去頭尾，斜切薄片（圖１）。粉皮切寬條（圖３）半鍋水燒開，把四季豆川燙１分鐘撈起，漂涼上撒少許鹽盛盤，再把粉皮川燙１０秒撈起（圖４），撒少許鹽及麻油，放在四季豆上。

❸參照本頁「凉拌三絲」做法❸，把炒好的肉絲置粉皮上。

❹鍋內留油３大匙，炒香葱段後撈出葱段棄置，再入紅辣椒略炒有香味，隨入②料燒沸，澆沸在肉絲上，食時拌勻。

蛋白質‥‥‥‥‥２４克
脂質‥‥‥‥‥‥‥５５克
醣質‥‥‥‥‥‥‥９２克
熱量‥‥‥‥‥９７０仟卡
Protein. 24g
Fat 55g
Carbohydrate 92g
970 Kcal

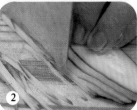

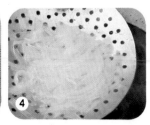

Three-Flavor Tossed Salad   Peking 6 servings

6 oz. boneless pork loin

① {
1 T. soy sauce
1 T. water
½ T. cornstarch
}

½ C. oil for frying
2 gherkin cucumbers*
5 vermicelli sheets*¹

② {
1½ T. soy sauce
1 t. sugar
½ T. rice vinegar
¼ t. MSG
½ T. sesame oil
¼ C. stock or water
}

❶ Remove any fat or muscle from the pork loin and shred. Mix with ① and marinate for at least 20 minutes. Heat ② until boiling and set aside.

❷ Grate the cucumbers or slice and shred them by hand (fig. 2). Add ¼ tsp. salt and rinse lightly in cold water. Drain and pat dry. Cut the vermicelli sheets into wide strips (fig. 3). Blanch the strips for 10 seconds. Remove and refresh in cold water. Drain and let cool (fig. 4). Sprinkle with ¼ tsp. salt. Arrange the vermicelli strips on a platter with the cucumber shreds on top.

❸ Heat pan and add oil, heat to 275°F. Add the pork shreds and mix to separate. After the meat changes color (for about 2 minutes), remove and drain. Place the meat on top of the cucumber shreds. Pour mixture ② over all. The salad should have 3-levels. Toss lightly before eating.

■ For added spiciness, sprinkle some chili oil over the salad.
"Mustard sauce" or "Sesame sauce" may be used instead of mixture ② .
Mustard sauce: Blend 1 Tbsp. rice vinegar, 1 Tbsp. soy sauce, ½ tsp. salt, 1 tsp. sugar, ⅛ tsp. black pepper, ½ Tbsp. sesame oil, 1 Tbsp. mustard paste and 2 Tbsp. warm water. To prepare mustard paste, see "Shrimp with Mustard Sauce" P. 186 for directions.
Sesame sauce: Blend 1 Tbsp. rice vinegar, 1 Tbsp. sesame paste, 1 Tbsp. soy sauce, ½ tsp. salt, 1 tsp. sugar, ½ Tbsp. sesame oil and 2 Tbsp. warm water.

* If gherkin cucumbers are unavailable, substitute 1 gourmet, seedless cucumber.
*¹ If fresh vermicelli sheets are unavailable, substitute dried. Reduce the quantity and soak in warm water until soft. Use as directed.

Spicy Pork and Green Bean Salad

6 oz. boneless pork loin
① same as above
6 ¼ -inch sections green onion
½ C. oil for frying
6 oz. fresh green beans
5 vermicelli sheets*¹
1 hot red pepper
② same as above

❶ Prepare the pork loin as directed in Step ❶ of the recipe shown above. Cut the red pepper in half, remove the seeds and mince.

❷ Snap the ends of the green beans and slice diagonally. Cut into thin slices (fig. 1). Cut the vermicelli sheets into strips (fig. 3). Heat 6 C. of water until boiling and blanch the green beans for 1 minute. Remove, refresh in cold water, and drain. Sprinkle with ¼ tsp. salt. Arrange the green beans on a serving plate. Blanch the vermicelli strips for 10 seconds and remove (fig. 4). Refresh in cold water, drain, sprinkle with ¼ tsp. salt and ¼ tsp. sesame oil. Arrange the strips on top of the green beans.

❸ Cook the pork as directed in step ❸ of the recipe shown above. Arrange the pork shreds on top of the vermicelli strips.

❹ Heat pan and add 3 Tbsp. oil, heat until very hot. Add the green onion sections and stir-fry until fragrant. Remove the green onions (and discard). Add the red pepper and stir-fry over low heat until fragrant. Add mixture ② and heat until boiling. Pour over the meat shreds and serve. Toss lightly before eating.

蜜汁排骨

廣東菜　　4人份

小排骨………半斤
① 酒…………1小匙
　 醬油…………½大匙
　 太白粉…1½大匙
　「炸油」………3杯
　 番茄醬……2大匙
　 糖…………2大匙
② 白醋…………1大匙
　 鹽…………⅓小匙
　 太白粉……1小匙
　 水…………3大匙

❶ 小排骨洗淨，拭乾水份，按肋骨條切開（圖1），再剁成3公分之塊狀，調入①料攪拌後，醃約30分鐘（圖2），炸前加太白粉拌勻（圖3）。把②料調在碗內備用（圖4）。

❷ 鍋熱，加「炸油」3杯燒熱(375℉)，將排骨下鍋炸15秒，用鍋鏟拌動，續用中火炸約3分鐘，撈出，再將油燒熱（400℉），重炸排骨約30秒，呈金黃色酥脆時撈起。

❸ 鍋內留油3大匙，入②料燒滾，放進炸好的排骨拌勻即可。

五香排骨

小排骨………半斤
　 酒…………1小匙
　 醬油…………1小匙
　 鹽…………¼小匙
① 糖…………½小匙
　 白醋…………½小匙
　 五香粉……⅛小匙
　 蛋黃…………1個
　 太白粉……2大匙
　「炸油」………3杯

❶ 排骨處理：參照本頁蜜汁排骨做法❶；將①料改用①料拌醃，炸前加入太白粉拌勻。

❷ 鍋熱，加「炸油」3杯燒熱（375℉），下排骨炸15秒，用鍋鏟拌動，以中火炸約3分鐘撈起，用大火再將油燒熱（400℉）重炸排骨約30秒，呈金黃色至酥脆時撈起盛盤。

■ 將小排骨改用豬里肌或豬腿肉亦可，做法同上。

蛋白質‥‥‥‥‥‥３３克
脂質‥‥‥‥‥‥１００克
醣質‥‥‥‥‥‥‥４０克
熱量‥‥‥‥１１９８仟卡
Portein. 33g
Fat 100g
Carbohydrate 40g
1,198 Kcal

 ① 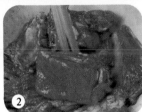 ② 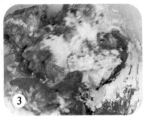 ③ 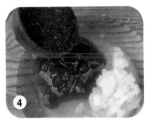 ④

Sweet and Sour Spareribs   Cantonese 4 servings

¾ lb. spareribs

① {
1 t. rice wine
½ T. soy sauce

1½T. cornstarch

3 C. oil for frying

② {
2 T. catsup
2 T. sugar
1 T. rice vinegar
⅓ t. salt
1 t. cornstarch
3 T. water

❶ Rinse the spareribs and pat dry. Cut the ribs to seperate them (fig. 1) and cut into sections 1-1½ inches in length. (There should be roughly 16 sections.) Add mixture ① and let marinate for about 30 minutes (fig. 2). Dredge each section in the cornstarch and coat thoroughly (fig. 3). Prepare mixture ② and place in a small bowl (fig. 4).

❷ Heat pan and oil to 375°F. Add the spareribs and deep-fry about 15 seconds, then mix to separate. Continue frying over medium heat for 3 minutes. Remove and reheat oil to 400°F. Add the spareribs and fry for 30 seconds until golden and crisp. Remove and drain.

❸ Heat pan and 3 Tbsp. of oil until hot. Add ② and heat until boiling. Add the spareribs and toss to coat the pork with the sauce. Remove and place on serving platter. Serve immediately.

Five-Spice Spareribs

¾ lb. spareribs

[1] {
1 t. rice wine
1 t. soy sauce
¼ t. salt
½ t. sugar
½ t. rice vinegar
⅛ t. five-spice powder
    （五香粉）
1 egg yolk
2 T. cornstarch
3 C. oil for frying

❶ Prepare the spareribs as directed in step 1 of the recipe above, substituting mixture [1] for ① .

❷ Heat pan and oil frying to 375°F. Add the spareribs and fry for 15 seconds, then mix to separate. Continue frying over medium heat for 3 minutes and remove. Reheat oil to 400°F and add the spareribs. Fry for 30 seconds until golden and crisp. Remove drain and arrange on serving plate. Serve.

■ Boneless pork loin or pork picnic shoulder may be substituted for the spareribs. Prepare as directed in the recipe above.

四喜丸子 北方菜　6 人份

前腿肉⋯⋯⋯半斤
（或絞肉）

① 酒⋯⋯⋯⋯1 小匙
　鹽⋯⋯⋯⋯$\frac{1}{4}$ 小匙
　味精⋯⋯⋯$\frac{1}{4}$ 小匙
　糖⋯⋯⋯⋯$\frac{1}{2}$ 小匙
　葱末⋯⋯⋯1 小匙
　薑末⋯⋯⋯1 小匙
　蛋⋯⋯⋯⋯$\frac{1}{2}$ 個
　太白粉⋯⋯1 大匙
　水⋯⋯⋯⋯3 大匙

② 醬油⋯⋯⋯1 大匙
　太白粉⋯⋯$\frac{1}{2}$ 大匙
　水⋯⋯⋯⋯1 大匙

③ 醬油⋯⋯⋯2 大匙
　糖⋯⋯⋯⋯$\frac{1}{2}$ 大匙
　水（或湯）⋯⋯1 杯

④ 太白粉⋯⋯1 小匙
　水⋯⋯⋯⋯1 大匙

青江菜⋯⋯⋯半斤

❶ 前腿肉（去皮）剁碎成絨狀。如購現成絞肉時，需再剁細，成肉絨（約 1～2 分鐘）。

❷ 將肉絨調①料拌勻（圖 1），再將水分 3 次加入，順同一方向仔細攪拌（圖 2），至肉絨有黏性（約 3 分鐘），然後做成 4 個大肉丸，下煎前把肉丸用手抹勻②料（圖 3），煎出色澤較美觀（不抹亦可）。

❸ 鍋熱，加油 4 大匙燒熱，將做好的肉丸下鍋，兩面煎呈金黃色（圖 4），加③料蓋緊鍋蓋燒滾後，改小火燜煮約 1 小時，見肉丸十分軟嫩時，將肉丸盛盤，其湯汁約剩$\frac{1}{3}$ 杯，以④料勾芡，澆淋肉丸上。

❹ 青江菜去老葉洗淨切半（小的不切），以 2 大匙油炒熟並加鹽、味精各$\frac{1}{4}$ 小匙，取出圍邊。

■ 絞肉加水的多寡，以肉的肥瘦來決定，肉肥及冰過的絞肉水加得少，肉瘦水就多加。

■ 可改用絞好的牛肉，除調①料拌勻後，照上法加水攪至肉黏外，再加入洋葱末 4 大匙或芹菜末 2 大匙，甚至兩種同加亦可，其他調味及做法同上。

蛋白質 · · · · · · · · · · · · ５１克
脂質 · · · · · · · · · · · · · １３３克
醣質 · · · · · · · · · · · · · · １６克
熱量 · · · · · · · · １４７１仟卡
Portein 51g
Fat 133g
Carbohydrate. 16g
1,471 Kcal

Simmered Lion's Head   Peking 6 servings

¾ lb. ground pork

①
1 t. rice wine
¼ t. salt
¼ t. MSG
½ t. sugar
1 t. minced green onion
1 t. minced ginger
½ egg
1 T. cornstarch
3 T. water

②
1 T. soy sauce
½ T. cornstarch
1 T. water

③
2 T. soy sauce
½ T. sugar
1 C. water or stock

④
1 t. cornstarch
1 T. water

¾ lb. green vegetable*

❶ Finely mince the ground pork.

❷ Mix the ground pork with ① (fig. 1), then add the water gradually while mixing. Stir continuously in one direction (fig. 2) until the meat mixture is sticky (for about 3 minutes). Shape into 4 balls. Dip each meat ball in mixture ② to add color (fig. 3).

❸ Heat pan (a frying pan may be used) and add 4 Tbsp. of oil. Fry the pork balls on all sides until golden (fig. 4). Add mixture ③, cover and heat until boiling. Reduce the heat and simmer for about 1 hour, or until ⅓ cup of the liquid remains and the meat is very tender. Remove the meat balls to a serving plate. Thicken the cooking liquid with mixture ④ and pour over the meat balls.

❹ Trim any old leaves and tough skin from the green vegetable. Rinse thoroughly and drain. Cut each stalk in half. Leave any small stalks whole. Heat pan and add 2 Tbsp. oil, heat until very hot. Add the vegetable and stir-fry until wilted. Add ¼ tsp. salt and ¼ tsp. MSG. Remove the vegetable and arrange around the edge of the meat balls.

* The Chinese green vegetable which is illustrated is available at a Chinese market. If unavailable, substitute Chinese cabbage.

■ The amount of water added to the pork should vary in proportion to the fat content. Decrease the amount if the pork is very fat and increase, if the pork is lean. The water helps to tenderize the meat. If the pork has been frozen, decrease the amount of water.

■ Ground beef may be substituted for the ground pork. Mix ground beef with ①, then add the water gradually. Stir continuously in one direction until the mixture becomes sticky (for about 3 minutes). Add 4 Tbsp. minced onion and/or 2 Tbsp. minced celery. Proceed as directed in the recipe above.

醬爆肉

四川菜　　4 人份

猪腿肉⋯⋯⋯6 兩
① 葱⋯⋯⋯⋯1 枝
　薑⋯⋯⋯⋯2 片
　水⋯⋯⋯⋯4 杯
芥蘭⋯⋯⋯⋯6 兩
五香豆干⋯⋯1 兩
② 酒⋯⋯⋯⋯$\frac{1}{2}$大匙
　甜麵醬⋯⋯1 大匙
　醬油⋯⋯1 $\frac{1}{2}$大匙
　糖⋯⋯⋯⋯1 小匙
　味精⋯⋯⋯$\frac{1}{4}$小匙
　麻油⋯⋯⋯$\frac{1}{2}$小匙
　水⋯⋯⋯⋯1 大匙
　油⋯⋯⋯⋯3 大匙

❶ 猪腿肉洗淨，整塊放入鍋内，加①料（水需淹蓋肉面），燒沸改小火煮約２０分鐘撈出待凉，去皮再切薄片（圖１、２）。五香豆干片切大薄片（圖３）。
❷ 芥蘭菜去老葉，取６公分長段，入沸水中燙煮約２分鐘撈起，速浸入冷水内漂凉瀝乾備用。
❸ 鍋熱，加油２大匙燒熱，把肉片、豆干片下鍋，用中火爆炒數下，鏟至鍋邊，倒入②料（預先拌勻）炒香，加芥蘭菜炒熟，將各料拌勻（圖４），最後淋油１大匙（以增光澤），即可盛盤。

醬爆牛肉

嫩牛肉⋯⋯⋯6 兩
① 醬油⋯⋯⋯1 大匙
　太白粉⋯⋯$\frac{1}{2}$大匙
　水⋯⋯⋯⋯3 大匙
芥蘭菜⋯⋯⋯6 兩
②料
油⋯⋯⋯⋯4 大匙

❶ 嫩牛肉横紋切肉片，加①料拌勻，醃３０分鐘。芥蘭菜處理：參照本頁「醬爆肉」做法❷。
❷ 鍋熱，加油２大匙，下牛肉片大火爆炒３０秒剛熟速鏟出，再加油１大匙，放入芥蘭菜及預先調勻的②料，隨下牛肉片拌勻，淋油（以增光澤）即可盛盤。

醬爆雞丁

雞肉⋯⋯⋯⋯6 兩
「油」⋯⋯⋯⋯$\frac{1}{2}$杯
葱段（３公分）6 枝
青椒⋯⋯⋯⋯1 個
紅辣椒⋯⋯⋯1 條
②料

❶ 雞肉、青椒及紅辣椒處理和調味，請參照第７４頁「麻辣子雞」做法❶、❷。
❷ 鍋熱，加油半杯燒熱（３００℉），入雞丁迅速用鍋鏟撥散，以大火泡炒見肉色轉白，約３０秒撈出，鍋内留油３大匙爆香葱段及青、紅椒，隨入雞丁及②料（預先拌勻）炒熟即成。

蛋白質 ·············· ４５克
脂質 ············· １０６克
醣質 ··············· １６克
熱量 ········ １１９０仟卡
Portein. 45g
Fat 106g
Carbohydrate. 16g
1,190 Kcal

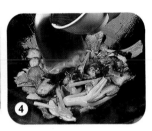

Stir-Fried Pork with Sweet Bean Sauce

Szechuan 4 servings

½ lb. fresh ham

① { 1 stalk green onion
2 slices ginger root
4 C. water

½ lb. Chinese broccoli*

1½ oz. spicy dried bean curd*¹

2 T. oil for frying

② { ½ T. rice wine
1 T. sweet bean paste
1½ T. soy sauce
1 t. sugar
¼ t. MSG
½ t. sesame oil
1 T. water

❶ Rinse the pork, drain and place in a pot with mixture ① . (Add more water, if necessary, to cover the pork.) Heat until boiling, cover and simmer for 20 minutes over low heat. Remove the meat and let cool. Cut into thin slices (fig. 1 and 2). Cut the dried bean curd into thin slices (fig. 3).

❷ Remove any old leaves and tough skin from the green vegetable. Cut into sections 2½-inch in length and blanch for 2 minutes. Remove and refresh in cold water. Remove and drain.

❸ Heat pan and add 2 Tbsp. oil, heat until very hot. Add the sliced pork and bean curd. Stir-fry briefly and push to the side of the pan. Add ② and stir-fry quickly to retain the crisp texture and bright green color. Toss lightly (fig. 4), sprinkle with 1 Tbsp. oil (for sheen), and toss again. Remove to serving plate and serve.

* If unavailable, substitute with broccoli or bok choy.

*¹ If unavailable, substitute 2 squares fresh bean curd, slice and fry until golden. Use as directed in Step ❸ .

Stir-Fried Beef with Sweet Bean Sauce

½ lb. flank steak or sirloin

½ lb. Chinese broccoli

4 T. oil for frying

⬜1 { 1 T. soy sauce
½ T. cornstarch
3 T. water
② same as above

❶ Cut the meat into thin slices. Add mixture ⬜1 and marinate for 20 minutes. Prepare the vegetable as directed in Step ❷ of the above recipe.

❷ Heat pan and add 2 Tbsp. oil, heat until hot. Add the beef slices and stir-fry quickly (for about 30 seconds). When the meat changes color, remove immediately. Reheat pan and add 1 Tbsp. oil until hot. Add the broccoli and mixture ② . Cook briefly and add the beef slices. Add 1 Tbsp. oil and toss lightly. Remove to a serving plate and serve.

Stir-Fried Chicken with Sweet Bean Sauce

½ lb. boneless chicken meat

1 C. oil for frying

6 1-inch sections green onion

1 green pepper

1 hot red pepper

②same as above

❶ Prepare the chicken, green pepper and hot red pepper as directed in Steps ❶ and ❷ "Spicy Fried Chicken," P. 74.

❷ Heat pan and add oil, heat to 300°F. Add the chicken and deep-fry for 30 seconds, until the color changes. Remove and drain. Drain all but 3 Tbsp. oil from pan and reheat until very hot. Add the green onion sections and stir-fry until fragrant. Add the green pepper, red pepper, chicken pieces and ② . Stir-fry briefly to coat the ingredients with the sauce. Remove and serve.

粉蒸肉

家常菜　6人份

前腿肉‥‥‥‥6兩		
（或五花肉）		
酒‥‥‥‥‥1小匙		
甜麵醬‥‥‥1大匙		
醬油‥‥‥‥1大匙		
① 味精‥‥‥‥¼小匙		
糖‥‥‥‥‥1小匙		
麻油‥‥‥‥1小匙		
水‥‥‥‥‥2大匙		
蔥、薑末各½大匙		
紅辣椒（切碎）1條		
蒸肉粉‥‥‥1½包		
洋芋‥‥‥‥1個		
蒸肉粉‥‥‥½包		
② 鹽‥‥‥‥‥¼小匙		
蔥花‥‥‥‥½大匙		

❶ 前腿肉切成4公分×3公分×0.3公分之長方塊，調入①料及蔥、薑末、紅辣椒末拌勻醃約30分鐘，並需常常翻拌，蒸前再拌上1½包的蒸肉粉（圖1）。

❷ 洋芋去皮切滾刀塊，加②料拌勻。

❸ 蒸籠擺法：洋芋擺在蒸籠底，腿肉置其上，水燒開大火蒸約1小時，趁熱灑上蔥花後與蒸籠一齊端出。

　蒸碗擺法：腿肉擺在碗底，洋芋置其上，水燒開，大火蒸約1小時，將蒸碗上覆菜盤；用雙手壓緊碗盤後倒扣在盤內。

■ 粉蒸肉材料，如選用瘦肉，蒸好灑上蔥花再澆淋滾燙油1大匙，食時較滑嫩。

■ 蒸肉粉做法：米1杯洗淨入淨鍋加八角1朵，花椒粒半小匙（約10粒）以小火炒黃，待涼碾磨成粗粉狀即成。

粉蒸牛肉

改用牛肉，份量做法同上，所蒸時間應延至2小時。

粉蒸雞．鴨

用雞腿或鴨肉12兩，其調味，做法同上，所蒸時間約1小時半。

荷葉粉蒸肉．牛肉．雞．鴨

❶ 豬肉・牛肉・雞・鴨等均剁塊，拌①料蔥薑末及紅辣椒醃泡30分鐘，蒸時拌上蒸肉粉。（洋芋免用）。

❷ 荷葉（新鮮或乾的，乾荷葉中藥店有售）需先用熱水燙軟，切小塊（圖2、3）再把已拌好蒸肉粉之材料，用荷葉包裹好（圖4），水開大火蒸1小時。

■ 除豬肉、牛肉、雞、鴨外，排骨、肥腸、魚均可照以上方法蒸製。洋芋也可用番薯（地瓜）、南瓜、青豆仁代替。

蛋白質 …………… ３５克
脂質 …………… １１６克
醣質 …………… ５０克
熱量 ……… １４０３仟卡
Portein. 35g
Fat 116g
Carbohydrate 50g
1,403 Kcal

 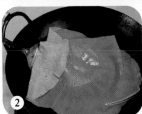 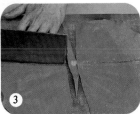 

Steamed Pork in Rice Powder

Family-style
6 servings

½ lb. fresh ham or pork picnic
    shoulder
① {
1 t. rice wine
1 T. sweet bean paste （甜麵醬）
1 T. soy sauce
¼ t. MSG
1 t. sugar
1 t. sesame oil
2 T. water
}
½ T. minced green onion
½ T. minced ginger
1 red hot pepper, minced (optional)
1½ pkg. rice powder* (about 1 cup)
1 potato （蒸肉粉）
② {
½ pkg. rice powder* (about ⅓ cup) （蒸肉粉）
¼ t. slat
}
½ T. minced green onion

❶ Cut the meat into thin slices about 1½-inch across. Place in a bowl with mixture ① , ½ Tbsp. minced green onion, ginger and hot pepper. Marinate for about 30 minutes. Stir frequently. Dredge the pork slices in the fragrant rice powder (fig. 1).

❷ Peel the potato and cut into bite-size pieces. Mix with ② .

❸ If placing ingredients directly into a metal steamer, arrange the potatoes on the bottom of the steamer and place the meat slices on top. Cover and steam for 1 hour over high heat. Remove and sprinkle the remaining minced green onion on top. Serve immediately in the steamer; or, if steaming in a heatproof bowl, arrange the ham slices in the bottom of the bowl and place the potatoes on top. Place in a steamer, cover and steam for 1 hour over high heat. Invert meat and potatoes onto a serving platter so that the meat slices are on top. Sprinkle with the minced green onion and serve.

* To prepare fragrant rice powder, mix 1 C. long-grain rice with 1 star anise and ½ tsp. Szechuan peppercorns. Stir-fry mixture (no oil) over low heat until golden. Remove and pulverize to a powder in a blender.

■ If the pork slices are very lean, sprinkle the minced green onions and 1 Tbsp. hot oil over the pork. (The oil will tenderize the meat and give it a sheen). Do this just before serving.

Steamed Beef with Rice Powder

Substitute tenderloin of beef for the pork. Prepare recipe as directed above, but increase the cooking time to 2 hours.

Steamed Chicken or Duck with Rice Powder

Substitute 1 lb. chicken legs or duckling for the pork. Prepare fhe recipe as directed above, but increase the cooking time to 1½ hours.

Lotus Leaf Pork, Beef, Chicken or Duck in Fragrant Rice Powder

❶ Cut the meat (½ lb.) into bite-size pieces. Mix with ① , green onion, ginger, red pepper, and marinate for 30 minutes. Dredge the meat pieces in the rice powder. Omit the potato.

❷ Soak 10 dried lotus leaves (available at a Chinese grocery store) in hot water until tender (for about 15 minutes). Cut the leaves into 5-inch squares (fig. 2, 3). The pieces should be large enough to hold the meat. Place a piece of meat in the lotus leaf and wrap it up (fig. 4). Place in steamer, cover and steam for 1 hour. Remove and serve.

■ Spareribs, fish fillets may be substituted for the meat. Sweet potato, squash and green beans may be substituted for the potato.

荷葉餅
Mandarin Pancakes

木須肉
Mu Hsu Pork

木須肉

北方菜　　4人份

里肌肉………4兩

①
醬油………2小匙
水…………1½大匙
太白粉……1小匙
葱薑末各…1小匙
（圖1）

②
韮黃…………2兩
（或菠菜、包心菜）
濕木耳……4大匙
熟筍絲………½杯
蛋…………2個

③
酒…………1小匙
醬油………1大匙
鹽…………½小匙
味精………¼小匙

❶ 里肌肉切絲（圖2）調①料拌醃10分鐘，下鍋前加油2小匙拌勻（炒時肉易於拌開）。韮黃（菠菜）切4公分長段（圖3）。濕木耳去蒂，切成細絲（圖4）。蛋放碗內打散備用。

❷ 鍋熱，加油4大匙燒熱，立即入肉絲迅速以鍋鏟拌開，用中火炒至肉色轉白後，鏟至鍋邊，入葱薑炒香，再將蛋液倒入炒至剛熟（凝固），隨加入②料及③料以大火拌炒約1分鐘，盛盤，可用荷葉餅，先塗抹甜麵醬（或海山醬），包捲此菜而食。

荷葉餅（又名單餅）

麵粉…………2杯
滾水…………⅔杯
水…………3大匙
（或蛋……1個）
油…………1大匙

❶ 麵粉沖入滾水，用筷子攪拌再加水（或蛋）拌勻，揉合成麵糰擱置10分鐘，謂之「醒麵」。

❷ 將麵糰置板上，揉至十分光滑再搓成長條，用刀分切16小塊，每小塊用手掌心由切口面壓扁成小圓餅，每兩塊疊在一起（疊前中間應先抹油），再趕成圓薄餅（直徑約16公分）。

❸ 鍋燒熱將餅置鍋內（不須擦油）以慢火烙烤約30秒鐘，翻面再烙30秒至兩面均有金黃斑點，中間稍鼓起後取出，甩打一下揭開成兩張荷葉餅。

■ 烙好之荷葉餅一張張疊放盤內，並用白布蓋上，以防冷後變硬。

蛋白質···········４２克
脂質············１０１克
醣質·············３０克
熱量·······１１２４仟卡

Protein. 42g
Fat 101g
Carbohydrate. 30g
1,124 Kcal

1

2

3

4

Mu Hsu Pork

Peking 4 servings

6 oz. boneless pork loin

① {
2 t. soy sauce
1½T. water
1 t. cornstarch
1 t. minced green onion
1 t. minced ginger
} (fig. 1)

② {
3 oz.Chinese leeks*
3 pre-softened wood ears
½ C. shreeded bamboo
2 eggs shoot, blanced

③ {
1 t. rice wine
1 T. soy sauce
½ t. salt
¼ t. MSG

❶ Remove any fat or muscle from the pork loin, shred (fig. 2) and mix with ① . Marinate for 10 minutes. Before cooking, add 2 tsp. oil to prevent the shreds from sticking together. Cut the Chinese leeks into 1¼-inch lengths (fig. 3). Remove any hard ends from the wood ears and shred (fig. 4). Beat the eggs lightly until frothy.

❷ Heat pan and add 4 Tbsp. oil, heat until very hot. Add the pork shreds and lower the heat to medium. Stir-fry quickly to separate the shreds. When the meat changes color, push to the side of the pan. Add the green onions, ginger and stir-fry until fragrant. Add the eggs and stir-fry for 15 seconds until just set. Add mixtures ② and ③ , toss lightly for 1 minute over high heat, and remove to a serving platter. Serve immediately.

"Mu Hsu Pork" may be served alone or wrapped in Mandarin Pancakes with sweet bean sauce or hoisin sauce.

Mandarin Pancakes

2 C. flour
⅔C. boiling water
3 T. cold water (or 1 egg)
1 T. oil (sesame oil, peanut oil or lard)

❶ Place flour in a bowl and add the boiling water. Mix thoroughly and add the cold water (or egg) to form a rough dough. Let stand for 10 minutes, covered with a damp cloth.

❷ Place dough on counter. Knead until smooth and elastic. Roll out to a sausage-shaped roll about 10-inch long and cut into 16 pieces. With a cut-surface down facing counter, press each section to a 1-inch circle. Brush one surface lightly with sesame oil. Place 2 circles together (oiled surfaces together) and press to seal. Roll out each double circle to a 6-inch thin pancake.
Heat a no-stick frying pan until hot. Fry pancake in the ungreased skillet twirling constantly, for about 30 seconds over low heat until small golden bubbles appear on top, and the pancake puffs. Flip over and fry for another 30 seconds. Remove and pull apart the pancakes. Arrange on a serving plate.

■ If not being used immediately, cover the pancakes a damp cloth so that they will not dry out. To reheat, steam for 5 minutes over high heat.

北平肴肉

北方菜　12人份

猪蹄膀‧‧‧‧‧‧‧1個
（或腿肉‧‧‧‧‧1斤）
① 葱‧‧‧‧‧‧‧‧‧‧‧‧‧‧4枝
　蕈‧‧‧‧‧‧‧‧‧‧‧‧‧‧3片
　大蒜‧‧‧‧‧‧‧‧‧‧‧3粒
　花椒粒‧‧‧‧1小匙
　八角‧‧‧‧‧‧‧‧‧‧‧1朵
　桂皮‧‧‧‧‧‧‧‧‧‧‧1塊
　猪肉皮‧‧‧‧‧‧‧6兩
　（或膠粉‧‧‧1½包）
　白蘿蔔（切塊）1條
② 酒‧‧‧‧‧‧‧‧‧‧‧‧2大匙
　醬油‧‧‧‧‧‧‧‧4大匙
　鹽‧‧‧‧‧‧‧‧‧‧‧1小匙
　糖‧‧‧‧‧‧‧‧‧‧半小匙
　水‧‧‧‧‧‧‧‧‧‧‧‧‧7杯

牛腱肉‧‧‧‧‧‧‧‧1斤
牛筋‧‧‧‧‧‧‧‧12兩
白蘿蔔（切塊）1條
①料　②料

羊後腿肉‧‧‧‧‧1斤
猪肉皮‧‧‧‧‧‧‧6兩
（或膠粉‧‧‧1½包）
白蘿蔔（切塊）1條
①料　②料

❶ 將整塊猪肉及猪肉皮（切小塊）洗淨置於鍋內加入清水須淹蓋過肉面，大火燒煮2分鐘後，將水倒棄，再加①、②料及白蘿蔔（圖1），用大火燒沸改小火續煮約1小時，撈出猪肉，將肉皮及白蘿蔔繼續燒煮至汁剩1杯半時，用紗布或篩子過濾後湯汁留用（圖2）。

❷ 將猪肉切塊（或手撕）舖在飯盒（圖3），再倒入湯汁（圖4），待涼擺入冰箱內冷凍（約需1小時），吃時切塊，以少許嫩薑絲或甜麵醬蘸食。

■ 如用膠粉代替猪肉皮，可將1½包膠粉加冷水¼杯泡約10分鐘使其溶解。在猪肉撈出後，湯汁繼續煮至剩1杯半時，加入已溶的膠粉調勻，其他做法相同。

■ 盤飾：參照第11頁，辣椒類盤飾。

牛肉凍

❶ 牛腱肉、牛筋、白蘿蔔及①、②料一齊燒煮約2小時（至筋肉極爛）撈出牛腱肉。牛筋切碎再入鍋煮至湯汁剩1杯半時用篩子或紗布過濾湯汁留用。

❷ 做法參照北平肴肉❷。

羊羔

❶ 做法參照北平肴肉做法❶。

❷ 將羊肉撕下肉皮舖在飯盒底（四方模型）肉撕或切成長條，排列在肉皮上，再倒入湯汁，待涼冷凍即成。

蛋白質‥‥‥‥‥‥‥‥８８克
脂質‥‥‥‥‥‥‥‥１９０克
醣質‥‥‥‥‥‥‥‥１９０克
熱量‥‥‥‥２０８２仟卡
Protein. 88g
Fat 190g
Carbohydrate. 190g
2,082 Kcal

Peking-Style Pork in Aspic Peking 12 servings

1⅓ lbs. fresh ham or pork
    picnic shoulder

① {
4 stalks green onions
3 slices ginger
3 cloves garlic
1 t. Szechuan peppercorns
1 star anise
1 cinnamon stick (or ¼ tsp. cinnamon)
}

1½ envelopes unflavored gelatin
1 Chinese radish* (cut into bite-size pieces)

② {
2 T. rice wine
4 T. soy sauce
1 t. salt
½ t. sugar
7 C. water
}

❶ Rinse the pork, drain and place in a pot with water to cover. Heat until boiling and blanch 2 minutes over high heat. Remove, drain and discard the water. Return the pork to the pot, with ① , ② and the radish pieces (fig. 1). Heat until boiling and reduce heat to low, cover and simmer for about 1 hour. Remove pork and let cool. Continue cooking liquid with the radish, until it is reduced to 1½ cups.

❷ Remove the radish (discard) and strain the liquid (fig. 2). Cut the pork into bite-size pieces (fig. 3).

❸ Add the gelatin to ¼ cup cold water and let it soften. Heat slowly until dissolved.
Heat the strained liquid until boiling and let it simmer for 2 minutes. Add the dissolved gelatin.

❹ Arrange the pork pieces in a square pan or mold. Pour the strained liquid into the mold (fig. 4) and let cool to room temperate. Refrigerate for at least 2 hours until firm. Cut into squares and arrange on a serving platter. Serve with shredded ginger, sweet bean sauce or hoisin sauce.

* If Chinese radish is unavailable, omit.
■ Garnish: See "Vegetable Garnish," P. 11.

Beef in Aspic

1⅓ lbs. beef (chuck or stewing meat)
1 lb. beef tendons (optional)*
1 Chinese radish, cut into bite-size pieces (optional)
① same as above
② same as above

❶ Place beef, beef tendons, and radish pieces in a pot, with mixture ① and ②. Heat until boiling, reduce heat to low and cook for 2 hours until the beef is very tender. Remove the beef and mince the tendons. Return the tendons to the liquid and cook until the liquid is reduced to 1½ cups. Strain the liquid.

❷ Prepare the remaining steps as directed in Steps ❷ , ❸ and ❹ of the recipe shown above.

* If unavailable, substitute 1½ envelopes unflavored gelatin and prepare as directed in Steps ❷ and ❸ of the recipe shown above.

Lamb in Aspic

1⅓ lbs. leg of lamb meat
1½ envelopes unflavored gelatin
1 Chinese radish, cut into pieces
① same as above
② same as above

❶ Prepare recipe as directed in Steps ❶ - ❸ of "Peking-Style Pork in Aspic."

❷ Remove the skin from the lamb and use hands to tear into shreds, or dice. Arrange the skin in the mold and place the meat on top. Prepare the remaining steps as directed in Step ❹ of "Peking-Style Pork in Aspic."

葱烤排骨　　　　　　　　　　廣東菜　　6人份

小排骨……１２兩
葱花…………８條
（長７公分）

①
酒…………１大匙
醬油………１大匙
鹽…………１小匙
糖…………１大匙
海山醬……１大匙
（或番茄醬）
五香粉……½小匙
蒜頭(拍破)…３粒

❶選購肥肉較少之排骨，洗淨後拭乾，盛碗內調①料拌勻（圖１），醃１小時以上，醃泡時須常常翻拌，使其入味。

❷烤箱燒至４５０℉，烤盤加水１杯置於烤箱底層（便於接排骨所滴下之油漬，以防冒煙弄髒烤箱），將排骨放在鐵絲網上（圖２），擺進烤箱中層（圖３），烤約３０分鐘，試以牙籤或叉子插入無血水流出即熟，且表面呈焦紅色即可取出，按肋骨分切成單條（圖４）排列盤內，每間隔插上葱花即可。

生煎排骨

大排骨……１２兩
①料（五香粉改用胡椒粉，海山醬免用）
太白粉……１大匙

②
醬油………１小匙
辣醬油……１大匙
糖…………１小匙
麻油………１小匙

❶大排骨切１公分厚片（約６片），用刀背搥鬆，調①料拌勻醃３０分鐘，下鍋前加太白粉拌勻。

❷鍋熱，加油４大匙燒熱，移開鍋將排骨一塊塊放入鍋內，再把鍋重移爐上，中火煎熟（約３分鐘），改大火續煎１分鐘使兩面呈金黃色，淋入②料拌勻再澆麻油即成。

蛋白質‥‥‥‥‥‥４８克
脂質‥‥‥‥‥‥１０４克
醣質‥‥‥‥‥‥‥１４克
熱量‥‥‥‥１２０１仟卡
Protein. 48g
Fat 104g
Carbohydrate 14g
1,201 Kcal

Roasted Spareribs with Green Onions

Cantonese 6 servings

1 lb. small spareribs
8 2-inch sections green onion

① {
1 T. rice wine
1 T. soy sauce
1 t. salt
1 T. sugar
1 T. hoisin sauce (or catsup)
⅛ t. five-spice powder
3 cloves garlic, smashed
}

❶ Select relatively lean spareribs. Rinse ribs, drain and pat dry. Place in a large bowl with mixture ① (fig. 1) and marinate for at least 1 hour. Mix frequently so that the spareribs will marinate evenly.

❷ Preheat the oven to 450°F. Pour 1 C. water in a large shallow roasting pan, then place on lowest rack of oven to collect the drippings from the spareribs and to keep the oven clean. Arrange the spareribs on a wire rack (fig. 2), place on the middle rack of the oven (fig. 3). Bake for 30 minutes, baste occasionally. To test for doneness, prick with a fork or toothpick; if the resulting liquid is clear, the spareribs are cooked. (They should be a deep, golden brown.) Cut into individual ribs (fig. 4) and arrange on a serving platter. Place a green onion section between each sparerib and serve.

Deep-Fried Spareribs

1 lb. spareribs prepare
mixture ① , omit
the hoisin sauce and
substitute ⅛ tsp. black
pepper for the five spice
powder

② {
1 t. soy sauce
1 T. hot soy sauce or Worcestershire sauce
1 t. sugar
1 t. sesame oil
}

❶ Cut the ribs, through the bones, into sections ½-inch thick (about 6). Use the blunt edge of the cleaver, to pound lightly to tenderize. Marinate in ① for 30 minutes. Dredge the ribs in the cornstarch.

❷ Heat pan and add 4 Tbsp. oil, heat until very hot. Remove pan from the heat and add the ribs. Return the pan to the heat. Fry 3 minutes over medium heat. Increase the heat to high and fry for 1 more minute until the ribs are golden. Sprinkle mixture ② over the ribs. Sprinkle the sesame oil on top and mix to coat the spareribs lightly with the sauce. Remove to a serving platter and serve.

肉丸子

絞肉…………6兩
① 鹽…………半小匙
味精………¼小匙
糖…………2小匙
胡椒粉……⅛小匙
蛋…………半個
麵粉………3大匙

② 洋葱(切碎)…半杯
紅蘿蔔(切碎)¼杯
「炸油」……4杯
椒鹽………半小匙

❶ 買回的絞肉須再剁得更碎（圖１），調入①料仔細攪拌約２分鐘至有膠黏性再加②料拌勻即為「肉漿」（圖２）。

❷ 肉丸子做法有兩種：
蒸法：將「肉漿」用手擠成１６個小肉丸置蒸盤，（蒸盤上須先抹油）（參照圖４擠法），水開大火蒸１０～１２分鐘即熟。
炸法：「炸油」４杯燒熱（３００℉）熄火，再將「肉漿」用手擠成小丸子約１６個，全部放入油鍋內，重將火點燃，以大火炸約３分鐘呈金黃色撈出盛盤，蘸椒鹽食之。

■ 椒鹽製法：參照第１５４頁「鹽酥魚」。

雀巢丸子

絞肉…………6兩
①料　②料
「炸油」………4杯
乾米粉………2兩
（或粉絲）

❶ 請參照本頁「肉丸子」做法❶，作成「肉漿」。將乾米粉用手弄碎（圖３），肉漿擠成丸子沾滾乾米粉待炸（圖４）。

❷ 「炸油」４杯燒熱（３７５℉），炸約４秒鐘視米粉泡鬆時撈出，熄火，使溫度降熱（２５０℉），再將肉丸放入用小火續炸約３分鐘，先撈出一個切開，若熟即可全部撈出。

蛋白質‥‥‥‥‥‥３９克
脂質‥‥‥‥‥‥１０５克
醣質‥‥‥‥‥‥‥‥３４克
熱量‥‥‥‥‥１２４９仟卡
Portein 39g
Fat 105g
Carbohydrate 34g
1,249 Kcal

Chinese-Style Meat Balls Family-Style 6 servings

① ½ 1b. ground pork

①
- ½ t. salt
- ¼ t. MSG
- 2 t. sugar
- ⅛ t. black pepper
- ½ egg
- 3 T. flour

②
- ½ C. chopped onions
- ¼ C. chopped raw, carrot
- 4 C. oil for frying
- ½ T. Szechuan peppercorn salt*

❶ Mince the ground pork to a smooth paste (fig. 1). Add mixture ① , stir in one continuous direction for about 2 minutes, to mix the ingredients thoroughly. Add mixture ② and mix until the ingredients are evenly combined (fig 2).

❷ To form meat balls, use one of the following methods:

a. **To steam:** Take some of the meat mixture into the palm of the hand and squeeze out balls through the index finger and thumb (fig. 4). Use a spoon, dipped in water, to help form the meat balls. Place the meat balls on a lightly-oiled heatproof plate. Place in steamer, cover, and steam for 10-12 minutes over high heat. Remove and serve with the Szechuan peppercorn salt.

b. **To deep-fry:** Heat pan and add oil for frying, heat to 300°F. Turn off the heat. Squeeze out the meat paste (as directed above) to form approximately 16 balls. Place in the oil and turn the heat to high. Deep-fry for 3 minutes, until golden. Remove, drain and serve with the peppercorn salt.

* To prepare Szechuan peppercorn salt, see "Crisp Savory Fish" P. 154.

Bird's Nest Meat Balls

½ 1b. ground pork
① same as above
② same as above
4 C. oil for frying
3 oz. dried rice noodles or collophane noodles

❶ To prepare meat mixture, see step ❶ of the recipe above. Break the dried rice noodles into ½-inch lengths (fig.3). Make meat balls by hand as directed in the recipe shown above. Roll the meat balls in the rice noodles (fig. 4).

❷ Heat pan and for oil for frying, heat to 375°F. Add the meat balls and deep-fry for about 4 seconds, until the rice noodles puff up. Remove and turn off the heat. Let the oil cool to 250°F and add the meat balls. Deep-fry over low heat for about 3 minutes and test one meat ball for doneness by cutting open. If meat is cooked, remove, drain and serve.

123

紅燴牛尾

北方菜　　6人份

牛尾…………1斤
洋蔥…………半個
番茄…………1個
① 酒……………1大匙
醬油…………2大匙
黑豆瓣醬…1大匙
番茄醬………2大匙
糖……………½大匙
水……………4杯
② 太白粉………1小匙
水……………1大匙

❶用刀將牛毛及污垢刮除(圖1)，洗淨剁塊。
　剁法：找出牛尾關節，在關節處切開(圖2)，亦可請牛肉
　店代切成小塊，然後在開水內燙煮2分鐘撈起待用。
❷洋蔥、番茄切塊(圖3)。
❸鍋熱，加油2大匙燒熱，將洋蔥炒香，再加番茄同炒約30
　秒(圖4)，倒入快鍋內，加①料及牛尾蓋緊鍋蓋，以中火
　燒煮約1小時，至肉熟透變軟，湯汁變稠約剩半杯，以②
　料勾芡即可盛盤。
■如用普通鍋燒煮時，①料內之水要酌加變6杯，燒煮時間
　延為2～3小時。

紅燒牛尾

牛尾…………1斤
紅蘿蔔………1條
洋蔥(切小片)¼杯
① 酒……………2大匙
醬油(深色)5大匙
糖……………1大匙
蔥……………2枝
薑……………2片
八角…………1顆
桂皮…………1小片
水……………5杯
②料

❶牛尾處理法，參照本頁「紅燴牛尾」做法❶。紅蘿蔔切滾
　刀塊。
❷鍋熱，油2大匙燒熱，將洋蔥炒香加①料及牛尾倒入快鍋
　蓋鍋燒煮50分鐘，至肉熟透變軟，湯汁約剩1½杯(不
　夠加水)，加入紅蘿蔔燒煮約10分鐘，再以②料勾芡即
　可。
■如尾毛過多，可先置爐上將毛燒淨，皮略帶焦黃色，再用
　刀將污垢及燒焦處刮除並洗淨，剁塊或買現成去皮之牛尾。
■除牛尾外，可選用牛腩、筋條、腱子肉……等。燒煮方法
　同上。

蛋白質‥‥‥‥‥‥‥４１克
脂質‥‥‥‥‥‥‥‥４３克
醣質‥‥‥‥‥‥‥‥１８克
熱量‥‥‥‥‥‥６２５仟卡
Protein 41g
Fat 43g
Carbohydrate. 18g
625 Kcal

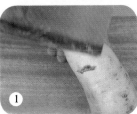   

Stewed Ox Tail
Peking 6 servings

❶ Use a cleaver to scrape any hair from the ox tail (fig. 1). Rinse thoroughly and cut into 1-inch sections.

Cutting method: With fingers, feel for joints in the tail and cut into pieces at each joint (fig. 2), or ask the butcher to cut the ox tail into 1-inch sections. Blanch the sections for 2 minutes and remove.

❷ Cut the onion and tomato into bite-size pieces (fig. 3).

❸ Heat pan and add 2 Tbsp. oil, heat until very hot. Add the onions and stir-fry until fragrant, then add the tomatoes and stir-fry for another 30 seconds (fig. 4). Pour the mixture into a pressure cooker, add ① and the ox tail*. Cover and cook over medium heat for 1 hour until the ox tail is very tender and about ½ C. of the liquid remains. Add ② to thicken the sauce. Serve.

Red-Cooked Ox Tail

❶ Follow step ❶ above. Peel the carrot and cut into bite-size pieces.

❷ Heat pan, add 2 Tbsp. oil, heat until very hot. Add the onion and stir-fry until fragrant. Add ① and the ox tail. Pour the mixture into a pressure cooker, cover and cook for 50 minutes, until ox tail is tender*, and the liquid is reduced to approximately 1½C. (add some water if necessary). Add the carrot pieces, uncover and continue to cook for another 10 minutes. Add mixture ② to thicken and remove to serving plate. Serve.

* If no pressure cooker is unavailable, increase the water to 6 C., place the mixture in a heavy casserole and cook for 2-3 hours over medium heat until the ox tail is tender and the liquid has reduced to the appropriate quantity.

■ Stew meat or tongue may be substituted for the ox tail. Prepare as directed above.

1⅓ lbs. ox tail

½ onion

1 tomato

① {
1 T. rice wine
2 T. soy sauce
1 T. black soy bean paste
2 T.catsup
½ T. sugar
4 C. water
}

② {
1 t. cornstarch
1 T. water
}

1⅓ lbs. ox tail

1 carrot

¼ C. onion, diced

① {
2 T. rice wine
5 T. soy sauce
1 T. sugar
2 Stalks green onion
2 slices ginger
1 star anise
1 stick cinnamon peel
5 C. water
}

② same as above

中式牛排

廣東菜　　6人份

牛腓脷………半斤
（或嫩牛肉）

①{
酒…………½大匙
醬油………１大匙
嫩精………¼小匙
（或小蘇打）
胡椒粉……⅛小匙
紅蘿蔔汁…１大匙
葱（拍扁）……２枝
薑（拍扁）……２片
太白粉……１大匙
水…………３大匙
}

洋葱絲………½杯
紅辣椒（切碎）１條

②{
辣醬油……１大匙
番茄醬……１大匙
糖…………½大匙
鹽…………½小匙
檸檬汁……１小匙
（或白醋）
太白粉……１小匙
水…………３大匙
}

玉蘭菜……１２兩
（青花菜）

❶ 牛肉洗淨，橫紋切成１公分厚片，約切６片，每片用刀背搥鬆（圖１），加①料拌勻（圖２），醃約２小時，其間須時時翻拌使其入味。

❷ 玉蘭菜取花頭部份，在開水內燙煮２分鐘撈起，泡入冷水漂涼瀝乾。

❸ 鍋燒極熱，加油５大匙，放進牛肉片，以中火煎至兩面呈金黃色鏟出（圖３）。

❹ 鍋熱，油３大匙燒熱，將洋葱炒香，下紅辣椒及已煎過的牛肉片，下酒半大匙邊炒邊淋②料，以大火炒至汁將收乾，再加油１大匙（增光澤）拌勻盛盤。

❺ 熱鍋，加油２大匙燒熱，隨入燙過之玉蘭菜，鹽¼小匙炒拌（圖４）１分鐘取出圍盤裝飾。

■ 除玉蘭菜外，可選用時令蔬菜，如青江菜、豆苗、菠菜、空心菜……等。

蛋白質‥‥‥‥‥‥‥71克
脂質‥‥‥‥‥‥‥‥80克
醣質‥‥‥‥‥‥‥‥45克
熱量‥‥‥‥‥1162仟卡
Protein. 71g
Fat 80g
Carbohydrate. 45g
1,162 Kcal

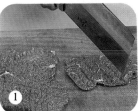

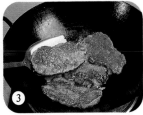

Sliced Steak with Chinese Broccoli

Cantonese 6 servings

¾ lb. flank steak or tenderloin
of beef

① {
½ T. rice wine
1 T. soy sauce
¼ t. meat tenderizer or
baking soda
⅛ t. black pepper
1 T. fresh carrot juice
2 stalks green onion,
smashed
2 slices ginger, smashed
1 T. cornstarch
3 T. water
}

½ C. shredded onions
1 hot red pepper, minced
½ T. rice wine

② {
½ T. vinegar
1 T. catsup
½ T. sugar
½ t. salt
1 t. lemon juice or rice
vinegar
1 t. cornstarch
3 T. water
}

1 lb. broccoli

❶ Remove any fat or muscle from the beef and rinse lightly. Cut the meat, across the grain, into 6½-inch thick slices. Pound each piece with the blunt edge of the cleaver to tenderize (fig. 1). Add ① (fig. 2) and marinate for 2 hours. Stir occasionally.

❷ Divide the broccoli flowerets into sections. (Discard the stem.) Cook the flowerets for 2 minutes in boiling water and remove. Refresh in cold water and drain. Heat pan and add 2 Tbsp. oil, heat until very hot. Add the broccoli flowerets and ¼ tsp. salt (fig. 4). Stir-fry for about 1 minute and remove. Arrange the flowerets around the edge of the platter, surrounding the beef mixture. Serve hot.

❸ Heat pan until very hot. Add 5 Tbsp. oil, and place the meat slices flat in the pan. Fry over medium heat until both sides are brown. Remove. (fig. 3).

❹ Heat pan and add 3 Tbsp. oil. Add the onions and stir-fry until fragrant. Add the minced red pepper, beef slices and rice wine. Stir-fry over high heat while adding mixture ② . Toss lightly until the liquid is almost dry, then add 1 Tbsp. oil. Toss again and remove to a serving plate.

■ Broccoli may be substituted with another green vegetable of choice. Revise the cooking time accordingly.

芥蘭牛肉

廣東菜　6人份

嫩牛肉………6兩

①
酒…………1小匙
醬油…………1大匙
嫩精…………$\frac{1}{4}$小匙
（或小蘇打）
太白粉……1大匙
水…………3大匙

葱段（2公分）6枝
薑片………6小片
芥蘭菜………半斤
「油」………$\frac{1}{2}$杯

②
蠔油………2大匙
（或醬油）
味精………$\frac{1}{4}$小匙
糖…………$\frac{1}{2}$小匙
太白粉……$\frac{1}{2}$小匙
水…………1大匙

嫩牛肉…………6兩
①料
葱段（2公分）……6枝
青菜……………6兩
②料
（蠔油改沙茶醬1大匙）

❶ 牛肉橫紋（不順紋）切3公分寬薄片（圖1），加①料拌勻醃約30分鐘（圖2），下鍋前加油1大匙攪拌，炒時肉片易於散開。

❷ 芥蘭菜去除老葉取嫩菜薳約4公分長段（圖3、4）。用開水燙煮約1分鐘撈出，立刻泡入冷水內漂涼，瀝乾水份備用。

❸ 鍋熱，加「油」半杯燒熱（275℉），把牛肉片倒入，馬上用鍋鏟或筷子撥散，以大火泡炒見肉色變，約20秒撈出，鍋內留油3大匙燒熱，將葱薑炒香，放入芥蘭菜炒約30秒，下酒半大匙及牛肉片和②料炒勻盛盤。

■ 家常做法，芥蘭菜不必先燙煮，可直接用油炒，再加酒、鹽、糖各$\frac{1}{4}$小匙炒熟。

■ 如牛肉很嫩，可不必加嫩精或小蘇打醃。

沙茶牛肉

❶ 參照本頁「芥蘭牛肉」做法❶、❷、❸。

■ 青菜：以空心菜、豆苗、小白菜、菠菜……等任選一種炒熟鋪盤，再擺上炒好之牛肉片即成。

蛋白質 …………… ５０克
脂質 ……………… ５９克
醣質 ……………… ２１克
熱量 ………… ８１６仟卡
Protein 50g
Fat 59g
Carbohydrate 21g
816 Kcal

Stir-Fried Beef with Chinese Broccoli

Cantonese 6 servings

½ lb. sirloin or tenderloin of beef

①
- 1 t. rice wine
- 1 T. soy sauce
- ¼ t. meat tenderizer or baking soda
- 1 T. cornstarch
- 3 T. water

½ C. oil for frying
6 ¾-inch green onion sections
6 thin slices ginger
½ lb. Chinese broccoli*
½ T. rice wine

②
- 2 T. oyster souce or soy sauce
- ¼ t. MSG
- ½ t. sugar
- ½ t. cornstarch
- 1 T. water

❶ Remove any fat or muscle from the beef and cut, across the grain, into 1¼-inch thick slices (fig. 1). Add ① and marinate for 30 minutes (fig. 2). Before (stir-frying, add 1 Tbsp. oil and toss lightly. To prevent the meat from sticking together).

❷ Remove any old leaves and peel the tough skin from the Chinese broccoli. Cut into 1½-inch sections (fig. 3, 4). Blanch for about 1 minute. Remove and refresh in cold water. Drain.

❸ Heat pan and add ½C. oil, heat to medium hot (275°F). Add the beef and stir to prevent slices from sticking together. Stir-fry over medium heat for about 20 seconds until the meat changes color. Remove and drain. Remove all but 3 (Tbsp. oil from pan and heat until very hot. Add the green onion and ginger, stir-fry until fragrant. Add the Chinese broccoli and stir-fry) for another 30 seconds. Add the rice wine, beef, mixture ②, and toss lightly. Remove to serving plate and serve hot.

* If Chinese broccoli is unavailable, substitute regular broccoli or spinach.

■ In home cooking, blanching the broccoli may be omitted. Stir-fry in the pan with ¼ tsp. rice wine, ¼ tsp. salt and ¼ tsp. sugar until tender. Prepare remaining steps as directed above.

Stir-Fried Saucy Beef

½ lb. sirloin or tenderloin of beef
① same as above
6 ¾-inch green onion sections
½ lb. green vegetable*
Substitute 1 T. Yakitori barbecue sauce*[1] (沙茶醬) for oyster sauce and prepare ② as above.

❶ To prepare, proceed as directed in the recipe above.
Yakitori barbecue sauce is a combination of peanut oil, peanut powder, green onion oil, coriander seed, garlic powder, hot pepper powder, star anise, Szechuan brown peppercorns and dried shrimp mixed together to a smooth paste. It may be purchased in a Chinese grocery store. If unavailable, substitute with ⅓ tsp. pepper or 1 tsp. hot chili paste (辣椒醬).

* Any green vegetable may accompany this dish. Stir-fry until cooked or tender, arrange on a serving platter and portion the meat mixture on top.

滑蛋牛肉　　　　　廣東菜　　6人份

嫩牛肉………３兩
①料
　薑酒汁……½大匙
　醬油………½大匙
　鹽…………¼小匙
　糖…………½小匙
　嫩精………¼小匙
　（或小蘇打）
　太白粉……１大匙
　水…………２大匙
雞蛋…………５個
②料
　鹽…………½小匙
　味精………¼小匙
蔥粒…………２大匙
（０.５公分）

❶ 牛肉洗淨，橫紋切成薄片，加①料拌勻，醃１小時，下鍋前加油１大匙攪拌，使肉片易於炒開。

❷ 鍋熱，加「油」半杯燒熱（２７５℉），放進牛肉片，迅速用鍋鏟泡炒約１０秒，見牛肉色變撈出。

❸ 雞蛋加②料打散後，加入泡過油的牛肉片拌勻（圖２），鍋熱，加油５大匙燒熱，倒進蛋汁牛肉片，以中火拌炒至蛋剛凝固（圖３），灑入蔥粒後盛盤（圖４）。

■ 薑酒汁：薑拍碎加酒擠出的汁（圖１）。

滑蛋蝦仁

蝦仁…………３兩
１料
　鹽…………⅛小匙
　酒…………¼小匙
　太白粉……１小匙
雞蛋…………５個
②料
蔥粒………２大匙
（０.５公分）

❶ 蝦仁加少許鹽拌一拌，用水洗盡黏液，拭乾水份，調①料拌勻醃２０分鐘以上。

❷ 鍋熱，加「油」半杯燒熱（２７５℉），放入蝦仁泡炒，見蝦色變且熟約３０秒，撈出倒入蛋汁內（雞蛋加②料預先打散）。油５大匙燒熱倒進蛋汁蝦仁，以中火拌炒至蛋剛凝固，灑入蔥粒即成。

蛋白質‥‥‥‥‥‥‥‥５３克
脂質‥‥‥‥‥‥‥‥‥‥８４克
醣質‥‥‥‥‥‥‥‥‥‥１１克
熱量‥‥‥‥‥‥‥‥１０２９仟卡
Protein 53g
Fat 84g
Carbohydrate 11g
1,029 Kcal

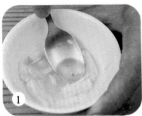

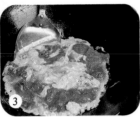

Stir-Fried Eggs with Beef Cantonese 6 servings

<table>
<tr><td>4</td><td>oz.</td><td>sirloin or tenderloin
of beef</td></tr>
<tr><td>½</td><td>T.</td><td>ginger-wine* (fig. 1)</td></tr>
<tr><td>½</td><td>T.</td><td>soy sauce</td></tr>
<tr><td>¼</td><td>t.</td><td>salt</td></tr>
<tr><td>½</td><td>t.</td><td>sugar</td></tr>
<tr><td>¼</td><td>t.</td><td>meat tenderizer or
baking soda</td></tr>
<tr><td>1</td><td>T.</td><td>cornstarch</td></tr>
<tr><td>2</td><td>T.</td><td>water</td></tr>
<tr><td>5</td><td></td><td>eggs</td></tr>
<tr><td>½</td><td>t.</td><td>salt</td></tr>
<tr><td>¼</td><td>t.</td><td>MSG</td></tr>
<tr><td>2</td><td>T.</td><td>diced green onions</td></tr>
</table>

(The bracket ① groups: ginger-wine, soy sauce, salt, sugar, meat tenderizer, cornstarch, water. The bracket ② groups: salt, MSG.)

❶ Remove any fat or muscle from the beef and rinse lightly. Cut the beef, against the grain, into thin slices. Add ① and marinate for 1 hour. Before stir-frying, add 1 Tbsp. oil and toss lightly.

❷ Heat pan and add ½C. oil, heat to 275°F. Add the beef and stir with a spatula to separate the slices. Stir-fry quickly over medium heat until the meat begins to change color. After about 10 seconds, remove and drain. (The meat should be medium-rare.)

❸ Add mixture ② to the eggs and beat lightly. Fold the meat slices into the egg mixture (fig. 2). Heat pan and add 5 Tbsp. oil, heat until very hot. Add the egg mixture. Stir-fry over medium heat until the eggs are scrambled and slightly set. (fig. 3). Sprinkle the diced green onions on top (fig. 4). Remove to a serving plate and serve hot.

* Ginger-wine: mash 1 slice of ginger, add to ½ Tbsp. rice wine, and squeeze out then liquid. Use the liquid as directed above.

Stir-Fried Eggs with Shrimp

❶ Devein the shrimp, mix with a pinch of salt and rinse lightly. Drain and pat dry. Add ☐ and marinate for at least 20 minutes. Set aside.

❷ Heat pan and add ½C oil, heat to medium hot (275°F). Add the shrimp and deep-fry for about 30 seconds, until the color changes and the shrimp are cooked. Remove and drain. Add mixture ②to the eggs and beat lightly. Fold the cooked shrimp into the egg mixture. Heat pan and add 5 Tbsp. oil, heat until very hot. Add the egg mixture and stir-fry over medium heat until the eggs are scrambled and slightly set. Sprinkle the green onions over the top and toss lightly. Remove to a serving platter and serve hot.

<table>
<tr><td>4</td><td>oz.</td><td>raw, shelled shrimp</td></tr>
<tr><td>⅛</td><td>t.</td><td>salt</td></tr>
<tr><td>¼</td><td>t.</td><td>rice wine</td></tr>
<tr><td>1</td><td>t.</td><td>cornstarch</td></tr>
<tr><td>5</td><td></td><td>eggs</td></tr>
<tr><td>②</td><td></td><td>same as above</td></tr>
<tr><td>2</td><td>T.</td><td>diced green onions</td></tr>
</table>

(The bracket ☐ groups: salt, rice wine, cornstarch.)

葱爆牛肉

四川菜　4 人份

嫩牛肉⋯⋯⋯4 兩

①
酒⋯⋯⋯⋯ 1 小匙
醬油⋯⋯⋯ $\frac{1}{2}$ 大匙
太白粉⋯⋯ $\frac{1}{2}$ 大匙
水⋯⋯⋯⋯ 2 大匙

葱⋯⋯⋯⋯⋯ 2 兩

②
酒⋯⋯⋯⋯ 1 小匙
醬油⋯⋯⋯ 1 大匙
味精⋯⋯⋯ $\frac{1}{4}$ 小匙
糖⋯⋯⋯⋯ $\frac{1}{2}$ 小匙
胡椒粉⋯⋯ $\frac{1}{8}$ 小匙
太白粉⋯⋯ $\frac{1}{2}$ 大匙
水⋯⋯⋯⋯ 2 大匙

嫩牛肉⋯⋯⋯⋯⋯4 兩
①料
②料
嫩薑絲⋯⋯⋯⋯⋯ $\frac{1}{2}$ 杯

❶ 牛肉洗淨橫紋切片或切絲，加①料拌勻（圖1），醃約２０分鐘，下鍋前加油１大匙攪拌，炒時肉絲易於撥散。葱切３公分長段（圖２），如葱太粗可由中間剖切兩半。

❷ 鍋熱，加「油」半杯燒熱（２７５℉），倒入牛肉片迅速用鍋鏟撥散，以大火泡炒見肉色變，約２０秒撈起（圖３），鍋內留油３大匙燒熱，入葱段以大火爆炒約１０秒，加入牛肉及②料拌炒（圖４），最後淋麻油１小匙（以增色香）即可盛盤。

■ 若牛肉不夠嫩，可在①料內加嫩精 $\frac{1}{4}$ 小匙或小蘇打 $\frac{1}{8}$ 小匙拌勻醃泡。

薑芽牛肉

❶ 參照本頁「葱爆牛肉」做法❶、❷。祇將葱段改用嫩薑絲。

蛋白質‥‥‥‥‥‥２８克
脂質‥‥‥‥‥‥‥‥５４克
醣質‥‥‥‥‥‥‥‥‥‥２克
熱量‥‥‥‥‥‥６１３仟卡
Protein. 28g
Fat 54g
Carbohydrate 2g
613 Kcal

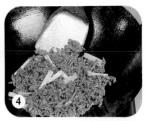

Stir-Fried Beef with Green Onions

Szechuan 4 servings

6 oz. flank steak or sirloin

① {
1 t. rice wine
½ T. soy sauce
½ T. cornstarch
2 T. water
}

4 stalks green onion

② {
1 t. rice wine
1 T. soy sauce
¼ t. MSG
½ t. sugar
⅛ t. black pepper
½ T. cornstarch
2 T. water
}

1 t. sesame oil

❶ Remove any fat or muscle from the beef and slice against the grain. Shred finely and mix with ① . Marinate for about 20 minutes (fig. 1). Before stir-frying, add 1 Tbsp. oil and toss lightly. (The oil will prevent the shreds from sticking together during frying). Cut the green onion stalks into I-inch sections (fig. 2). If the stalks are thick, split in half lengthwise.

❷ Heat pan and add ½C. oil, heat until hot (about 275°F). Add the beef shreds and stir-fry over medium heat, use chopsticks or a spatula to separate the shreds. When the meat changes color (about 20 seconds later), remove and drain (fig. 3). Heat pan and add 3 Tbsp. oil, heat until very hot. Add the green onion sections and stir-fry for about 10 seconds until fragrant. Add the beef, mixture ② and toss lightly (fig. 4). Sprinkle 1 tsp. sesame oil over the stir-fried mixture (added for sheen). Toss lightly and remove to a serving platter. Serve.

■ To further tenderize the beef, add ¼ tsp. meat tenderizer or ⅛ tsp. baking soda to mixture ① .

Stir-Fried Beef with Ginger

❶ Substitute ½ C. ginger slices or shreds for the green onion sections. Prepare as directed in the recipe above.

6 oz. flank steak or sirloin

① same as above

② same as above

½ C. ginger, sliced or shredded

魚香牛肉絲

四川菜　　6 人份

嫩牛肉⋯⋯⋯6 兩

① 酒⋯⋯⋯⋯$\frac{1}{2}$ 大匙
醬油⋯⋯⋯2 小匙
太白粉⋯⋯1 大匙
水⋯⋯⋯⋯3 大匙

荸薺（2 兩）⋯6 個
乾木耳⋯⋯⋯5 朵
「油」⋯⋯⋯⋯$\frac{1}{2}$ 杯

② 辣豆瓣醬⋯2 小匙
葱、薑、蒜末
（各）⋯⋯⋯1 大匙

③ 醬油⋯⋯⋯1 大匙
味精⋯⋯⋯$\frac{1}{4}$ 小匙
糖⋯⋯⋯⋯2 小匙
黑醋⋯⋯⋯1 小匙
太白粉⋯⋯1 小匙
水⋯⋯⋯1 $\frac{1}{2}$ 大匙

❶ 牛肉洗淨，橫紋先切薄片（圖 1），再切成細絲（圖 2）。加①料拌勻，醃 2 0 分鐘以上，下鍋前加油 2 大匙攪拌，泡油時肉絲易於撥散。

❷ 荸薺去皮切碎。乾木耳用溫水泡軟去蒂切碎（圖 3）。

❸ 鍋熱，加「油」半杯燒熱（2 7 5℉），倒入牛肉絲迅速用鍋鏟撥散，以大火泡炒見肉色變，約 2 0 秒撈起，鍋內留油 3 大匙燒熱，將②料爆香，加荸薺、木耳略炒，續入牛肉絲，下酒半大匙及③料，迅速用大火拌炒（圖 4），即可盛盤。用荷葉餅包捲而食另有一番風味。

■ 如牛肉不夠嫩時，可在①料內加嫩精 $\frac{1}{4}$ 小匙或小蘇打 $\frac{1}{8}$ 小匙醃泡 3 0 分鐘以上。

■ 荷葉餅：做法參照第 1 1 6 頁。

蛋白質‥‥‥‥‥‥48克
脂質‥‥‥‥‥‥‥59克
醣質‥‥‥‥‥‥‥41克
熱量‥‥‥‥‥818仟卡
Protein. 48g
Fat 59g
Carbohydrate. 41g
818 Kcal

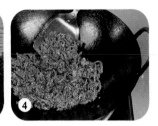

Fish-Flavored Shredded Beef Szechuan 6 servings

½ lb. flank steak or sirloin

① ½ T. rice wine
   2 t. soy sauce
   1 T. cornstarch
   3 T. water

   6 water chestnuts
   5 dried wood ears
   ½ C. oil for frying

② 2 t. hot chili paste
   1 T. minced green onions
   1 T. minced ginger
   1 T. minced garlic

   1 T. soy sauce
   ¼ t. MSG
   2 t. sugar
③ 1 t. black vinegar or Worcester-
         shire sauce
   1 t. cornstarch
   1½ T. water

❶ Remove any fat or muscle from the beef. Rinse and slice thinly against the grain (fig. 1), then shred finely (fig. 2). Add ① and marinate for at least 20 minutes. Set aside. Before stir-frying, add 2 Tbsp. oil (This will prevent the shreds from sticking together).

❷ Mince the water chestnuts. Soften the dried wood ears in warm water, remove any hard ends and chop. Set aside (fig. 3).

❸ Heat pan and Add ½C. oil, heat to 275°F. Add the beef and immediately mix with a spatula to separate the shreds. When the meat changes color (about 20 seconds), remove from the pan and drain. Drain all but 3 Tbsp. oil from pan and heat until very hot. Add ② and stir-fry until fragrant. Add the water chestnuts and wood ears. Stir-fry briefly. Add the wine, beef and ③, stir-fry over high heat until the ingredients are mixed and coated with the sauce (fig. 4). Remove to a serving plate and serve.

■ To further tenderize the beef, add ¼ tsp. meat tenderizer or ⅛ tsp. baking soda to mixture ①.

■ Mandarin pancakes: refer to p. 116 for preparation.

家常牛肉絲

四川菜　　6 人份

	嫩牛肉‥‥‥‥6 兩	
	醬油‥‥‥‥‥1 大匙	
①	太白粉‥‥‥‥½ 大匙	
	水‥‥‥‥‥‥3 大匙	
	芹菜‥‥‥‥‥3 兩	
	辣豆瓣醬‥‥1 小匙	
	蒜苗‥‥‥‥‥1 枝	
②	紅辣椒‥‥‥‥1 條	
	薑絲‥‥‥‥‥1 大匙	
	「油」‥‥‥‥½ 杯	
	酒‥‥‥‥‥‥1 大匙	
	醬油‥‥‥‥‥1 大匙	
	黑醋‥‥‥‥‥1 小匙	
	味精‥‥‥‥‥¼ 小匙	
③	鹽‥‥‥‥‥‥¼ 小匙	
	糖‥‥‥‥‥‥¼ 小匙	
	太白粉‥‥‥‥1 小匙	
	水‥‥‥‥‥‥1 小匙	

❶ 牛肉橫紋切薄片（圖１），再切成細絲（圖２），加①料拌勻，醃３０分鐘以上，炒前加油２大匙拌開。

❷ 芹菜摘除葉，洗淨後用刀面在菜梗上拍破（圖３），並切３公分長段。蒜苗斜切片。辣椒剖開去籽切細絲（圖４）。

❸ 鍋熱，加「油」半杯燒熱（２７５℉），入牛肉絲迅速用鍋鏟撥散，以大火泡炒見肉色變，約２０秒撈出，留油３大匙將辣豆瓣醬炒香，入②料略炒，續下芹菜及牛肉絲和③料，以大火爆炒即成。

陳皮牛肉

	牛肉‥‥‥‥‥1 斤	
	酒‥‥‥‥‥‥2 大匙	
⒈	鹽‥‥‥‥‥‥2 小匙	
	硝‥‥‥‥‥‥1 小匙	
	「炸油」‥‥‥3 杯	
	花椒粒‥‥‥‥１０粒	
⒉	八角‥‥‥‥‥半朶	
	陳皮絲‥‥‥1 大匙	
	干辣椒‥‥‥‥5 條	
	酒‥‥‥‥‥‥1 大匙	
	味精‥‥‥‥‥½ 小匙	
⒊	糖‥‥‥‥‥‥3 大匙	
	酒釀‥‥‥‥‥2 大匙	
	醋‥‥‥‥‥‥½ 大匙	
	麻油‥‥‥‥‥1 小匙	

❶ 牛肉橫紋切薄片，加⒈料拌勻置冰箱內醃一夜。干辣椒用剪刀斜剪約２公分長呈菱形，去籽備用。

❷ 鍋熱，加「炸油」３杯燒熱（３７５℉），下牛肉片以中火泡炸約６分鐘後，改大火炸１分鐘，至肉片水份將乾撈出。

❸ 鍋熱，加麻油２大匙，用小火將干辣椒炒香呈淡褐色即可盛出。原鍋加麻油３大匙燒溫，將⒉料以小火炒香，下陳皮絲略炒，加水１杯及牛肉片和⒊料燒沸，以小火燜煮至汁剩⅓，隨入干辣椒炒至汁乾，最後淋醋及麻油拌勻即可盛盤。

■ 此道⒈料內有硝，其目的為防腐及肉色紅較美觀，如家庭做可免用硝。將成品待涼密封置冰箱冷藏，可保存一星期。

■ 陳皮：就是陳年的橘子皮，橘皮經曬乾，涼後密封保藏，橘皮有油越陳越香，利用此香味來除肉（牛肉、羊肉…）腥味。如曬得太乾，用溫水稍泡軟。

蛋白質‥‥‥‥‥４４克
脂質‥‥‥‥‥‥４３克
醣質‥‥‥‥‥‥‥１１克
熱量‥‥‥‥‥‥６１６仟卡

Protein 44g
Fat 43g
Carbohydrate. 11g
616 Kcal

Home-Style Cooked Beef Shreds

Szechuan
6 servings

½ lb. flank steak or sirloin

①
- 1 T. soy sauce
- ½ T. cornstarch
- 3 T. water

3 stalks celery
1 t. hot chili paste

②
- 1 stalk fresh garlic
- 1 red hot pepper
- 1 T. shredded ginger root

½ C. oil for frying
1 T. rice wine

③
- 1 T. soy sauce
- 1 t. black vinegar or worcester-shire sauce
- ¼ t. MSG
- ¼ t. salt
- ¼ t. sugar
- 1 t. cornstarch
- 1 t. water

1⅓ lb. flank steak or sirloin

[1]
- 2 T. rice wine
- 1 t. salt

3 C. oil for frying

[2]
- 10 Szechuan peppercorns
- ½ star anise

1 piece dried tangerine peel, the size of a quarter*
5 dried red peppers

[3]
- 1 T. rice wine
- ½ t. MSG
- 3 T. sugar
- 2 T. fermented wine rice*¹

½ T. rice vinegar
6 T. sesame oil

❶ Remove any fat or muscle from the beef. Cut into thin slices (fig. 1) and shred (fig. 2). Mix with ① and marinate 30 minutes. Before stir-frying, add 2 Tbsp. oil, to prevent the shreds from sticking together.

❷ Remove any leaves and peel the celery. Rinse lightly, drain and flatten with the blade of a cleaver (fig. 3). Cut into I-inch sections. Diagonally slice fresh garlic. Halve red pepper, remove seeds and shred (fig. 4).

❸ Heat pan and add oil for frying, heat to 250°F. Add beef shreds and stir-fry for 20 seconds, until almost cooked. Remove and drain. Remove all but 3 Tbsp. oil from pan and reheat. Add the chili paste, ② and stir-fry until fragrant. Add the celery, beef shreds and ③ . Stir-fry over high heat and remove to a serving plate. Serve.

Cinnamon-Flavored Beef

❶ Remove any fat and muscle from the beef. Cut into thin slices. Add [1] and marinate over night. Diagonally cut the dried red peppers into ¼-inch section. Remove seeds.

❷ Heat pan and add oil for frying, heat to 375°F. Add the beef slices and cook for 6 minutes over medium heat. Turn heat to high and cook for 1 additional minute (until the beef is dry). Remove and drain.

❸ Heat pan and add 2 Tbsp. sesame oil, heat until hot. Add the dried red pepper and cook over low heat until black. Remove the dried peppers and retain. Add 3 additional tablespoons of sesame oil and heat to medium. Add [2] and cook until fragrant over low heat. Add the tangerine peel, 1 C. water, beef slices and mixture [3] . Heat until boiling, reduce heat and simmer covered unitl the liquid has reduced to ⅓ of the original quantity. Add the dried red peppers and stir-fry until the mixture is dry. Sprinkle the vinegar and sesame oil over the mixture. Toss lightly and remove to a serving plate. Serve.

* Soften the tangerine peel in warm water for 1 hour. Remove and shred.

*¹ If unavailable, substitute rice wine.

■ If refrigerated, this dish will keep for 1 week.

乾煎黃魚

江浙菜　　6人份

黃魚1條約12兩

① 薑酒汁……½大匙
　鹽…………2小匙
　味精………¼小匙
　麵粉………2大匙
　「油」………5大匙

② 薑末………1小匙
　白醋………2小匙

❶ 魚去鱗及內臟，洗淨拭乾水份，在魚身之兩面，切斜刀紋（圖1），再把①料抹勻魚身內外，醃1小時以上。
❷ 將醃過之黃魚兩面撒上麵粉待煎（圖2）。
❸ 鍋燒至極熱，再加油5大匙，俟油沸滾時手提魚尾，順鍋邊將魚放入（圖3），用中火煎呈金黃色約2分鐘（圖4），然後翻面，續煎另一面至魚肉熟透鏟出（用筷子容易插入即熟）。
❹ 食時沾用②料，魚皮酥肉嫩，鮮美可口。
■ 薑酒汁：薑拍碎加酒擠出的汁。
■ 除黃魚外，其他新鮮而刺少之魚均可代用。
■ 盤飾：參照第3頁，番茄類盤飾第2種。

椒盬黃魚

黃魚1條………12兩
①料
太白粉(或麵粉)1大匙
「炸油」…………4杯
葱花……………1大匙
椒鹽……………½大匙

❶ 參照本頁「乾煎黃魚」做法❶、❷。
❷ 「炸油」4杯燒熱（375°F），將魚提着魚尾放入，用中火炸約3分鐘後改大火炸1分鐘，至魚皮兩面呈金黃色肉熟酥脆撈起，上灑葱花及椒鹽（或將椒鹽另置小碟一齊上桌以供沾食）。

138

蛋白質‥‥‥‥‥‥‥８８克
脂質‥‥‥‥‥‥‥‥５６克
醣質‥‥‥‥‥‥‥‥２２克
熱量‥‥‥‥‥‥‥９７６仟卡
Protein. 88g
Fat 56g
Carbohydrate. 22g
976 Kcal

Pan-Fried Yellow Fish *Chekiang-Kiangsu 6 servings*

1 whole firm white-fleshed fish* (about 1½ lbs.)

① ½ T. ginger-wine*[1]
   2 t. salt
   ¼ t. MSG

2 T. flour

5 T. oil for frying

② 1 t. minced ginger
   2 t. rice vinegar

❶ Gut and scale the fish, leave the head intact. Score both sides of the fish with diagonal cuts about 1½-inch apart (fig. 1). Rub mixture ① over both sides of the fish and inside the stomach. Marinate for about 1 hour.

❷ Dust the fish generously with flour, make sure that the scoring is completely coated (fig. 2).

❸ Heat pan until very hot. Add the oil and heat until almost smoking. Holding the fish by its tail, slide it down the side to the bottom of the pan (fig. 3). Fry each side of the fish for about 2 minutes, until golden, turn once. (The meat should flake.) Remove, drain and arrange on a serving platter.

❹ Prepare mixture ② and place in a serving bowl. When eating, dip the fish meat into mixture ②.

* Yellow fish is traditionally used in this dish. If it is unavailable, substitute sea bass, pickeral or lake trout.

*[1] To prepare ginger-wine, mash 2 slices fresh ginger root and add to ½ tablespoon rice wine. Pinch the ginger, to imbibe the rice wine with the ginger flavor. Remove the ginger slices and use as directed.

■ Garnish: See "Vegetable Garnish," p. 3.

Pan-Fried Yellow Fish with Szechuan Peppercorn Salt

1 whole firm, white-fleshed fish (about 1½ lbs.)

① same as above

1 T. cornstarch or flour

4 C. oil for frying

1 T. minced green onion

1½ T. Szechuan peppercorn salt

❶ Prepare steps ❶ and ❷ as directed in the recipe above.

❷ Heat pan and add oil, heat to about 375°F. Hold the fish by its tail, lower it into the oil. Deep-dry the fish for about 4 minutes over medium heat until golden. Turn heat to high and fry an additional minute, until the skin is crisp and the meat golden. Remove and drain. Arrange the fish on a serving platter. Sprinkle the fish with the minced green onion and Szechuan peppercorn salt, or the salt may be served in a small bowl and served separately for dipping.

139

清蒸魚

活草魚１條約１斤

①{
薑酒汁……１大匙
鹽…………２小匙
味精………$\frac{1}{4}$小匙
}

②{
葱絲………４大匙
嫩薑絲……２大匙
紅辣椒(切絲)１條
胡椒………$\frac{1}{8}$小匙
油…………３大匙
}

❶ 魚去鱗除鰓及內臟後洗淨，在魚腹由頭至尾剖開，深觸及魚大骨邊，使魚背相連攤開，用刀刮除魚肚之黑薄膜（圖１，黑膜有腥味）。在魚肉厚處剁２、３刀並斬斷大骨（圖２），或在正面魚背肉厚處劃兩刀，深約厚度之一半（剁或劃刀目的是容易熟及入味），將①料抹勻魚身（圖３），醃３０分鐘以上。

❷ 將魚置於盤內魚背朝上，水燒開放入蒸籠(鍋)內，大火蒸１０分鐘，視魚眼突出轉白，或用筷子、刀叉在肉厚處易於插入即熟，取出上灑②料，再澆淋滾燙之熱油３大匙，使迸出響聲且散發葱薑的香味（圖４）。

■ 薑酒汁：薑拍碎加酒擠出的汁。

■ 選用較無腥味之新鮮魚類，尤以活魚爲佳。鯰魚也很適宜。

西湖醋魚

活草魚１條約１斤

①料　　　　②料
葱……………２枝
薑……………２片

③{
酒…………１大匙
水…………６杯
}

④{
醬油………３大匙
糖…………３大匙
黑醋………３大匙
鹽…………$\frac{1}{4}$小匙
川魚湯………１杯
太白粉……１大匙
}

❶ 魚的處理參照本頁清蒸魚做法❶。

❷ 鍋熱，加油１大匙燒熱，將葱薑炒香，下③料燒沸，將醃好的魚下鍋魚腹朝底，蓋鍋川煮待沸速予熄火，再燜約８分鐘，取出置盤，上灑②料，把④料燒開加油後澆淋在魚身上即成。

蛋白質 ············· ７７克
脂質 ················ ６３克
醣質 ················· ２克
熱量 ·········· ９０９仟卡

Protein 77g
Fat 63g
Carbohydrate 2g
909 Kcal

① ② ③ ④

Steamed Trout Chekiang-Kiangsu 6 servings

1 whole trout* (about 1⅓ lbs.)

① ⎰ 1 T. ginger-wine*¹
  ⎱ 2 t. salt
  ¼ t. MSG

② ⎰ 4 T. shredded green onions
  ⎟ 2 T. shredded ginger
  ⎟ 1 shredded hot red pepper
  ⎱ ⅛ t. black pepper

3 T. oil for frying

1 whole trout (about 1⅓ lbs.)

① same as above

② same as above

2 stalks green onions

2 slices ginger

③ ⎰ 1 T. rice wine
  ⎱ 6 C. water

④ ⎰ 3 T. soy sauce
  ⎟ 3 T. sugar
  ⎟ 3 T. balck vinegar or Worce-
  ⎟   stershire sauce
  ⎟ ¼ t. salt
  ⎟ 1 C. fish stock
  ⎱ 1 T. cornstarch

1 T. oil

❶ Scale, remove the gills, and gut the fish. Rinse thoroughly and drain. Cut the fish open from head to tail along the stomach side. Scrape away any dried blood (fig. 1) with the corner of the cleaver, score the fish with 2-3 cuts in the thickest section of the fish, slice through the backbone (fig. 2). This will enable the meat to cook evenly. Rub mixture ① inside and over the outside of the fish (fig. 3). Marinate for at least 20 minutes.

❷ Place the fish, skin-side up, on a lightly-oiled heatproof plate. Place in steamer, cover and steam for 10 minutes over high heat. When the meat flakes at the thickest section, when prodded with a chopstick or fork, the fish is cooked. Remove and sprinkle ② over the fish. Heat 3 Tbsp. oil until smoking and pour over ② (fig. 4). The hot oil will bring out the flavor of the green onion and ginger. Serve immediately.

* If fresh trout is unavailable, choose the freshest fish available. Perch, flounder, pickerel, or sea bass may be substituted.

*¹ Ginger-wine: Mash a slice of ginger and add to 1 Tbsp. wine. Pinch the ginger to imbibe the wine with the ginger flavor. Remove the ginger slice and use the wine as directed.

West Lake Fish

❶ To prepare the fish, follow step ❶ of the recipe shown above. Add 1 Tbsp. oil, heat until very hot. Add the green onion, ginger and stir-fry until fragrant. Add mixture ③ and heat until boiling. Add the fish, spread open and cover. Heat until boiling. Immediately, turn off the heat. Let stand for about 8 minutes. Remove the fish to a serving platter. Sprinkle ② over the fish. Heat ④ until boiling. Add the oil to make the sauce shiny and toss lightly. Pour the sauce over the fish and serve.

上海魚丸

江浙菜　　12人份

海鰻中段約 1 斤半
（淨肉 8 兩）

鹽…………… 1 小匙

① 葱（拍碎）…… 4 枝
　 薑（拍碎）…… 4 片
　 酒…………… 1 大匙
　 水…………… 1 杯

蛋白………… 1 只

② 鹽…………… 1 小匙
　 酒…………… 1 小匙
　 味精………… ½ 小匙

③ 太白粉……… 1 大匙
　 水…………… 2 大匙

豆苗………… 4 兩

❶ 海鰻洗淨，由脊背剖切去除脊骨，片開成二片（參照紅糟酥魚圖 1 ），切去魚腹多脂處。

❷ 魚皮向下，用刀背將魚肉處搥鬆（圖 1 ），再以刀面刮下肉泥（圖 2 ），剩下的魚皮、筋、骨等丟棄。

❸ 淨肉剁成泥狀，放入大碗中，加入鹽 1 小匙再將①料少量多次的加入，邊加邊用手快速攪拌至有膠黏性，再加蛋白（使色白而光澤）拌成「魚漿」（圖 3 ）。

❹ 鍋熱，加水 6 杯，熄火將「魚漿」用手擠成一個個魚丸放入鍋內，俟全部擠完後開火，以中火燒煮，用鍋鏟或大湯勺在魚丸面上撥動滾熟（圖 4 ）撈出，湯汁 3 杯留用。

❺ 魚湯（或高湯）3 杯加②料及魚丸燒沸，以③料芶芡，豆苗墊底，沖入滾熱的湯及魚丸即可食用。

■ ①料內葱薑需在水內用手擠出汁後撈棄。初學者可酌量減少水，以防魚漿不易成膠黏狀，若魚漿無法成膠狀時可酌加鹽繼續攪拌。此魚丸加水多較滑嫩。

■ 魚丸除上述做法外，並可依個人喜愛做為火鍋配菜、湯菜、雜燴配菜……等。

蛋白質 ············· ６２克
脂質 ··············· ３７克
醣質 ················· ４克
熱量 ··········· ６３５仟卡
Protein 62g
Fat 37g
Carbohydrate. 49g
635 Kcal

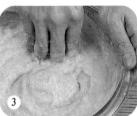

Shanghai-Style Fish Balls Chekiang-Kiangsu 12 servings

⅔ lb. white fish fillets
1 t. salt

① {
4 stalks green onion, smashed
4 slices ginger, smashed
1 T. rice wine
¾ C. water*

1 egg white

② {
1 t. salt
1 t. rice wine
½ t. MSG

③ {
1 T. cornstarch
2 T. water

⅓ lb. green vegetable*¹, trimmed
and cleaned

❶ Rinse the fish and drain well.

❷ Place the fillets skin-side down on the counter and lightly pound the meat with the blunt edge of the cleaver (fig. 1). Scrape the meat from the skin with the sharp edge (fig. 2). Discard the skin and bones.

❸ Mince the meat to a smooth paste, by hand or machine. Place in a bowl and stir in one continuous direction. Add 1 tsp. salt and continue mixing. Remove the green onion and ginger from mixture ① after squeezing to imbibe the wine with the flavors. Add mixture ① gradually to the fish paste, stir constantly. Add the egg white and mix for another 5 minutes until the fish paste is completely homogenous (fig. 3).

❹ Heat pan and add 6 C. cold water. Turn off the heat. Take a handful of fish paste and squeeze through the thumb and index finger 1-inch in diameter. Use a soup spoon dipped in water to separate by making a fist and form into balls and place directly into the water. Turn on the heat and cook until the balls rise to the surface. Turn the balls with a spatula while cooking (fig. 4). Remove the fish balls and drain. Retain 3 C. of the cooking liquid.

❺ Heat pan and add 3 C. of the retained cooking liquid. Add ② and the fish balls. Heat until boiling and add ③ to thicken. Arrange the green vegetable in the bottom of a serving bowl and pour the hot soup on top. Serve.

* The amount of water in mixture ① depends on the moistness of the fish. Add more water to the fish paste if necessary.

*¹ The vegetable which is illustrated is available at a Chinese market. If unavailable, substitute spinach or watercress.

■ A novice may reduce the amount of water in mixture ① . (Too much water makes the fish paste difficult to form into balls.) If the fish paste has too much water, add some salt and continue mixing before forming into balls.

■ Fish balls may also be served in a "Fire Pot," with various soups, etc., according to personal taste.

大蒜燒鯰魚

四川菜　　6 人份

鯰魚 2 條⋯⋯ 1 斤
（或土殺）

大蒜⋯⋯⋯ 1 6 粒

薑末⋯⋯⋯ 1 小匙

酒⋯⋯⋯⋯ $\frac{1}{2}$ 大匙

① 醬油⋯⋯⋯ 2 大匙
　味精⋯⋯⋯ $\frac{1}{4}$ 小匙
　糖⋯⋯⋯⋯ 2 小匙
　胡椒⋯⋯⋯ $\frac{1}{4}$ 小匙
　鎮江醋⋯⋯ $\frac{1}{2}$ 大匙
　水⋯⋯⋯⋯ 1 杯

② 太白粉⋯⋯ 1 小匙
　水⋯⋯⋯⋯ $\frac{1}{2}$ 大匙

蒜苗⋯⋯⋯ 1 大匙
（或蔥絲）

❶ 鯰魚去內臟洗淨瀝乾，切成 3 公分之塊狀（圖1）。大蒜去皮。蒜苗先將蒜白部份斜切，蒜葉切絲備用（圖2）。

❷ 油 3 大匙燒熱，下大蒜粒炒香，再放入蒜白、薑末及鯰魚煎約 1 分鐘，下酒及①料（圖3），蓋鍋以小火燜煮約 1 0 分鐘，用②料勾芡，最後加油 1 大匙拌勻，上灑蒜苗（圖4），盛盤趁熱送席。

或將鯰魚煎約 1 分鐘後移入砂鍋燜煮，其他做法同上，可與砂鍋一齊端出。

■ 如喜食辣味者，可加辣豆瓣醬半大匙。

冬菇燒鯰魚

大蒜免用，改冬菇4朵泡軟去蒂切半，與鯰魚一齊燒煮，其調味及做法同上。

栗子燒鯰魚

大蒜免，改用栗子一罐或乾栗 1 2 粒（乾栗先用熱水泡約 1 小時至軟，用牙籤挑出夾縫中之薄皮），與鯰魚一齊燜煮，其調味及做法同上。

蛋白質‥‥‥‥‥‥６７克
脂質‥‥‥‥‥‥‥４６克
醣質‥‥‥‥‥‥‥３０克
熱量‥‥‥‥‥‥８４３仟卡
Protein. 67g
Fat 46g
Carbohydrate. 30g
843 Kcal

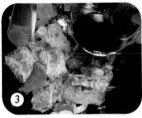

Fried Fish with Garlic   Szechuan 6 servings

2 whole fish (combined weight
   equal to about 1⅓ lbs.)
16 cloves garlic
1 t. minced ginger
½ T. rice wine
   2 T. soy sauce
   ¼ t. MSG
   2 t. sugar
① ¼ t. black pepper
   ½ T. rice vinegar
   1 C. water
② { 1 t. cornstarch
   { ½ T. water
1 stalk leek or scallion

❶ Scale the fish, remove the gills and entrails. Rinse thoroughly and drain. Cut the body, through bones into 1-inch sections (fig. 1). Peel the garlic cloves and separate the green and white sections of the leek. Cut the white section diagonally into ¼-inch sections. Shred the green section (fig. 2).

❷ Heat pan and add 3 Tbsp. oil, heat until very hot. Add the garlic, white section of the leek and stir-fry until fragrant. Add the ginger and fish. Fry on both sides until golden for about 1 minute. Add the rice wine, mixture ① (fig. 3) and cover. Heat until boiling, reduce heat and simmer for about 10 minutes over low heat. Add mixture ② to thicken. Add 1 Tbsp. oil, toss lightly and sprinkle the green shredded section of the leek on top and serve. Remove to a serving platter and serve immediately.

■ The fish may be pan-fried until golden on both sides, placed in a casserole cooked as directed above.

■ One-half tablespoon of hot chili paste (辣椒醬) may be added to the sauce to make this dish spicy.

Fried Fish with Black Mushrooms
Substitute 4 Chinese black mushrooms for the garlic. Soak until soft, remove the stems and cut the caps in half. Cook together with the fish. Prepare the recipe as directed above.

Fried Fish with Chestnuts
Substitute 1 can chestnuts or 12 dried chestnuts (栗子), for the garlic cloves. Soften the dry chestnuts for 1 hour in hot water to cover. Remove any tough skin with a toothpick and cook with the fish. Prepare the recipe as directed above.

紅糟酥魚　　臺灣菜　　6人份

海鰻‧‧‧‧‧‧‧‧１２兩
（或淨魚肉半斤）

① 薑酒汁‧‧‧‧‧$\frac{1}{2}$大匙
紅糟‧‧‧‧‧‧‧‧‧$\frac{1}{2}$大匙
味精‧‧‧‧‧‧‧‧$\frac{1}{4}$小匙
糖‧‧‧‧‧‧‧‧‧‧‧１小匙

「炸油」‧‧‧‧‧‧‧３杯

酥炸粉
麵粉‧‧‧‧‧‧‧‧‧‧１杯
發泡粉‧‧‧‧‧‧‧１小匙
紅糟‧‧‧‧‧‧‧‧$\frac{1}{2}$大匙
油‧‧‧‧‧‧‧‧‧‧‧‧１大匙
水‧‧‧‧‧‧‧‧‧‧‧$\frac{3}{4}$杯

椒鹽‧‧‧‧‧‧‧‧$\frac{1}{2}$大匙

❶ 海鰻由脊背剖切開，順大骨邊切取魚肉（圖１），將魚肉切成１公分×３公分長條（圖２），調上①料拌勻，醃約２０分鐘。

❷ 酥炸粉調法：麵粉、發泡粉一齊預先篩過，再加紅糟、油及水調勻成濃稠狀即成（圖３），酥炸粉調好後，宜在３０分鐘內使用。

❸ 「炸油」３杯燒熱（３００℉），將醃過魚條在「酥炸粉」內沾滾，再放入油鍋（圖４），中火炸２分鐘，再改大火炸１分鐘呈金黃色，肉熟皮脆時撈出盛盤，食時沾椒鹽。

■ 魚肉：除海鰻外，石斑魚、勉魚‧‧‧‧‧‧等刺少魚肉皆可。

■ 薑酒汁：薑拍碎加酒擠出的汁。椒鹽做法可參照第１５４頁「鹽酥魚」。

■ 盤飾：參照第１７頁，黃瓜類盤飾第２種。

酒釀酥魚

■ 將①料及酥炸粉內之紅糟各改用酒釀１$\frac{1}{2}$大匙外，其他材料、做法同上。

酥炸魚條

①料及酥炸粉內之紅糟免用，其他調味做法同上。

■ 酥炸粉除炸魚外，炸蝦、雞肉、豬肉均適宜。

146

蛋白質‥‥‥‥‥‥６０克
脂質‥‥‥‥‥‥‥５４克
醣質‥‥‥‥‥‥‥６１克
熱量‥‥‥‥‥９７２仟卡

Protein. 60g
Fat 54g
Carbohydrate. 61g
972 Kcal

   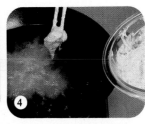

Deep-Fried Fish with Red Fermented Rice
Taiwanese 6 servings

1 lb. fish fillets*
① {
½ T. ginger-wine*[1]
½ T. red fermented rice*[2]
¼ t. MSG
1 t. sugar
}
3 C. oil for frying

Batter {
1 C. flour
1 t. baking powder
½ T. red fermented rice
1 T. oil
¾ C. water
}
½ T. Szechuan peppercorn salt

❶ Cut open the fish along the backbone and remove the filets (fig. 1). Remove the skin from the filets and cut into rectangular pieces 1¼-inch in length and ⅜-inch thick (fig. 2). Mix with ① and marinate for 20 minutes.

❷ Prepare the batter: Sift the flour and baking powder together. Add the red fermented rice, oil and water. Whisk vigorously to form a smooth batter (fig. 3). The batter should be used within 30 minutes of mixing.

❸ Heat pan and add oil for frying, heat to 300°F. Coat the fish slices with the batter and immerse in the hot oil (fig. 4). Deep-fry for 2 minutes over medium heat. Turn the heat to high and deep-fry for 1 additional minute until the pieces are golden and crisp. Remove and drain. Arrange the pieces on a serving platter and serve with the Szechuan peppercorn salt.

* A firm-fleshed fish with few bones is recommended, such as had-dock, sea bass, or pickerel.

*[1] To prepare ginger-wine, mash 1 slice fresh ginger root and add to ½ Tbsp. rice wine. Pinch the ginger to imbibe the wine with its flavor. Remove the ginger slices and use as directed.

*[2] Red fermented rice is a Chinese condiment made from fermented rice which is used in seasoning and coloring poultry and meat. It may be purchased at a Chinese grocery store.

■ Garnish: See "Vegetable Garnish," P. 17.

Deep-Fried Fish with Fermented Wine Rice

Substitute ½ Tbsp. fermented wine rice for the red fermented rice in mixture ① and the batter. Prepare the recipe as directed above.

Deep-Fried Fish Slices in Batter

Omit the red fermented rice in mixture ① and in the batter. Prepare the recipe as directed above.

■ Shrimp or pork loin may be substituted for the fish and batter-fry as directed in recipe shown above.

147

烤魚片

台灣菜　　6人份

| 魚肉‥‥‥‥‥１２兩 |
| 味噌‥‥‥‥‥‥‥６兩 |
| （或甜麵醬） |

① ⎰糖‥‥‥‥‥‥‥６大匙
　⎱酒‥‥‥‥‥‥‥３大匙
　⎱冷開水‥‥‥‥３大匙

❶ 魚肉洗淨擦乾水份，切成３大片（圖１）。

❷ 味噌（或甜麵醬）調入①料拌勻（圖２），塗抹魚片醃泡一天（圖３）。烘烤前將魚片取出洗淨，拭乾水份。

❸ 烤法：烤箱燒至４５０℉，將魚片置中層烤約２０分鐘，至魚片表面呈金黃色即可置盤。食時可擠檸檬汁數滴（圖４），更爲香醇。

　煎法：鍋燒熱加油３大匙，隨入魚片以小火煎約２分半鐘，翻面再煎２分半鐘至魚肉熟透（用鍋鏟易於插入魚身），並呈金黃色即成。

■ 如顏色不夠紅時，可刷上醬油烘烤，顏色較紅。

■ 宜用旗魚、石斑魚、馬加魚‥‥‥等大型刺少的魚類。

■ 國內甜麵醬和味噌鹹度相差無幾，故①料內用糖份量相同。如在國外甜麵醬可能已加工滲糖，故需酌量減少或免加糖。

■ 此種醬汁經燒沸擱冷後，可醃泡白蘿蔔、菜心及大頭菜（切條）等蔬菜。但已浸泡魚之醬汁，因有腥味不宜使用。

蛋白質‥‥‥‥‥‥１１５克
脂質‥‥‥‥‥‥‥‥‥２０克
醣質‥‥‥‥‥‥‥‥‥４２克
熱量‥‥‥‥‥‥‥８２３仟卡
Protein. 115g
Fat 20g
Carbohydrate. 42g
823 Kcal

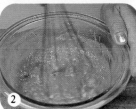

Baked Fish Slices　　　Taiwanese 6 servings

1　lb. fresh fish, mid-section of
　　the body*
½　lb. miso or sweet bean
　　paste*¹
① { 6　T.　sugar
　　3　T.　rice wine
　　3　T.　water

❶ Rinse the fish and pat dry. Cut the fish into steaks or slices 1-inch thick (fig. 1).

❷ Blend the miso or sweet bean paste with mixture ① (fig. 2). Rub the mixture over the outside of the fish slices and marinate for 8 hours or overnight in the refrigerator (fig. 3). Before baking, rinse the fish off and pat dry. Cook the fish by using either of the following methods:

❸ To bake: Preheat the oven to 450°F. Set the fish on a broiler pan and place the pan in the center shelf of the oven. Bake for about 20 minutes, or until the fish is golden and flakes. Remove and place on a serving plate. Before eating, squeeze fresh lemon juice over the fish steaks (fig. 4).

To pan-fry: Heat pan and add 3 Tbsp. oil, heat until hot. Add the fish slices and cook for about 2½ minutes over low heat. Turn the fish slices over and cook for another 2½ minutes, until the fish is golden brown and flakes when prodded with a fork or chopstick. Remove and arrange on a serving plate. Serve with lemon wedges, as directed above.

* Sword fish, scrod or blue fish may be used, depending on the availability.

*¹ Sweet bean paste (甜麵醬) and miso may vary in saltiness. If using canned sweet bean paste in which sugar has been added, reduce the sugar in mixture ① or omit, according to personal taste.

■ To give the fish steaks more color, brush lightly with soy sauce before baking.

■ This marinade (mixture ①) is equally delicious with Chinese radishes or cucumbers. To prepare: Cut the vegetables lengthwise. Heat mixture ① until boiling, let cool and pour over the vegetables. Marinate for least 8 hours and serve. Refrigerated vegetables will keep for 1 week. Discard the marinade used for fish and use a fresh batch for vegetables.

豆瓣煎魚

四川菜　　6人份

魚片（３片）１２兩
辣豆瓣醬…１大匙
①⎰葱末………１大匙　⎱（圖
　⎱薑末………１大匙　⎰１
　⎱蒜末………１大匙　⎰）
酒…………１大匙
②⎰鹽…………½小匙
　⎱味精………¼小匙
　⎱醬油………½大匙
　⎱糖…………½大匙
　⎱鎮江醋……１大匙
　⎱水……………½杯
③⎰太白粉……半大匙
　⎱水…………１大匙
　⎱葱末………１大匙

❶鍋熱，加油３大匙燒熱，放入魚片，用中火煎至兩面呈金黃色約２分鐘（圖２），將魚片鏟至鍋邊，把辣豆瓣醬炒香，再加①料（圖３），拌炒發出香味，再下酒及②料與魚一齊用中火燒煮約３分鐘，至汁剩一半（圖４），以③料勾成薄糊狀後置盤，上灑葱末即成。

豆瓣蝦段

明蝦（４條）…半斤
薑酒汁………１小匙
太白粉………½大匙
「炸油」………３杯
辣豆瓣醬…１大匙
①料
②料（水改３大匙）
③⎰太白粉……１小匙
　⎱水……………½大匙

❶明蝦的處理法，參照第１８８頁「醋烹蝦段」做法❶。
❷「炸油」３杯燒熱（３７５℉），放入已沾太白粉之蝦段，大火炸１５秒，用鍋鏟拌開，續炸１分鐘撈出置盤。
❸鍋熱，加油３大匙燒熱，炒香辣豆瓣醬，再入①料拌炒至發出香味時，下酒１大匙及②料燒沸，以③料勾汁即為沾料，或澆淋在炸過的蝦段上，趁熱食用。
■薑酒汁：薑片拍碎加酒擠出的汁。

蛋白質··········１０７克
脂質·············６６克
醣質············１１克
熱量·······１０４５仟卡
Protein 107g
Fat 66g
Carbohydrate 11g
1,045 Kcal

   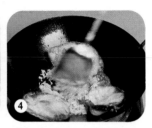

Braised Fish Slices in Hot Sauce

Szechuan
6 servings

1 lb. fish, cut into 3 steaks, 1-inch thick
1 T. hot chili paste

① {
1 T. minced green onion
1 T. minced ginger
1 T. minced garlic
} (fig 1)

1 T. rice wine

② {
½ t. salt
¼ t. MSG
½ T. soy sauce
½ T. sugar
1 T. rice vinegar
½ C. water
}

③ {
½ T. cornstarch
1 T. water
}

1 T. minced green onion

❶ Heat pan and add 3 Tbsp. oil, heat until very hot. Add the fish sections and fry about for 2 minutes on both sides over medium heat, or until golden (fig. 2). Push the fish to one side of the pan and add the hot chili paste. Stir-fry until fragrant and add mixture ① (fig. 3). Continue to stir-fry briefly, then add ② and push the fish slices back to the center of the pan. Cook for about 3 minutes over medium heat, or until the liquid is reduced to half of the original amount (fig. 4). Add mixture ③ to thicken and remove to a serving platter. Sprinkle the minced green onion on top and serve.

Fried Prawns in Hot Sauce

4-6 prawns or scampi (about ¾ lb.)
1 t. ginger-wine*
½ T. cornstarch
3 C. oil for frying
1 T. hot chili paste
① same as above
② same as above, but decrease the water to 3 Tbsp.

③ {
1 t. cornstarch
½ T. water
}

❶ To prepare the prawns, see p. 189. Step ❶ "Sweet and Sour Prawns." Dredge the prawns in the cornstarch.

❷ Heat pan and add oil, heat to 375°F. Add the prawn sections and deep-fry for 15 seconds over high heat, use a spatula to separate the pieces. Continue to fry for 1 minute, remove, drain and arrange on a serving platter.

❸ Remove all but 3 Tbsp. oil from pan and reheat until very hot. Add the hot chili paste and stir-fry until fragrant. Add mixture ①, stir-fry briefly, then add mixture ②. Heat until boiling and add ③ to thicken. Pour into a finger bowl and serve on the side as a dipping sauce, or pour directly over the prawn slices. Serve immediately.

* Ginger-wine: Place 1 slice mashed ginger in 1 tsp. rice wine. Pinch to imbibe the wine with the ginger flavor. Remove the ginger slice and use the liquid as directed above.

雪菜肉絲蒸魚
Steamed Fish with Pork
and Red-in-snow

雪菜筍絲
Stir-Fried Red-S
and Bamboo Sh

雪菜肉絲蒸魚

江浙菜　　6人份

鱈魚1塊…12兩
①{
薑酒汁……1大匙
鹽………1小匙
味精………½小匙
胡椒………⅛小匙
}
里肌肉………2兩
（或瘦肉）
②{
太白粉……½小匙
水………½大匙
}
雪裡紅（切碎）½杯
紅辣椒……½大匙
（切絲）
醬油………½大匙
雞油………1大匙
（或沙拉油）

❶ 鱈魚洗淨拭乾水份，在肉厚處劃刀使其入味（圖1），盛盤調入①料醃20分鐘。里肌肉切絲調②料拌勻，醃20分鐘。

❷ 熱鍋，加油2大匙燒熱，先炒肉絲，肉色轉白加入雪裡紅拌炒，即刻鏟出灑在魚身上，並放入紅辣椒，淋醬油半大匙及雞油1大匙（圖2），水燒開罷進蒸籠（鍋）內，大火蒸10分鐘（視魚大小，以筷子或刀叉輕易插入即熟），趁熱送席。

冬菇肉絲蒸魚

將雪裡紅改冬菇3朵，泡軟切絲，其他調味，做法同上。
■ 除鱈魚外，可選用較無腥味之魚類為宜。

雪裡紅………半斤
筍…………1枝
紅辣椒………1條
①{
醬油………1大匙
糖…………1小匙
味精………¼小匙
}

雪菜筍絲

❶ 雪裡紅漂洗淨，用手擠乾水份（圖3），切0.5公分長段，筍切絲及辣椒去籽切絲（圖4）。

❷ 油4大匙燒熱，用大火炒雪裡紅及筍絲（約1分鐘），再入紅辣椒絲及①料炒勻即成。

雪筍肉絲

做法與雪菜筍絲同，僅加入肉絲即可。
■ 雪裡紅醃製法：油菜洗淨晾乾或曬乾，加鹽揉搓，放入盆內醃透約一天便可使用。

152

蛋白質‥‥‥‥‥‥２０５克
脂質‥‥‥‥‥‥‥‥６４克
醣質‥‥‥‥‥‥‥‥１７克
熱量‥‥‥‥１５２３仟卡
Protein 205g
Fat 64g
Carbohydrate 17g
1,523 Kcal

Steamed Fish with Pork and Red-in-Snow

Chekiang-Kiangsu
6 servings

1 lb. fresh fish fillets*

①
- 1 T. ginger-wine*[1]
- 1 t. salt
- ½ t. MSG
- ⅛ t. black pepper

3 oz. boneless pork loin

②
- ½ t. cornstarch
- ½ T. water

½ C. red-in-snow*[2], rinsed and minced

½ T. shredded hot red pepper

½ T. soy sauce

1 T. rendered chicken fat (or peanut oil)

❶ Rinse the fish fillets and pat dry. Score the fish fillets diagonally, on both sides so that the flavor of the marinade will permeate the fish (fig. 1). Place the fish on a lightly-oiled heatproof plate and rub with mixture ① . Marinate for 20 minutes. Remove any fat or muscle from the pork loin and mix with②.

❷ Heat pan and add 2 Tbsp. oil, heat until very hot. Add the shredded pork and stir-fry until it changes color. Add the red-in-snow and toss lightly. Remove and cover the fish with the stir-fried mixture. Sprinkle with the shredded red pepper, soy sauce and chicken fat (fig. 2). Place the fish in a steamer, cover and steam over high heat for about 10 minutes. (Adjust the steaming time in proportion to the thickness of the fillets.) If the fish flakes when prodded with a chopstick or a fork, it is cooked. Remove and serve immediately.

* Any firm-fleshed fish with few bones may be used.

*[1] To prepare ginger-wine, place 2 slices mashed ginger in 1 Tbsp. rice wine. Pinch to imbibe the wine with the ginger flavor. Remove the slices and use the liquid as directed above.

*[2] Red-in-snow (雪裡紅) is a seasoning made from a salted vegetable. It is available in cans at any Chinese grocery store.

Steamed Fish with Prok and Mushrooms

Substitute 3 Chinese black mushrooms for the red-in-snow in the recipe shown above.
Soak the black mushrooms in warm water until soft. Remove the stems, discard and shred the caps. Prepare the recipe as directed in the recipe shown above.

Stir-Fried Red-in-Snow and Bamboo Shoots

¾ lb. or 2 cans red-in-snow

1 bamboo shoot, blanched

1 hot red pepper

①
- 1 T. soy sauce
- 1 t. sugar
- ¼ t. MSG

❶ Rinse the red-in-snow thoroughly. Squeeze out the excess water (fig. 3). Cut into ¼-inch lengths. Shred the bamboo shoot. Remove the seeds from the red pepper and shred (fig. 4).

❷ Heat pan and add 4 Tbsp. oil, heat until very hot. Add the red-in-snow, bamboo shoot and stir-fry over high heat for 1 minute. Add the red pepper and mixture ① . Toss lightly and remove to serving platter. Serve.

Stir-Fried Pork with Red-in-Snow

Shred ¼ lb. boneless pork and stir-fry until cooked with the red-in-snow, bamboo shoot, etc., as directed in the recipe above shown above.

153

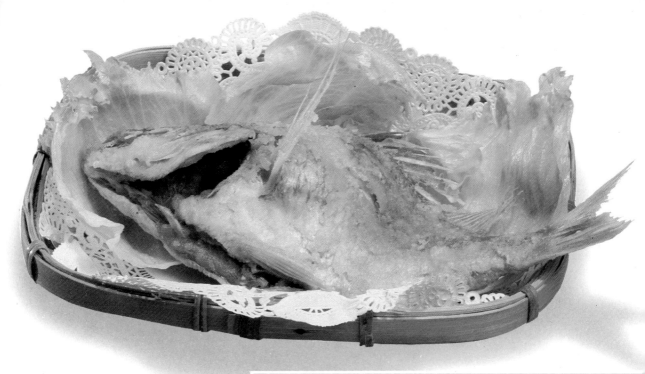

塩酥魚

鮮魚（1條）12兩

① ┌ 薑酒汁……1大匙
　├ 鹽…………1小匙
　└ 味精………¼小匙

太白粉……1大匙

「炸油」………4杯

椒 ┌ 花椒粉……½小匙
鹽 └ 鹽…………1大匙

生菜…………1棵

❶ 魚去鱗及內臟，洗淨後拭乾水份，在魚背肉厚處，各劃2直刀（圖1），用鐵針或竹籤由魚頭貫穿魚身至魚尾，使尾端往上翹起固定形狀（圖2）。

❷ 將①料抹勻魚身內外醃30分鐘以上，炸前灑太白粉1大匙（圖3）。

❸ 「炸油」4杯燒熱（375℉），提着魚尾順鍋放入，用中火炸3分鐘，然後改大火炸30秒，至魚皮呈金黃肉熟酥脆撈出，瀝乾油（圖4）。

❹ 盤內先舖上生菜（先拭乾水），擺上炸酥的魚並灑少許椒鹽，或將椒鹽另置小碟一齊端出沾食。

■ 椒鹽做法：乾淨鍋燒熱，放入花椒粒1小匙炒至淡褐色，酥時取出碾成粉末即為「花椒粉」；再加鹽1大匙拌勻即成「花椒鹽」簡稱「椒鹽」。亦可用胡椒粉拌鹽或五香粉拌鹽，均供油炸食物沾用。

■ 薑酒汁：薑拍碎加酒擠出的汁。

■ 此道菜肴可覆蓋魚網裝飾；做法參考第30頁，蘿蔔類盤飾第6種。

蛋白質 ·············· ９１克	
脂質 ················· ３６克	
醣質 ················· １４克	
熱量 ·········· ７５７仟卡	

Protein. 91g
Fat 36g
Carbohydrate. 14g
757 Kcal

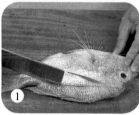

Savory Fried Fish

Taiwanese 6 servings

1 whole fresh fish* (about 1 lb.)
① { ½ T. ginger-wine*¹
    1 t. salt
    ¼ t. MSG
1 T. cornstarch
4 C. oil for frying
Szechuan peppercorn salt:*²
½ t. Szechuan peppercorns
1 T. salt
4 leaves leafy lettuce

❶ Scale and gut the fish. Rinse thoroughly and pat dry. Score the fish in 2 places along the backbone, at the thickest section of the fish (fig. 1). Insert a metal or bamboo skewer from the mouth through the tail end of the fish, to prevent the fish from curling in the hot oil (fig. 2).

❷ Rub mixture ① inside the scores, stomach and along the outside. Marinate for at least 30 minutes. Dust the fish with the cornstarch (fig. 3).

❸ Heat pan and add oil, heat to 375°F. Hold the fish by the tail, slowly lower into the hot oil. Deep-fry for about 3 minutes over medium heat. Turn the heat to high and continue to deep-fry for about 30 seconds until the skin is golden brown. Remove and drain (fig. 4).

❹ Rinse the lettuce leaves and drain. Arrange the leaves on the bottom of the serving platter and place the fish on top. Sprinkle with the Szechuan peppercorn salt, or serve separately in a small finger bowl for dipping. Serve.

* Any whole firm-fleshed fresh fish may be used.

*¹ To prepare the ginger-wine, mash 1 slice fresh ginger-root and add to ½ tablespoon rice wine. Pinch the ginger to imbibe the rice wine with the ginger flavor. Remove the ginger slices and use as directed.

*² To prepare the Szechuan peppercorn salt: Heat a pan until hot (no oil). Add the peppercorns and stir-fry for about 5 minutes over high heat (turning constantly), until they darken and become crisp. Remove and pulverize in a blender to a smooth powder. Mix with the salt and serve as a dip with deep-fried foods. Five-spice salt may also be served with the fish.

松子全魚

江浙菜　　12人份

鯉魚1條…1斤半

① 酒…………1大匙
　　蔥…………2枝
　　薑…………2片
　　鹽…………1小匙
　　胡椒粉………少許

蛋黃…………1個
太白粉………1杯
「炸油」………4杯
松子…………1兩
洋蔥丁………$\frac{1}{2}$杯

② 糖…………5大匙
　　醋…………4大匙
　　番茄醬……4大匙
　　水…………4大匙
　　鹽…………$\frac{1}{4}$小匙
　　太白粉……1小匙

❶ 魚去鱗及內臟洗淨，切下魚頭，由下顎剖切使魚頭展開。
　　魚由脊背邊剖開，去除脊骨，尾部保留（圖1）。

❷ 魚皮朝下在肉面每隔約1.5公分斜切交叉成菱型花刀（圖
　　2），調①料抹勻醃30分鐘，下鍋前沾裹蛋黃及太白粉
　　，劃刀處需塗抹勻，魚頭亦沾太白粉後備炸（圖3）。

❸ 鍋熱，加「炸油」4杯，冷油即將松子下鍋，用鍋鏟不停攪動
　　，以中火炸呈金黃色撈起瀝淨油。仍將原油燒熱（350℉）
　　，將魚身捲成筒狀使菱形花紋張開入鍋，以大火炸約3分
　　鐘呈金黃色，肉熟皮酥撈出（圖4），魚頭下鍋炸熟置盤排
　　成魚狀。

❹ 鍋熱，加油2大匙將洋蔥丁炒香，入②料燒沸，淋油1大
　　匙(以增光澤)，即可澆在炸好的魚上，並灑松子即成。

■ 如無松子可免用。

蛋白質·········１０４克
脂質················７６克
醣質···········１０９克
熱量·······１５５０仟卡
Protein. 104g
Fat 76g
Carbohydrate. 109g
1,550 Kcal

Sweet and Sour Fish with Pine Nuts
Chekiang-Kiangsu 12 servings

1 whole fish* (about 2 lbs.)

① {
1 T. rice wine
2 stalks green onion
2 slices ginger
½ t. salt
¼ t. black pepper
}

1 egg yolk
1 C. cornstarch
4 C. oil for frying
1 oz. pine nuts*[1]
½ C. chopped onion

② {
5 T. sugar
4 T. rice vinegar
4 T. catsup
4 T. water
¼ t. salt
1 t. cornstarch
}

1 T. oil

❶ Scale and cut the fish. If the head is still remaining, cut open, along the chin. Make an incision along the backbone and cut down into the body, along the bone to separate the filet from the bone, cut to the tail. Turn over and repeat for the opposite side (fig. 1). Remove the backbone. (The fish should still be connected at the tail end).

❷ Score the filet meat lengthwise at every ½-inch and crosswise, to form a diamond pattern (fig. 2). Add mixture ① and marinate for 30 minutes. Before frying, coat the filets with the egg yolk and dredge in the cornstarch. Make sure that the fish is coated throughout. If using the fish head, coat it as well (fig. 3).

❸ Heat Pan and add oil, heat to 200°F. Add the pine nuts and deep-fry over medium heat until golden brown, stir continuously. Remove and drain. Reheat oil to 350°F. Roll the fish into a semi-circle shape so that the scoring is exposed and the meat "flowers" out. Place in the oil and deep-fry for 3 minutes over high heat until golden. (The meat should be flaky and the skin, crisp.) Remove and drain (fig. 4). Deep-fry the fish head until golden. Remove, drain and reconstruct the whole fish on a serving platter.

❹ Heat pan and add 2 Tbsp. oil, heat until very hot. Add the onions and stir-fry until fragrant. Add mixture ② and heat until boiling. Add 1 Tbsp. oil and toss lightly. Pour the sauce over the fish and sprinkle with the pine seeds. Serve immediately.

* The fish in the illustration is carp, however pickerel, sea bass or lake trout is recommended. One and one-third pounds of fish filets may be substituted for the whole fish. Prepare as directed in Step ❷

*[1] If unavailable, omit.

元寶鯽魚

鯽魚２條‥‥１２兩
絞肉‥‥‥‥‥６兩
① 葱、薑末(各)½大匙
鹽‥‥‥‥‥¼小匙
水‥‥‥‥‥２大匙
太白粉‥‥‥½大匙
葱段‥‥‥‥１０枝
（１０公分）
② 酒‥‥‥‥‥１大匙
醬油‥‥‥‥３大匙
味精‥‥‥‥¼小匙
糖‥‥‥‥‥１大匙
黑醋‥‥‥‥½大匙
水‥‥‥‥‥１½杯
③ 太白粉‥‥‥１小匙
水‥‥‥‥‥１大匙

❶ 鯽魚去鱗除鰓，由背部順大骨邊剖開（圖１），挖除內臟（圖２），使腹部相連洗淨待塞。
如所購之魚已先在腹部剖開亦可，即由腹部塞入，但所塞之肉絨經烹煮後魚腹易於張開，暴露肉絨。
❷ 絞肉與①料攪拌至膠黏狀即成肉絨，將肉絨由魚背剖開處塞進腹內（圖３）。
❸ 烹調有炸、煎後紅燒的兩種方法：
炸法：鍋熱，加「炸油」３杯燒熱（３５０℉），魚下鍋炸約１分鐘呈金黃色撈出，鍋內留油２大匙炒香葱段，入已過油的魚及②料蓋鍋燒沸，以小火燜煮２０分鐘至熟透（圖４），再以③料勾芡，淋下油１大匙盛盤。
煎法：鍋熱，加油６大匙燒熱，魚落鍋用中火將魚兩面煎呈金黃色，鏟至鍋邊，入葱段炒香加②料蓋鍋燒沸，以小火燜煮約２０分鐘至熟透，以③料勾芡，淋油１大匙置盤。

葱燒鯽魚

鯽魚２條‥‥１２兩
葱段‥‥‥‥１０枝
②料　　　　③料

❶ 鯽魚去鱗，由腹部剖開除內臟，洗淨。
❷ 鍋熱，加油６大匙燒熱，葱段炒香，把魚落鍋煎至兩面呈金黃色，入②料用小火燜煮約１０分鐘至熟透，以③料勾芡淋油１大匙盛盤。

蛋白質⋯⋯⋯⋯⋯⋯７７克
脂質⋯⋯⋯⋯⋯⋯１０７克
醣質⋯⋯⋯⋯⋯⋯⋯１５克
熱量⋯⋯⋯⋯１３４６仟卡
Protein 77g
Fat 107g
Carbohydrate 15g
1,346 Kcal

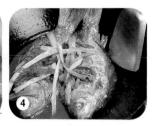

Braised Butterfish with Stuffing

Chekiang-Kiangsu 6 servings

2 whole butterfish*, about ½ lb. each

½ lb. ground pork or beef

1 T. cornstarch

① ½ T. minced green onions
½ T. minced ginger
¼ t. salt
2 T. water
½ T. cornstarch

10 (4-inch) sections green onion

② 1 T. rice wine
3 T. soy sauce
¼ t. MSG
1 T. sugar
½ T. black vinegar or Worcestershire sauce
1½ C. water

③ 1 t. cornstarch
1 T. water

1 T. oil

❶ Scale the fish and remove the gills, leave the stomach intact*[1]. Make a long incision along the back of the fish and slice to make a pocket for the stuffing (fig. 1). Remove the entrails through the incision (fig. 2) and rinse thoroughly. Drain and pat dry. Sprinkle the cavity with the cornstarch.

❷ Chop the ground meat to a smooth paste and add mixture ① . Mix thoroughly, stir in one continuous motion until the mixture is smooth (stuffing). Stuff the mixture into the fish (fig. 3).

❸ The fish may be prepared by either of the following methods:

To deep-fry: Heat pan and add 3 C. oil, heat to 350°F. Add the fish and deep-fry for about 1 minute, until golden. Remove, drain and remove all but 2 Tbsp. oil from the pan. Reheat until hot and add the green onion sections. Stir-fry until fragrant, then add the fish and mixture ② . Cover and heat until boiling. Cook for 20 minutes over low heat until the fish flakes and the stuffing is cooked. (fig. 4). Add mixture ③ to thicken the sauce and add 1 Tbsp. oil. Mix the sauce and remove to serving plate. Serve.

To pan-fry: Heat the pan and add 6 Tbsp. oil, heat until almost smoking. Add the fish and fry over medium heat until both sides are golden. Push the fish to the side of the pan, add the green onion sections and stir-fry until fragrant. Add mixture ② , push the fish back to the center and cover. Heat until boiling, reduce the heat to low and simmer for 20 minutes, until the fish meat flakes. Add mixture ③ to thicken, and 1 Tbsp. oil as directed above.

* If unavailable, substitute fresh trout.

*[1] If the belly of the fish is already slit open, stuff the fish through the stomach. Before steaming, close the opening with toothpicks.

Butterfish with Green Onions

2 whole butterfish, ½ lb. each

10 stalks green onion

② same as above

③ same as above

❶ Scale the fish and gut the fish through the stomach. Rinse thoroughly and drain.

❷ Heat pan and add 6 Tbsp. oil heat until very hot. Add the onions and stir-fry until fragrant. Add the fish, and fry on both sides until golden. Add ② , cover and cook over low heat for about 10 minutes, until the fish meat flakes. Add mixture ③ to thicken. Sprinkle 1 Tbsp. oil and toss lightly. Remove to plate and serve.

双冬燴海參

海參（３條）１２兩

① 酒…………½大匙
　 葱……………２枝
　 薑……………４片

水……………２杯

葱 ……………６枝

（３公分長段）

薑……………６片

冬菇(大)……３朵

筍……………１枝

酒…………１小匙

② 醬油………３大匙
　 糖…………１小匙
　 味精………¼小匙
　 高湯………¾杯

③ 太白粉……１大匙
　 水…………１大匙

麻油………½小匙

❶ 海參除內臟洗淨（圖１），每條直剖兩半再斜切４～６塊（圖２）。冬菇泡軟每朵切４片，筍切滾刀塊（圖３）。

❷ 鍋熱，加油１大匙，炒香①料後，加水燒沸，放入海參煨煮２分鐘撈起，以除去腥味，湯汁不用。

❸ 油３大匙燒熱，將葱、薑炒香隨入海參略炒，下酒１小匙加冬菇、筍及②料蓋鍋，以小火燒煮約１０分鐘至汁剩一半時，以③料勾芡（圖４），最後淋麻油即可盛盤。

■ 發乾海參的方法：

將海參盛乾淨鍋內加水浸泡半天，再置爐上蓋鍋以小火燒煮１～２小時（燒煮時要注意水須淹蓋海參面），熄火待鍋中水冷却始取出，重新換水再煮１～２小時（小火），照此法將海參煮軟發脹後，剪開腹部挖除腸筋及內壁黃皮刮下，重新換水再煮與浸泡，反覆數次至海參軟硬適度時即可使用。

蛋白質⋯⋯⋯⋯⋯ ３１克
脂質⋯⋯⋯⋯⋯⋯ ３５克
醣質⋯⋯⋯⋯⋯⋯ ２０克
熱量⋯⋯⋯⋯ ５２０仟卡
Protein. 31g
Fat 35g
Carbohydrate. 20g
520 Kcal

Braised Sea Cucumbers with Mushrooms

Cantonese 6 servings

3 pre-conditioned sea cucumbers (1 lb.)*

① ½ T. rice wine
2 stalks green onions
4 slices ginger

2 C. water
6 green onions (1¼-inch sections)
6 slices ginger
3 large Chinese black mushrooms
1 bamboo shoot
1 t. rice wine

② 3 T. soy sauce
1 t. sugar
¼ t. MSG
¾ C. stock

③ 1 T. cornstarch
1 T. water
½ t. sesame oil

❶ Remove the entrails from the sea cucumbers and rinse well (fig. 1). Cut each cucumber lengthwise in half, then diagonally cut into 4-6 sections (fig. 2). Soften the black mushrooms in warm water until soft, remove the stems and discard. Cut the caps in halves, then quarters. Blanch the bamboo shoot briefly, remove and refresh in cold water. Drain and roll-cut into bite-size pieces (fig. 3).

❷ Heat pan and add 1 Tbsp. oil, heat until very hot. Add mixture ① and stir-fry until fragrant. Add the water and heat until boiling. Add the sea cucumbers and cook for 2 minutes, then remove and drain. (This cooking removes the strong fishy flavor.) Discard the liquid.

❸ Heat pan and add 3 Tbsp. oil heat until very hot. Add the green onions, ginger and stir-fry until fragrant. Add the sea cucumbers, rice wine, black mushrooms, bamboo shoots and ② . Simmer covered for about 10 minutes over low heat, or until the liquid is reduced to half of the original amount. Add mixture ③ to thicken (fig. 4). Add the sesame oil, toss lightly and remove to a serving plate. Serve immediately.

* To pre-condition the dried sea cucumbers:
Place the sea cucumbers in a pot. Add cold water to cover and soak for 12 hours. Place over low heat and cook for 1-2 hours. Add more water, if necessary, so that the water always covers the cucumbers. Turn off the heat and remove the pot from the heat. Let cool until the water is room temperature. Drain the cucumbers, make a cut on one side, down the length of the cucumbers. Remove the entrails and scrape out the insides with the blade of a cleaver. Place the cucumbers in cold water to cover and soak for 1-2 hours. Use as directed in the recipe shown above.

五味九孔

台灣菜　　6人份

九孔…………半斤
① 酒…………1大匙
　 葱…………2枝
　 薑…………2片
　 水…………5杯
生菜…………1個
② 番茄醬……2大匙
　 黑醋………1大匙
　 醬油………1大匙
　 細糖………$\frac{1}{2}$大匙
　 味精………$\frac{1}{4}$小匙
　 麻油………1小匙
　 葱薑、蒜末、紅辣
　 椒末(各)…1小匙

❶ 刷子沾少許鹽將九孔之外殼及肉部刷淨（圖1），並用冷水沖洗瀝乾。
❷ ①料燒開，放入九孔（圖2），改小火煮約1分鐘熄火，浸泡約1分鐘至剛熟撈出，泡入冷開水待涼剝殼並去頭端之硬嘴（圖3），翻面再放回原殼上。
❸ 生菜剝開洗淨，切絲（圖4），置盤中，將九孔擺放在上面，再淋上已預先拌勻之②料即成。

蛤蜊…………半斤
①料
包生菜
②料

五味蛤蜊

❶ 包生菜切絲舖在盤底。
❷ 把①料燒開，放進蛤蜊川燙至蜊殼微開撈出，用手將蜊殼剝開，無肉之一邊剝除，連肉之一邊盛盤，再淋②料即成。
■ 蛤蜊吐沙法：參照第204頁「蛤蜊蒸蛋」做法❶。

蛋白質‥‥‥‥‥‥６７克
脂質‥‥‥‥‥‥‥‥９克
醣質‥‥‥‥‥‥‥３４克
熱量‥‥‥‥‥４８３仟卡
Protein. 67g
Fat 9g
Carbohydrate. 34g
483 Kcal

Five-Flavor Mussels

Taiwanese 6 servings

⅔ lb. fresh mussels*

① {
1 T. rice wine
2 stalks green onion, smashed
2 slices ginger, smashed
5 C. water
}

1 head lettuce

② {
2 T. catsup
1 T. black vinegar or
  Worcestershire sauce
1 T. soy sauce confectioners'
½ T. confectioners' sugar
¼ t. MSG
1 t. sesame oil
1 t. minced green onion
1 t. minced ginger
1 t. minced garlic
1 t. minced hot red pepper
}

⅔ lb. steamer clams
① same as above
1 head lettuce
② same as above

❶ Dip a brush in some salt and scrub the mussels and remove any black seaweed. (fig. 1). Rinse thoroughly in cold water and drain.

❷ Place mixture ① in a pan and heat until boiling. Add the mussels (fig. 2). Cover, simmer over low heat for 1 minute. Turn off the heat and let stand for 1 minute. Remove the mussels and refresh in cold water. Drain and open up the mussels. Remove the beard (fig. 3) and place the meat back into the shell.

❸ Rinse the lettuce and shred finely (fig. 4). Arrange the lettuce in the center of a serving plate. Place the mussels on top of the lettuce. Mix together the ingredients of ② and pour over the mussels.

* The seafood in the illustration (九孔) is a mollusk available in the Far East, similar in flavor to the mussel.

Five-Flavor Clams

❶ To rid the clams of sand, see step ❶ "Steamed Eggs with Clams" P. 204. Shred the lettuce.

❷ Place mixture ① in a pot and heat until boiling. Add the clams and cook for 2 minutes until the shells open. Remove and open the clams. Remove the black covering on the neck and return the clam to a half-shell. Discard the other shell. Arrange the shredded lettuce on a serving plate and place the clams on top. Mix the ingredients of ② and pour over the clams. Serve.

炸墨魚丸

台灣菜　　6人份

墨魚………１２兩
肥肉…………１兩
「炸油」………４杯
①{
薑酒汁……１小匙
鹽…………半小匙
味精………$\frac{1}{4}$小匙
蛋白…………１個
太白粉……１大匙
}
椒鹽………半大匙

❶墨魚除去頭、尾、內臟及薄膜（圖１），約剩６兩淨肉，用搥肉器之平面將墨魚肉搥成泥狀即為「墨魚漿」（圖２）。肥肉用刀剁爛。

❷「墨魚漿」調入①料，順同一方向仔細攪拌成膠狀約３分鐘，再入肥肉拌妥（圖３）。

❸鍋熱，入「炸油」４杯燒熱（275°F）熄火，將調好之「墨魚漿」用手抓起擠成丸子約８粒，全部放入油鍋內（圖４），重將火點燃，以中火炸約４分鐘，於丸子浮出油面時，用鍋鏟推動丸子炸勻呈金黃色撈起，瀝乾置盤，沾椒鹽食之。

■薑酒汁：薑拍碎加酒擠出的汁。

■椒鹽做法：參照第154頁「鹽酥魚」。

蛋白質‥‥‥‥‥‥４２克
脂質‥‥‥‥‥‥‥３６克
醣質‥‥‥‥‥‥‥‥８克
熱量‥‥‥‥‥‥５３４仟卡
Protein. 42g
Fat 36g
Carbohydrate 8g
534 Kcal

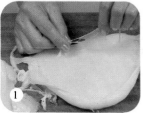  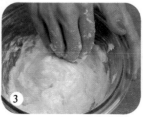 

Deep-Fried Squid Balls   Taiwanese 6 servings

1 lb. squid meat
1 T. pork fat
4 C. oil for frying

①{
1 t. ginger-wine*
½ t. salt
¼ t. MSG
1 egg white
1 T. cornstarch
½ T. Szechuan peppercorn salt*¹

❶ Clean the squid and remove the thin outer skin (fig. 1). Use, a meat mallet to pound the squid meat to a smooth paste (fig. 2); or it may be chopped by machine. Chop the pork fat to a smooth paste.

❷ Add mixture ① to the squid paste and mix continuously in one direction for about 3 minutes, or to a smooth, sticky consistency. Add the pork fat and continue to mix until completely blended (fig. 3).

❸ Heat pan and add oil, heat to 300°F. Turn off the heat. Take a handful of the squid paste and make a fist, squeeze the paste through the opening between the index finger and thumb. Shape into about 8 balls and place in the hot oil (fig. 4). Turn the heat to medium, and deep-fry for about 4 minutes, stir occasionally with a spatula or ladle. When the balls float to the surface and are golden brown, remove and drain. Arrange on a serving platter and serve with Szechuan peppercorn salt as a dip.

* To prepare ginger-wine, mash 1 slice fresh ginger root and add to 1 tsp. rice wine. Pinch the ginger to imbibe the rice wine with the ginger flavor. Remove the ginger slice and use as directed.

*¹ To prepare Szechuan peppercorn salt, see "Savory Fried Fish," P. 154.

炒鱔糊

江浙菜　　6 人份

鱔魚(燙熟)…6兩

「油」…………1 杯

① 味精………¼小匙
胡椒粉………少許
糖…………½小匙
醬油………3 大匙

② 太白粉……半大匙
水…………1 大匙

蒜末………1 大匙

胡椒粉……¼小匙

③ 油………1½大匙
麻油……1½大匙

嫩薑絲……2 大匙

香菜葉……2 大匙

❶ 鱔魚洗淨瀝乾,順直切開或用手撕成2～3條(圖1),
視鱔片的大小決定,整齊排列切約7公分長段(圖2)。

❷ 鍋熱,加油1杯燒熱(375℉),倒入鱔魚泡油約10
秒撈出;留油3大匙再入鱔魚,下酒半大匙及①料大火爆
炒,以②料勾芡(圖3),最後淋油1大匙拌勻盛盤,中
間挖成凹狀放進蒜末灑胡椒粉¼小匙。

❸ 將③料燒至極熱澆淋在蒜末上(圖4),使發出響聲迸發
蒜香,盤兩旁擺上嫩薑絲及香菜,食時一齊拌勻。

■家常食用酌加韭黃,以減少鱔魚的份量,較為經濟實用。

蛋白質 ⋯⋯⋯⋯⋯ ３７克
脂質 ⋯⋯⋯⋯⋯⋯ ４７克
醣質 ⋯⋯⋯⋯⋯⋯ １０克
熱量 ⋯⋯⋯⋯ ６１５仟卡
Protein 37g
Fat 47g
Carbohydrate. 10g
615 Kcal

Stir-Fried Eel

Chekiang-Kiangsu 6 servings

½ lb. thin eels (pre-cooked)

1 C. oil for frying

①
- ¼ t. MSG
- ¼ t. black pepper
- ½ t. sugar
- 3 T. soy sauce
- ½ T. rice wine

②
- ½ T. cornstarch
- 1 T. water

1 T. minced garlic

¼ t. black pepper

③
- 1½ T. oil for frying
- 1½ T. sesame oil

2 T. chopped fresh ginger

2 T. coriander

❶ Rinse the eels and drain. Cut or tear in halves or thirds depending on the size (fig. 1). Cut the sections into 2½-inch lengths (fig. 2).

❷ Heat pan and add oil, heat to 375°F. Add the eel sections and deep-fry for about 10 seconds. Remove and drain. Remove all but 3 Tbsp. of oil from pan and reheat until very hot. Add the eels, rice wine and mixture ① . Stir-fry briefly over high heat and add mixture ② to thicken (fig. 3). Add 1 Tbsp. oil and toss lightly. Remove to a serving plate. Make a well in the center of the stir-fried mixture and place the minced garlic in the well. Sprinkle the black pepper on top.

❸ Heat pan and add mixture ③ until smoking. Pour over the garlic (fig. 4); add the shredded ginger and coriander on both ends of the platter. Serve immediately and toss lightly before eating. (The hot oil will make a sizzling noise and intensify the flavor of the garlic.)

■ If preparing this dish at home, it is more economical to use ½ cup 2½-inch sections of Chinese chives for the eel sections. Reduce the quantity of eel to ⅓ lb.

蠔油鮑片

廣東菜　　6人份

鮑魚…………½缶

包生菜………1個

① ｛ 鹽…………½小匙
味精………¼小匙 ｝

葱薑末(各)1大匙

② ｛ 蠔油………2大匙
醬油………1大匙
味精………¼小匙
糖…………¼小匙
麻油………1小匙
鮑魚汁………½杯 ｝

③ ｛ 太白粉……½大匙
水…………1大匙 ｝

❶ 鮑魚切大薄片（圖1）。包生菜用手撕或刀切大塊（圖2）。把②料盛碗內備用。

❷ 鍋熱，加油3大匙燒熱，放入包生菜加①料用大火爆炒（圖3），瀝乾盛盤。

❸ 鍋熱，加油3大匙燒熱，炒香葱、薑末，下酒1小匙及②料燒開，以③料勾茨，隨入鮑片再拌炒1分鐘，最後澆上油1大匙（以增光澤），起鍋舖蓋包生菜上便成（圖4）。

■ 除包生菜外，豆苗、芥蘭菜、青江菜、包心菜…等均可。

蠔油芥蘭

芥蘭菜……12兩
②料（免用鮑魚汁）

❶ 芥蘭菜處理法：參照本頁「芥蘭牛肉」做法❷（餐廳所切芥蘭菜較長約10公分長段）。如菜梗太硬，把菜梗部份在滾水內燙煮時加小蘇打¼小匙。撈出芥蘭菜瀝乾水份，整齊排於盤內。

❷ 鍋內加油1大匙，入②料攪拌燒沸，淋於菜上即成。

■ 簡單法：燙好芥蘭置盤，淋上適量蠔油亦可。

蛋白質⋯⋯⋯⋯⋯３２克
脂質⋯⋯⋯⋯⋯⋯５０克
醣質⋯⋯⋯⋯⋯⋯３８克
熱量⋯⋯⋯⋯７０８仟卡
Protein. 32g
Fat 50g
Carbohydrate 38g
708 Kcal

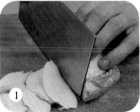
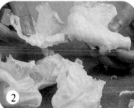

Stir-Fried Abalone with Oyster Sauce

Cantonese 6 servings

½ can abalone (about 5 oz.)

1 medium head Chinese cabbage*

① { ½ t. salt
   ¼ t. MSG

1 T. minced green onion

1 T. minced ginger

② { 2 T. oyster sauce
   1 T. soy sauce
   ¼ t. MSG
   ¼ t. sugar
   1 t. sesame oil
   ½ C. abalone liquid

③ { ½ T. cornstarch
   1 T. water

1 T. oil

❶ Drain the abalone (retain the liquid) and cut into thin slices (fig. 1). Tear the cabbage by hand or cut into 2-inch squares (fig. 2). Blend the ingredients of mixture ② and set aside.

❷ Heat pan and add 3 Tbsp. oil, heat until very hot. Add the cabbage sections and mixture ① . Stir-fry over high heat until tender and slightly wilted (fig. 3). Remove and place on a serving platter.

❸ Heat pan and add 3 Tbsp. oil, heat until very hot. Add the green onion, ginger and stir-fry until fragrant. Add the rice wine and mixture ② . Heat until the liquid boils then add ③ to thicken. Add the abalone slices and stir-fry for 1 minute. Add 1 Tbsp. oil to give the sauce a sheen, toss lightly and arrange on top of the cabbage (fig. 4). Serve immediately.

* Spinach, lettuce or broccoli may be substituted for the cabbage.

Chinese Broccoli with Oyster Sauce

1 lb. Chinese Broccoli

② same as above

   (take out abalone liquid)

❶ Remove any old leaves and peel the tough skin from the Chinese broccoli. Cut into 1½-inch sections (fig. 3, 4).* Blanch for about 1 minute. Remove and refresh in cold water. Drain.

❷ Heat pan and add 1 Tbsp. oil. (Add mixture ② , stir continuously. Let it come to a boil. Pour the sauce over the broccoli.)

* The broccoli may be cut into 3-inch sections, if desired.

■ Normal cooking, put the blanched Chinese Broccoli in a dish and pour some oyster sauce over the broccoli.

金菇生蠔

江浙菜　　6 人份

生蠔⋯⋯⋯⋯6 兩
薑酒汁⋯⋯⋯1 大匙
金菇⋯⋯⋯⋯1 缶
小黃瓜⋯⋯⋯2 條
① {
嫩薑⋯⋯⋯⋯6 片
葱⋯⋯⋯⋯⋯2 條
紅辣椒⋯⋯⋯1 條
}
② {
鹽⋯⋯⋯⋯⋯$\frac{3}{4}$ 小匙
味精⋯⋯⋯⋯$\frac{1}{4}$ 小匙
太白粉⋯⋯⋯$\frac{1}{2}$ 大匙
水⋯⋯⋯⋯⋯1 大匙
麻油⋯⋯⋯⋯$\frac{1}{2}$ 小匙
}

❶ 生蠔洗法：參照第180頁「酥蠔(一)」做法❶。把小黃瓜及①料全部切絲（圖1）。
❷ 生蠔加薑酒汁1大匙醃20分鐘。水3杯燒沸用大火將生蠔川燙15秒撈出瀝乾（圖2）。
❸ 鍋熱，加油3大匙燒熱，入①料炒香（圖3），下酒1大匙隨入金菇，小黃瓜絲及生蠔，用大火拌炒30秒（圖4），調入②料拌勻，最後淋麻油盛盤。
■ 除生蠔外，可用蛤蜊肉、蝦仁⋯⋯等。小黃瓜絲可改用芹菜、豆芽（摘除兩頭）也很相宜。

炒山瓜子

山瓜子⋯⋯⋯1 斤
① {
葱末⋯⋯⋯⋯1 小匙
蒜(拍碎)⋯⋯5 粒
紅辣椒絲⋯⋯$\frac{1}{2}$ 大匙
酒⋯⋯⋯⋯⋯2 大匙
薑絲⋯⋯⋯⋯$\frac{1}{4}$ 杯
}
② {
鹽⋯⋯⋯⋯⋯$\frac{1}{2}$ 小匙
味精⋯⋯⋯⋯$\frac{1}{4}$ 小匙
胡椒粉⋯⋯⋯$\frac{1}{4}$ 小匙
水⋯⋯⋯⋯⋯$\frac{1}{4}$ 杯
}

❶ 山瓜子洗淨備用。
❷ 鍋熱，加油2大匙燒熱，將①料炒香，放入山瓜子、酒、薑絲及②料以中火燜煮約2分鐘至殼開即可盛盤。
■ 台灣菜做法：將②料鹽改用醬油或蠔油1大匙半，烹調方法大致相同，惟最後加九層塔同炒，另有一番風味。
■ 購回山瓜子加水淹過山瓜子面靜置半天，使其吐沙再使用。

蛋白質 ‥‥‥‥‥‥‥ ２５克
脂質 ‥‥‥‥‥‥‥‥‥ ４６克
醣質 ‥‥‥‥‥‥‥‥‥ ２３克
熱量 ‥‥‥‥‥‥‥ ６６０仟卡

Protein. 25g
Fat 46g
Carbohydrate. 23g
660 Kcal

Stir-Fried Oysters with Golden Needle Mushrooms
Chekiang-Kiangsu 6 servings

½ lb. shucked oysters
1 T. ginger-wine*
1 13-oz. can golden needle mushrooms
2 gherkin cucumbers or 1 gourmet seedless cucumber

① {
6 slices ginger
2 stalks green onion
1 hot red pepper
1 T. rice wine

② {
¾ t. salt
¼ t. MSG
½ T. cornstarch
1 T. water

½ t. sesame oil

❶ Prepare the oysters as directed in Step ❶ "Crispy Fried Oysters," P. 180. Shred the cucumbers and ingredients of mixture ① (fig. 1). Drain the golden needle mushrooms and blanch briefly. Remove and refresh in cold water. Drain well.

❷ Mix the ginger-wine with the oysters and marinate for 20 minutes. Heat 3 C. water until boiling. Add the oysters and blanch for 30 seconds. Remove and drain (fig. 2).

❸ Heat pan and add 3 Tbsp. oil, heat until very hot. Add mixture ① and stir-fry until fragrant (fig. 3). Add the rice wine, golden needle mushrooms, cucumber shreds and the oysters. Stir-fry over high heat for 30 seconds (fig. 4). Add mixture ② and toss lightly. Sprinkle the sesame oil over the top and toss again. Remove to serving plate and serve immediately.

* To prepare ginger-wine, mash 2 slices fresh ginger root and add to 1 tablespoon rice wine. Pinch the ginger to imbibe the rice wine with the ginger flavor. Remove the ginger slices and use as directed.

■ Raw, shelled shrimp or shucked steamers may be substituted for the oysters. Shredded celery or bean sprouts may be substituted for the shredded cucumbers. If using bean sprouts, trim both ends.

Stir-Fried Clams

❶ Prepare the clams, to rid them of sand, as directed in Step ❶ "Steamed Eggs with Clams," P. 204. Remove and drain.

❷ Heat pan and add 2 Tbsp. oil, heat until very hot. Add mixture ① and stir-fry until fragrant. Add the clams, rice wine, ginger and mixture ②. Cook for 2 minutes over medium heat, or until the clams begin to open. Remove to a serving platter and serve.

■ To prepare Taiwanese-Style: Substitute 1½ Tbsp. soy sauce or oyster sauce for the salt in mixture ②. Prepare the recipe as directed above, but before removing from the pan, add ½ C. roughly chopped, fresh spearmint leaves. Toss lightly, remove to a serving platter and serve.

1⅓ lb. steamer clams

① {
1 t. minced green onion
5 garlic cloves, smashed
½ T. shredded hot red pepper
3 T. rice wine
¼ C. shredded ginger

② {
½ t. salt
¼ t. MSG
¼ t. black pepper
¼ C. water

171

碧綠鮮貝

廣東菜　　6 人份

鮮干貝⋯⋯⋯4 兩
薑酒汁⋯⋯$\frac{1}{2}$ 大匙
① 小蘇打⋯⋯$\frac{1}{2}$ 小匙
水⋯⋯⋯⋯4 大匙
芥蘭菜 ⋯⋯⋯半斤
（或青江菜）
酒⋯⋯⋯⋯$\frac{1}{2}$ 大匙
② 鹽⋯⋯⋯⋯$\frac{1}{4}$ 小匙
糖⋯⋯⋯⋯$\frac{1}{2}$ 小匙
葱段 ⋯⋯⋯⋯5 枝
（2 公分長）
薑片⋯⋯⋯5 小片
鹽⋯⋯⋯⋯$\frac{1}{2}$ 小匙
味精⋯⋯⋯$\frac{1}{4}$ 小匙
糖⋯⋯⋯⋯$\frac{1}{4}$ 小匙
③ 麻油⋯⋯⋯$\frac{1}{2}$ 小匙
太白粉⋯⋯$\frac{1}{2}$ 小匙
水⋯⋯⋯⋯2 大匙

❶ 鮮干貝切除表面硬筋（圖1），再橫紋切圓薄片（圖2），調上①料拌勻（圖3），醃 1 小時以上，然後用清水漂洗瀝乾（照此法處理，可使干貝爽脆）。

❷ 芥蘭菜剝除老葉洗淨並切 10～12 公分長段，在滾水內燙熟（約 1 分半鐘）撈出，放入冷水內泡涼後瀝乾。油 2 大匙燒熱，放進芥蘭菜及②料拌炒約 2 分鐘，鏟出盛盤。

❸ 水 5 杯燒開後熄火，將干貝下鍋川燙約 20 秒至熟撈出（圖4）。

❹ 油 2 大匙燒熱，先炒香葱薑，續入已燙過之干貝及③料炒勻，放在炒熟的芥蘭菜上即成。

■ 鮮干貝：直徑在 4 公分以下之鮮嫩干貝，①料內免用小蘇打及水醃泡。

■ 薑酒汁：薑片（最好老薑）拍碎加酒擠出的汁。例薑拍碎半大匙加酒半大匙擠出汁，即為薑酒汁半大匙。

蛋白質 · · · · · · · · · · · · · ２７克
脂質 · · · · · · · · · · · · · · · １６克
醣質 · · · · · · · · · · · · · · · １４克
熱量 · · · · · · · · · · · ３６３仟卡
Protein 27g
Fat 16g
Carbohydrate. 14g
363 Kcal

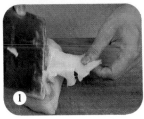   

Stir-Fried Scallops over Broccoli

Cantonese 6 servings

6 oz. fresh scallops*
½ T. ginger-wine*¹
¾ lb. Chinese broccoli
   (or any green vegetable)

① ½ T. rice wine
   ¼ t. salt
   ½ t. sugar

5 (¾-inch) green onion sections
5 slices ginger

② ½ t. salt
   ½ t. MSG
   ½ t. sugar
   ½ t. sesame oil
   ½ t. cornstarch
   2 T. water

❶ Cut away and remove outer hard skin of the scallops (fig. 1). Slice scallops against the grain into thin round pieces (fig. 2). Mix well with ginger-wine. (fig. 3). Marinate for at least 1 hour. Rinse with water and drain dry.

❷ Remove old leaves from Chinese broccoli, wash and cut into 2-inch lengths. Immerse in boiling water for about 1½ minutes and remove. Rinse in cold water, then drain. Heat wok and add 2 Tbsp. oil. Stir-fry Chinese broccoli with ① for about 2 minutes. Remove and arrange on serving platter.

❸ Boil 5 C. water, then turn off heat completely. Blanch scallops for about 20 seconds and remove (fig. 4).

❹ Heat wok and add 2 Tbsp. oil. Stir-fry green onions and ginger until fragrant. Add scallops along with ② , mixing well. Place on top of green vegetables and serve.

* The large scallops pictured above are found in the Far East. Use small, tender scallops as directed.

*¹ Preparation of ginger-wine: To ½ Tbsp. (2 slices) mashed old ginger, add ½ Tbsp. rice wine to make ½ Tbsp. of ginger wine.

173

紅油魷花

四川菜　　6 人份

① 墨魚或魷魚…１條
（淨重１２兩）

① 醬油………２大匙
味精………¼小匙
糖…………½大匙
鎮江醋……２小匙
葱薑末(各)½大匙
辣椒油…１½大匙
小黃瓜………３條

❶ 墨魚除內臟去薄膜，洗淨後拭乾，於內面每隔０.５～０.
７公分切一直條刀痕，深至墨魚厚度之一半（圖１），每
隔４公分寬切一長條（圖２），然後再橫切成斜薄片，泡入
冷水內（圖３，菜刀與墨魚成３０度所切之斜片，越斜切
出的片面越大）。

❷ 半鍋水燒開，將切好的墨魚片落鍋川燙１０秒，見肉色轉
白時即可撈出瀝乾（圖４）。

❸ 小黃瓜切薄片，加鹽半小匙醃１０分鐘後，以冷開水稍洗
並握乾，置盤，再將燙好之墨魚片整齊舖蓋上，最後淋上
調勻之①料即成。

■ 除小黃瓜外可用紅蘿蔔、芹菜、粉皮、筍（先煮熟冰涼後
切片）。

椒麻魷花

將①料改用椒麻汁：醬油２大匙、味精¼小匙，糖１小匙
、醋半大匙、麻油２大匙、花椒粒（切末）半大匙、葱薑
末各１大匙、其他材料、做法均同。

薑汁魷花

將①料改用嫩薑末２大匙，鹽半小匙、糖１小匙、白醋３
大匙、置於小碗內，作為沾料。

蒜泥魷花

將①料改用蒜泥汁：醬油露（膏）２大匙、味精¼小匙、
蒜末１小匙、糖、醋各１小匙、辣椒油１大匙，其他材料
、做法均同。

蛋白質 · · · · · · · · · · · · · ７９克
脂質 · · · · · · · · · · · · · · · ５克
醣質 · · · · · · · · · · · · · · １６克
熱量 · · · · · · · · · ４３３仟卡
Protein. 79g
Fat 5g
Carbohydate 16g
433 Kcal

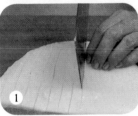

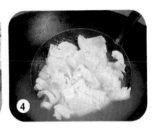

Spicy Squid with Chili Oil Szechuan 6 servings

1 lb. fresh squid
2 T. soy sauce
¼ t. MSG
½ T. sugar
① { 2 t. rice vinegar
½ T. minced green onion
½ T. minced ginger
1½ t. hot chili oil
3 gherkin cucumbers or 1 gourmet,
   seedless cucumber

❶ Remove the thin outer skin from the squid and rinse lightly. Drain and score the squid lengthwise at about every ¼-inch, on the inner side (fig. 1). Cut the squid in half, lengthwise. Diagonally cut the squid halves into thin slices, cut in a direction perpindicular to the scores (fig. 2). The sharper the angle of the edges, the larger the piece will appear once cooked. Place the cut pieces in cold water to cover and let stand for 5 minutes (fig. 3).

❷ Fill the wok with 6 C. water and heat until boiling. Add the squid sections and blanch for about 10 seconds or until the squid changes color. Remove and drain (fig. 4).

❸ Cut the cucumbers lengthwise in half, then cut into 3 sections, lengthwise. Cut each section into thin slices and toss with ½ tsp. salt. Let stand for 10 minutes. Rinse the cucumber slices with cold water. Squeeze out the excess water and arrange on a serving platter. Place the blanched squid pieces on top. Blend the ingredients of ① and pour over the top. Serve.

■ Pre-cooked carrot, celery, vermicelli sheets, all sliced, may also be used instead of cucumbers.

Spicy Squid with Sesame Sauce

Substitute the ingredients of ① for the following: 2 Tbsp. soy sauce, ¼ tsp. MSG, 1 tsp. sugar, ½ Tbsp. rice vinegar, 2 Tbsp. sesame oil, ½ Tbsp. crushed Szechuan peppercorns, 1 Tbsp. minced green onions, 1 Tbsp. minced ginger. Prepare the recipe as directed above.

Squid with Ginger

Substitute the ingredients of ① for the following: 2 Tbsp. minced ginger, ½ tsp. salt, 1 tsp. sugar, 3 Tbsp. rice vinegar. Mix in small bowl and use as dip for the squid and cucumber slices.

Squid with Garlic

Substitute the ingredients of ① for the following: 2 Tbsp. soy sauce, ¼ tsp. MSG, 1 Tbsp. minced garlic, 1 tsp. sugar, 1 tsp. rice vinegar, 1 Tbsp. chili oil. Mix in a bowl and serve as a dip with the squid and cucumber slices.

爆双花　　　　　　江浙菜　　6人份

鮮魷魚‥‥‥‥‥１條
（去頭鬚淨重５兩）
泡發魷魚‥‥‥‥１條
（去頭鬚淨重４兩）
① {
　葱末‥‥‥‥½大匙
　薑末‥‥‥‥½大匙
　蒜末‥‥‥½半大匙
　酒‥‥‥‥‥½大匙
② {
　鹽‥‥‥‥‥½小匙
　味精‥‥‥‥¼小匙
　太白粉‥‥‥１小匙
　水‥‥‥‥‥２大匙
麻油‥‥‥‥‥½小匙

❶ 將魷魚身上薄膜除去後，直切１～３刀成２～４片（視魷魚大小），然後在內面即內臟面切交叉之網狀花紋，並斜刀切塊（圖１、２、３、４）

❷ 水煮：水６杯燒開，將切好之魷魚下鍋川燙約１０秒，見色變而捲時撈出。

　泡油：「炸油」３杯燒熱（３７５℉），將魷魚下鍋泡炸１０秒撈起。

❸ 油３大匙燒熱，炒香①料，再加燙或泡油過之魷魚，下酒及②料用大火爆炒約３０秒，再淋半大匙油及半小匙麻油（以增色、香）鏟出置盤即可。

■ 發乾魷魚的方法：
　將乾魷魚置水中（水須蓋滿）浸泡約３小時，將水瀝乾，再加４大匙小蘇打粉及８杯清水，浸泡４小時至魷魚脹大後，瀝淨水，再加１５杯清水，浸泡６小時，並多次換水，以除腥味。

■ 如無乾魷魚，可增加鮮魷魚之數量至２條，如無鮮魷魚，亦可用墨魚代替。

■ 可將紅蘿蔔、竹筍、黃瓜、青椒等切薄片，加入同炒，以增美觀。

盐爆魷魚

魷魚‥‥‥‥‥２條
①料
　酒‥‥‥‥‥½大匙
② {
　鹽‥‥‥‥‥¼小匙
　味精‥‥‥‥¼小匙
　水‥‥‥‥‥２大匙
　香菜‥‥‥‥２大匙
　蝦油‥‥‥‥２大匙

❶ 魷魚任選一種使用（新鮮或泡發均可）做法參照「爆双花」做法❶、❷。

❷ 油３大匙燒熱，先炒香①料加入燙好魷魚並下酒及②料改大火爆炒約３０秒再淋油半大匙即可置盤，與另用小碟裝蝦油同上桌以供沾食。

■ 如無「泡發」的魷魚，均用鮮魷魚，做法相同，可省略「爆双花」做法❷。可適量加入紅蘿蔔、筍、小黃瓜、青椒、芹菜‥‥‥等配料。

蛋白質‥‥‥‥‥３１克
脂質‥‥‥‥‥‥‥‥３７克
醣質‥‥‥‥‥‥‥‥‥１克
熱量‥‥‥‥‥‥４６２仟卡
Protein. 31g
Fat 37g
Carbohydrate 1g
462 Kcal

 1
 2
 3
 4

Stir-Fried Squid Flowers Chekiang-Kiangsu 6 servings

7 oz. fresh squid
6 oz. pre-softened dried squid*

① { ½ T. minced green onion
    ½ T. minced ginger
    ½ T. minced garlic
½ T. rice wine

② { ½ t. salt
    ¼ t. MSG
    1 t. cornstarch
    2 T. water
½ T. oil
½ t. sesame oil

❶ Remove the thin outer skin from the squid and rinse lightly. Drain and cut the body lengthwise in half. Cut each half-section diagonally into 3-4 pieces, depending on the length of the squid. On the inner side (not the skin side), score the squid meat length wise and crosswise (figs. 1, 2, 3, 4). Repeat for the dried squid meat.

❷ Cook the squid using one of the following methods:
To boil: Heat 6 C. water until boiling. Add the squid sections (both fresh and dried) and blanch for about 10 seconds until the pieces "flower" and the color of the meat changes. Remove and drain.
To deep-fry: Heat 3 C. oil for frying to 375°F. Add the squid sections and deep-fry 10 seconds. Remove and drain.

❸ Heat pan and add 3 Tbsp. oil, heat until very hot. Add mixture ① and stir-fry until fragrant. Add the squid, rice wine and ② . Stir-fry for about 30 seconds over high heat. Add ½ Tbsp. oil and ½ tsp. sesame oil to give the sauce a sheen, and remove to serving platter. Serve.

* To soften 1-4 dried squid:
Place the squid in water to cover. Let stand for about 3 hours and remove. Drain water and add 4 Tbsp. baking soda and 8 C. water. Soak for 4 hours, or until the squid has expanded. Drain water and add 15 C. cold, fresh water. Soak for 6 hours, change the water several times to remove the fishy flavor. Use as directed above.

■ If dried squid is unavailable, increase the quantity of fresh squid to 13 oz. Cuttlefish may also be used, if squid is not available. Omit Step ❷ and follow the recipe as directed above.

■ Sliced carrots, bamboo shoot, cucumbers, green peppers, etc. may also be added to the dish.

Savory Fried Squid

2 dried or fresh squid (about 7 oz).
① same as above
½ T. rice wine
2 { ¼ t. salt
    ¼ t. MSG
    2 T. water
    2 T. chopped coriander or parsley
2 T. shrimp oil（蝦油）

❶ To prepare the dried or the fresh squid, follows Steps ❶ and ❷ as directed in the recipe above.

❷ Heat pan and add 3 Tbsp. oil, heat until very hot. Add mixture ① and stir-fry until fragrant. Add the blanched squid, wine and 2 . Cook for 30 seconds over high heat. Add ½ Tbsp. oil over the dish and toss lightly. Remove to a serving plate. Serve with the shrimp oil on the side and use as a dipping sauce.

醬爆青蟹

廣東菜　　12人份

活青蟹…1斤4兩
（2隻）

麵粉………3大匙

「炸油」………3杯

蔥薑末(各)1大匙

①{
酒…………1大匙

甜麵醬……1大匙

醬油……1½大匙

糖…………½大匙
}

高湯…………½杯

②{
太白粉……1小匙

水…………2小匙
}

❶ 活蟹處理法：用筷子1枝，從蟹口穿入（圖1），待2分鐘不動時，揭開蟹蓋（圖2），去除內臟及沙囊（圖3），內外刷洗乾淨（圖4），切塊（參照第198頁「海鮮粥」圖2），再沾麵粉備炸。把①料盛碗調勻備用。

❷ 「炸油」3杯燒熱（375℉），放入蟹塊，用大火炸約2分鐘呈淡黃色撈出，瀝淨油。

❸ 鍋熱，加油3大匙燒熱，先將蔥薑末炒香，再加①料拌炒數下，隨入蟹塊及高湯燒煮至汁剩一半時，以②料芶芡，最後淋油半大匙及麻油1小匙（以增色、香），拌勻盛盤端出。

■ 除青蟹外，海蟹亦可。

蛋白質 ·············· ４４克
脂質 ················· ４０克
醣質 ················· ２７克
熱量 ··········· ６６７仟卡
Protein 44g
Fat 40g
Carbohydrate. 27g
667 Kcal

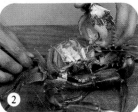

Stir-Fried Crab in Sweet Bean Sauce

Cantonese 12 servings

2 live hard-shelled crabs*
  (about ⅔ lb. apiece)
3 T. flour
3 C. oil for frying
1 T. minced green onion
1 T. minced ginger

① {
1 T. rice wine
1 T. sweet bean paste
1½T. soy sauce
½ T. sugar
}
½ C. stock

② {
1 t. cornstarch
2 t. water
}
½ T. oil
1 t. sesame oil

❶ To prepare the crab: Work a chopstick into the mouth of the crab and push the chopstick down into the heart (fig. 1). Wait for about 2 minutes, until the crab stops moving. Pull off the upper shell (fig. 2), remove the gills (fig. 3) and scrub thoroughly (fig. 4). Cut into serving pieces (see P. 198 "Seafood Congee," Step ❶ , fig. 2) and coat each with flour. Mix ingredients of ① together in small bowl.

❷ Heat pan and add oil, heat to 375°F. Add the crab pieces and deep-fry for 2 minutes over high heat until golden. Remove and drain.

❸ Heat pan and add 3 Tbsp. oil until very hot. Add the green onions, ginger and stir-fry until fragrant. Add mixture ① , the crab sections and the stock. Heat until boiling, then cook until the liquid is reduced to half of the original quantity, stir occasionally. Add mixture ② to thicken. Add ½ Tbsp. oil and sesame oil to give the sauce a sheen, toss lightly and remove to a serving plate. Serve immediately.

* If live crab is unavailable, substitute 1⅔ lbs. fresh or frozen crab or crab's legs.

酥蠔 (一)

福州菜　　6 人份

生蠔（蚵）…………６兩
薑酒汁…………１大匙
蕃薯粉或太白粉…½杯
「炸油」…………３杯
椒鹽…………１大匙

❶ 生蠔洗法：生蠔加鹽少許，輕輕攪拌，並撿出碎蠔殼，用
　 水漂洗至無黏液時，撈出瀝乾。

❷ 洗淨的生蠔加薑酒汁醃泡２０分鐘（圖１），再放入沸水
　 內燙至半熟約２０秒（圖２），撈出瀝乾。

❸ 將生蠔沾滾多量蕃薯粉備炸（圖３）。

❹ 鍋熱，將「炸油」３杯燒熱（３７５℉），生蠔落鍋，大火
　 炸呈金黃色約２分鐘（圖４），撈起盛盤，備椒鹽同上以
　 供沾食。

酥蠔 (二)

生蠔…………６兩
薑酒汁……１大匙
「炸油」………３杯
┌麵粉………４大匙
│發泡粉……¼小匙
1│水…………３大匙
│油…………½大匙
└椒鹽………½大匙

❶ 參照本頁酥蠔(一)做法❶、❷。

❷ 1料全部盛在大碗內，攪拌成糊狀，再將生蠔放入輕輕拌
　 勻備炸。

❸ 參照本頁酥蠔(一)做法❹。

■ 薑酒汁：薑拍碎加酒擠出的汁。

■ 椒鹽做法：參照第１５４頁「鹽酥魚」。

蛋白質 ················· ２４克
脂質 ·················· ３１克
醣質 ················· ３９克
熱量 ··········· ５９３仟卡
Protein. 24g
Fat 31g
Carbohydrate. 39g
593 Kcal

Crispy Deep-Fried Oysters I   Fukienese 6 servings

½ lb. shucked oysters
1 T. ginger-wine*
½ C. cornstarch or potato starch
3 C. oil for frying
1 T. Szechuan peppercorn salt*¹

❶ Clean the oysters by adding ¼ tsp. of salt to water and gently mix. Rinse lightly in water and drain.

❷ Add the ginger-wine to the oysters and marinate for 20 minutes (fig. 1). Blanch the oysters to cover for 20 seconds until partially cooked (fig. 2). Remove and drain.

❸ Dredge the oysters in the cornstarch (fig. 3).

❹ Heat pan and add oil, heat to 375°F. Add the oysters and deep-fry for 2 minutes over high heat, or until golden (fig. 4). Remove, drain and place on a serving platter. Serve with the Szechuan peppercorn salt.

* To prepare ginger-wine, smash 2 slices fresh ginger root and add to 1 tablespoon rice wine. Pinch the ginger, to imbibe the rice wine with the ginger flavor. Remove the ginger slices and use as directed.

*¹ To prepare Szechuan peppercorn salt: See note P. 154, "Crispy Savory Fish."

Crispy Fried Oysters II

½ lb. shucked oysters
1 T. ginger-wine
3 C. oil for frying

[1] { 4 T. flour
¼ t. baking soda
3 T. water
½ T. oil

½ T. Szechuan peppercorn salt

❶ To prepare the oysters, follow steps ❶ and ❷ of the recipe shown above.

❷ Blend the ingredients of mixture [1] to make a smooth batter. Add the oysters to the batter and mix gently.

❸ To deep-fry the oysters, follow Step ❹ of the recipe shown above.

鮮炸魷魚　　　　　　　　江浙菜　　6人份

鮮魷魚‥‥‥‥1 條
（去頭鬚淨重12兩）

① 酒‥‥‥‥‥1 小匙
鹽‥‥‥‥‥½ 小匙
味精‥‥‥‥¼ 小匙
葱（拍破）‥‥2 枝
薑‥‥‥‥‥2 片

玉米粉 ‥‥‥‥¾ 杯
（或麵粉）

「炸油」‥‥‥‥3 杯

❶ 魷魚僅用魚身，去除薄膜後，切法有兩種：

用字：將魷魚兩邊修齊，以6公分寬爲一單位，上下直切
條狀（圖1），用刀在魷魚兩側向中間等齊各剖入
2公分，剖時刀應與菜板平行（圖2），在中間所
留未切的2公分處劃兩直刀（兩刀相距約0.5公分
）深約厚度之一半（圖3），然後以0.8公分爲間
格橫切2刀深至魚身厚之一半，第三刀以同等間格
予於切斷，呈用字花形爲一片（圖4）。

條狀：視魚身大小先橫切成3片（每片寬約6公分 ）
然後每片由中央側面剖成2薄片，剖時刀應持平與
菜板平行（魚身薄的免剖），然後切0.5公分×6公
分之條狀 。

❷ 把切好的魷魚，調上①料拌勻醃約20分鐘。

❸ 醃過之魷魚滾沾多量玉米粉，使緊裹魚身待炸。

❹ 鍋熱，入「炸油」3杯燒熱（375℉），魷魚散開下鍋
並不停用鍋鏟攪動，以防相黏，炸約3分鐘呈金黃色撈出
，然後再將油燒熱（400℉），把魷魚重下鍋回炸約1
0秒，呈金黃酥脆撈出，瀝淨油置盤（此道爲香酥下酒菜）。

蛋白質‥‥‥‥‥‥‥８３克
脂質‥‥‥‥‥‥‥‥５０克
醣質‥‥‥‥‥‥‥‥７３克
熱量‥‥‥‥１０９２仟卡

Protein. 83g
Fat 50g
Carbohydrate. 73g
1,092 Kcal

1

2

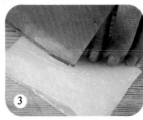

3

4

Fried Squid   Chekiang-Kiangsu 6 servings

1   lb. fresh squid (about 1⅓ lbs)
1   t. rice wine
½   t. salt
¼   t. MSG
2   stalks green onion, smashed
2   slices ginger, smashed
¾   C. cornstarch or flour
3   C. oil for frying

❶ Remove the thin membrane covering the squid and cut, use one of the
following methods:
shape*:   Trim the body of the squid to form to a rectangular shape.
Cut in half lengthwise to form 2 sections (fig. 1). On both
long sides of each squid section, slice halfway through the
thickness of the squid to a point two-thirds of the length
to the opposite edge (fig. 2). The cleaver should be parallel
to the cutting board while cutting. Make two scores lengthwise,
cutting halfway through the thickness about ⅕-inch from each
side of the center line (fig. 3). Turn the section to the horizontal
and make a cut on each edge about ½-inch from the end.
(The cut should extend from the edge to about three-quarter's
of the length to the center line.) Make 2 more cuts (on each
edge, similiar to the first cut) about ½-inch from the first cut.
At another ½-inch from the second cut, cut completely across
the squid section to separate the piece. Repeat this procedure
for the remaining length of the squid section.
Strips: Cut the squid sections crosswise into 2-3 pieces. If squid meat
is thick, cut in half through thickness with the cleaver parallel
to the cutting board. Cut each section into strips 2-inch wides.
❷ Mix squid pieces with ① and marinate for about 20 minutes.
❸ Dredge the squid pieces in the cornstarch, make sure that the surface is
completely coated.
❹ Heat pan and add oil for deep-frying, heat to 375°F. Add the squid
and mix continuously to prevent the pieces from sticking together.
Deep-fry for about 3 minutes until golden and remove. Reheat the
oil to 400°F and add the squid pieces. Deep-fry for about 10 seconds,
until crisp. Remove and drain excess oil. Place on a serving platter and
serve. (Excellent with wine).
* This Chinese character represents longevity.

雀巢酥蝦

廣東菜　　6 人份

鮮蝦…………半斤
（約３０條）
薑酒汁……$\frac{1}{2}$大匙
①{ 鹽…………$\frac{1}{2}$小匙
味精………$\frac{1}{4}$小匙
蒜末……１小匙
太白粉……１大匙
「炸油」……３杯
雀巢…………１個
生菜……６～８片
（或巴西利）

❶ 蝦剪除鬚爪，用牙籤在蝦背上挑除沙腸（若河蝦可免），洗淨瀝乾，調入①料拌勻，醃２０分鐘。
❷ 鍋熱，入「炸油」３杯燒熱（３７５℉），將蝦放入，用大火炸約１分半鐘，呈金黃酥脆時撈出放在雀巢上（雀巢底先舖生菜）。
■ 薑酒汁：薑片拍碎加酒擠出的汁。

雀巢雞丁

江浙菜　　6 人份

雞腿肉………半斤
①料
「油」…………１杯
蔥段（２公分）6枝
薑……………６片
③料
（鹽改醬油１大匙）
馬鈴薯………２個

❶ 雞腿肉先用刀背搥鬆，再切２公分四方丁，加①料拌勻醃３０分鐘。
❷ 鍋熱，加「油」半杯燒熱（２７５℉），放入雞丁迅速用鍋鏟撥散，以大火爆炒見肉色變且熟約１分鐘撈出，留油１大匙炒香蔥薑，再入雞肉及③料大火爆炒盛於雀巢上即成。
■ 「雀巢」做法參照第184頁。雀巢酥脆可與菜肴一齊吃。

雀巢

芋頭（或洋芋）1個
太白粉………$\frac{1}{2}$杯
1{ 鹽…………$\frac{1}{6}$小匙
「炸油」………６杯

❶ 芋頭或洋芋去皮（淨重約６兩），用刀切或刨成細絲，先泡在冷水內或在水籠頭下沖洗去漿，撈出瀝乾（圖１），放在盆內加 1 料拌勻待炸（圖２）。備兩枝漏杓。
❷ 「炸油」６杯燒熱（３７５℉），將其一漏杓沾油後杓內舖滿芋絲（圖３），另一枝沾油後覆壓其上，輕輕放進油鍋內（圖４），炸４～５分鐘，臨起鍋前改大火炸呈金黃色至酥脆時撈出，瀝淨油即成「雀巢」。
■ 雀巢也可不用，僅用生菜舖底，上覆酥蝦即可。

蛋白質‥‥‥‥‥‥３８克
脂質‥‥‥‥‥‥‥６２克
醣質‥‥‥‥‥‥‥８３克
熱量‥‥‥‥１０３９仟卡
Protein 38g
Fat 62g
Carbohydrate 83g
1,039 Kcal

   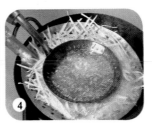

① ② ③ ④

Crispy Shrimp in Bird's Nest Cantonese 6 servings

¾ lb. small, raw shrimp

① { ½ T. ginger-wine*
½ t. salt
¼ t. MSG
1 t. minced garlic
1 T. cornstarch

3 C. oil for frying
1 "Bird's Nest," see recipe
   shown below
6-8 leafy lettuce leaves or parsley

⅔ lb. boned chicken leg
① same as above
1 C. oil for frying
6 1-inch sections green onion
6 slices ginger
③ same as above, but change salt to
1 T. soy sauce
2 medium potatoes

2 medium-size taro roots or
   potatoes

① { ½ C. cornstarch
½ t. salt

6 C. oil for frying

❶ Trim off any appendages remaining on the shrimp. Devein the shrimp with a toothpick. Rinse lightly and pat dry. Place in a bowl with mixture ① . Marinate for 20 minutes.

❷ Heat pan and add oil, heat to about 375°F. Add the shrimp and deep-fry about 1½ minutes. Remove and drain. Arrange the prepared "Bird's Nest" in the center of the platter and place the lettuce leaves around the outside of the platter. Place the shrimp on top of the bird's nest and serve immediately.

* To prepare ginger-wine: mash 1 slice ginger root and mix with 1 Tbsp. rice wine. Remove the ginger slice and use the liquid as directed.

Stir-Fried Chicken in Bird's Nest

❶ Pound the chicken with the blunt edge of the cleaver to tenderize. Dice into 1-inch pieces and add mixture ① . Marinate for about 30 minutes. Prepare the potatoes for "bird's nest" as directed in "Crispy Shrimp in Bird's Nest" P. 184. Place the bird's nest on a serving platter.

❷ Heat pan and add oil, heat to 275°F. Add the chicken and stir-fry for 1 minute over medium heat. Remove and drain. Remove all but 1 Tbsp. oil from pan and reheat until hot. Add the green onion, ginger and stir-fry until fragrant. Add the chicken, mixture ③ and toss lightly until the sauce has thickened. Remove and place on top of the bird's nest. Serve immediately.

"Bird's Nest"

❶ Peel the taro or potato. Cut into thin slices and shred finely. Place the shreds in a colander and rinse lightly with cold water. Drain thoroughly (fig. 1) and place the shreds in a bowl. Add mixture ① and toss lightly (fig. 2).

❷ Heat pan and add oil, heat to 350°F. Dip a 8-inch slotted strainer in the hot oil and remove. Arrange the taro shreds to line the strainer (fig. 3). Dip another strainer in the oil and place on top of the taro shreds. Submerge the taro-filled strainers in the hot oil (fig. 4) and deep-fry 4 to 5 minutes. Before removing, turn heat to high and cook until golden and crisp. Remove the fried "bird's nest" and drain on absorbent paper. Use as directed.

■ The "bird's nest" is an attractive garnish, but it may be omitted. When omitting, arrange the shrimp directly on the serving plate which has been garnished with the lettuce leaves.

盐蒸蝦 臺灣菜　6 人份

鮮蝦…………半斤
（約２０條）

① ┌ 酒…………½ 大匙
　 │ 鹽…………¼ 小匙
　 │ 葱…………２枝
　 └ 薑…………２片

沾料 ┌ 芥末醬…２小匙 ┐（圖
　　 │ 冷開水…½ 大匙 │ 4）
　　 └ 醬油……１小匙 ┘

❶ **蝦處理法**：鮮蝦剪除鬚爪，用牙籤在蝦背上挑除沙腸（若河蝦可免），洗淨瀝乾。

❷ **做法有三種**：

　蒸法：蝦盛盤內，調入①料拌勻，醃２０分鐘，水燒開擺進蒸籠或蒸鍋（圖１），大火蒸２分鐘，熄火燜１分鐘至嫩熟，食時蘸沾料鮮嫩可口。

　煮法：水２杯燒開加①料並放入鮮蝦燙煮１分鐘，熄火燜２分鐘至嫩熟，即可撈出置盤（圖２），食時蘸沾料。

　炊法：蝦洗淨不必瀝乾水份，放入鍋內加①料蓋鍋置爐上，用中火燜煮３０秒，蓋緊鍋蓋，提鍋上下搖動（圖３），再燜３０秒即可，置盤，食時蘸沾料。（因不另加水，爲恐水份蒸發，故蓋緊鍋蓋搖動，使蝦翻轉。）

■ **芥末醬做法**：芥末粉１大匙、酒１小匙、白醋¼ 小匙調勻蓋緊，擱置１０分鐘即可使用。（或用芥末粉１大匙、溫開水１¼ 小匙調勻蓋緊，擱置１０分鐘。）

■ **盤飾**：參照第５０頁，橙、檸檬類盤飾第１種。

油爆蝦

鮮蝦…………半斤
「炸油」………３杯

① ┌ 鹽…………½ 小匙
　 │ 味精………¼ 小匙
　 │ 葱花………２大匙
　 └ 麻油………１小匙

❶ 鮮蝦處理法同上。

❷ 「炸油」３杯燒熱（４００℉），放入蝦，大火炸約１分鐘撈出置大碗內，趁熱倒入①料，拌勻即可裝盤供食。

■ 蝦用海蝦或淡水蝦都可，以肥大新鮮爲佳。

蛋白質 ·············· ２７克
脂質 ················· 1 克
醣質 ················· 1 克
熱量 ·············· １２９仟卡
Protein 27g
Fat 1g
Carbohydrate 1g
129 Kcal

Shrimp with Mustard Sauce Taiwanese 6 servings

¾ lb. raw, fresh shrimp in shells*

① {
½ T. rice wine
¼ t. salt
2 stalks green onion, mashed
2 slices ginger, mashed
}

Dipping sauce:*1

2 t. prepared mustard
½ T. cold water } (fig. 4)
1 t. soy sauce

❶ Devein the shrimp with a toothpick. Rinse the shrimp lightly and drain.

❷ To cook, use any of the following methods:

To steam: Mix the shrimp with ① and marinate for 20 minutes. Place the shrimp on a heatproof plate (fig. 1); place in steamer and cover. Steam over high heat for 2 minutes. Turn off heat and let stand for 1 minute. (They should be "just" cooked and tender.) Arrange on a serving plate and serve with the dipping sauce.

To boil: Mix the shrimp with ① and marinate for 20 minutes. Boil 2 cups water and add the shrimp. Cook for 1 minute; turn off the heat and let stand covered for 2 minutes (fig. 2). Remove, drain, and arrange on a serving plate. Serve with dipping sauce.

To simmer: Rinse the shrimp lightly and immediately place in a pan with mixture ① . Cover and cook over medium heat for 30 seconds. Shake the wok lightly to toss the shrimp so that they will cook evenly (fig. 3). (Cover tightly while shaking the pan to prevent any steam from escaping.) Let stand covered for 30 seconds and remove. Arrange the cooked shrimp on a serving platter and serve with the mustard dipping sauce.

* Fresh shrimp are preferred for this dish, but if unavailable, substitute frozen shrimp.

*1 For added flavor, combine 1 Tbsp. dry mustard, 1 tsp. rice wine, and ¼ tsp. rice vinegar. Otherwise, blend 1 Tbsp. dry mustard with 1¼ tsp. warm water. Cover tightly, set aside for 10 minutes and use as directed.

■ Garnish: See "Vegetable Garnish", P. 50.

Quick-Fried Shrimp

¾ lb. fresh shrimp
3 C. oil for frying

1 {
½ t. salt
¼ t. MSG
2 T. minced green onions
1 t. sesame oil
}

❶ Prepare shrimp as directed in Step ❶ of the recipe shown above.

❷ Heat pan and add oil, heat to about 400°F. Add the shrimp and deep-fry for about 1 minute. Remove and drain. Toss immediately with mixture 1 and place on a serving platter. Serve.

醋烹蝦段　　　四川菜　6人份

明蝦（４條）…半斤
薑酒汁……½大匙
太白粉…１½大匙
「炸油」………３杯
①{
熟紅蘿蔔絲２大匙
熟筍絲……２大匙
冬菇絲……２大匙
青椒絲……２大匙
酒………½大匙
②{
白醋……１½大匙
糖………２大匙
鹽………½小匙
水………４大匙
太白粉……１小匙
麻油………１小匙

❶ 明蝦摘除蝦頭，洗淨拭乾，從蝦背剪開或刀切（圖１），深約蝦厚度之一半處，取出沙腸（圖２），橫放順每２節蝦殼接合處斜切成三段（圖３），調入薑酒汁半大匙醃２０分鐘，炸前沾太白粉（圖４）。

❷ 「炸油」３杯燒熱（３７５℉），放進蝦段大火炸１５秒用鍋鏟拌開，續炸１分鐘撈出；留油３大匙下①料拌炒數秒後，淋酒半大匙及②料燒沸續投入蝦段拌勻，最後淋麻油，以增色香，拌勻盛盤即成。

■ 薑酒汁：將薑片拍碎加酒擠出的汁。把②料之醋改檸檬汁其味道更佳。

醋溜蝦片

明蝦（或中蝦）半斤
①{
蛋白…………½個
太白粉……½大匙
太白粉…１½大匙
「炸油」………３杯
①料改切片
蒜（切片）……１粒
②料

❶ 蝦處理法參照第１９０頁「炒蝦球」做法❶，蝦背順直切一刀，攤開使腹部相連着成一大片，用刀在腹部輕剁數刀使筋斷，以防炸時捲成圓形，再橫切一刀成兩片，用①料醃約３０分鐘，炸前沾太白粉。

❷ 「炸油」３杯燒熱，放進蝦片，中火炸約１５秒，用鍋鏟拌開，續炸１５秒撈出，留油３大匙炒香蒜片隨入①料同炒，下酒半大匙及②料燒沸，即可熄火將蝦片落鍋拌勻淋油半大匙盛盤。

蛋白質・・・・・・・・・・・・・２７克
脂質・・・・・・・・・・・・・・・５２克
醣質・・・・・・・・・・・・・・・５１克
熱量・・・・・・・・・・・７６８仟卡

Protein 27g
Fat 52g
Carbohydrate 51g
768 Kcal

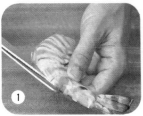

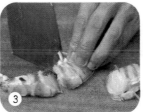

Sweet and Sour Prawns Szechuan 6 servings

¾ lb. fresh prawns or scampi
  (4-6)
½ T. ginger-wine*
1½T. cornstarch
3 C. oil for frying

①
{
2 T. shredded, cooked carrots
  shredded bamboo shoot
2 T. shredded pre-softened
  Chinese black mushroom
2 T. shredded green pepper
}

½ T. rice wine

②
{
1½T. rice vinegar*₁
2 T. sugar
½ t. salt
4 T. water
1 t. cornstarch
}

½ t. sesame oil
½ t. oil

¾ lb. prawns or scampi

①
{
½ egg white
1½T. cornstarch
}

3 C. oil for frying
① same as above,but slice the
  ingredients
1 clove garlic, minced
② same as above
½ t. oil

❶ Remove the heads from the prawns, if necessary and rinse lightly. Pat dry. Use scissors or a knife to slit each prawn down the back (fig. 1), pierce only halfway through the meat; devein (fig. 2). Cut each prawn on the diagonal, into 3 sections. Mix with the ginger-wine and marinate for 20 minutes. Coat each section with cornstarch before frying (fig. 4).

❷ Heat pan and add oil, heat to about 375°F. Add the prawns and deep-fry for about 15 seconds; stir to separate. Continue frying for one minute and remove. Drain all but 3 Tbsp. of oil from the pan and reheat. Add mixture ① and stir-fry briefly. Add rice wine and mixture ② . Heat until boiling and add the prawn sections. Toss lightly to coat the ingredients and add the sesame oil. Toss again and remove. Serve immediately.

* To prepare ginger-wine, mash 1 slice ginger root and mix with 1 Tbsp. rice wine. Remove the ginger slice and use the liquid as directed.

*₁ For a fresh flavor, substitute lemon juice for the rice vinegar in mixture ② .

Prawns Slices in Sour Sauce

❶ To pre-condition the prawns see Step ❶ "Deep-fried Prawns Balls," P. 190. Slice each prawn along the back; stop just short of the opposite edge. Open the prawns to lie flat on the counter. Score the surface of prawns to prevent curling during cooking. Cut each prawn lengthwise in half. Combine with mixture ① and marinate for 30 minutes. Coat the prawn sections with cornstarch.

❷ Heat pan and add oil, heat to 275°F. Add the prawn slices and fry 15 seconds; stir with a spatula to separate. Fry an additional 15 seconds and remove. Remove all but 3 Tbsp. of oil from the pan and reheat. Add the minced garlic, mixture ① and stir-fry until fragrant. Add the rice wine and mixture ② . Heat to boiling then turn off the heat. Add the prawn slices and toss lightly to coat the ingredients with the sauce. Dribble oil over the mixture; toss lightly and remove. Serve immediately.

炒蝦球

① 明蝦6條…12兩
　酒…………½大匙
① 鹽…………¼小匙
　蛋白………½個
　太白粉……1大匙

葱、薑末(各)1大匙
「油」…………1杯
乾木耳………6朵
小黃瓜………1條
酒……………1大匙
　鹽…………½小匙
　味精………¼小匙
② 麻油………1小匙
　太白粉……1小匙
　水…………4大匙

① 明蝦摘除蝦頭去殼，留尾端不剝(圖1)，洗淨拭乾，每條由蝦背順直剖切1～2刀，深至蝦厚度之一半(圖2)，抽出沙腸(圖3)，再橫切一刀成兩段(圖4)，調入①料拌勻醃20分鐘。

② 乾木耳泡軟去蒂，大朵的切成兩半。小黃瓜斜切薄片，或順直剖成4～6條，削去籽再橫切成4公分長段。

③ 鍋熱，加「油」1杯燒熱(275℉)，放入明蝦用中火泡油約10秒呈白色圓球狀且熟撈出，鍋內留油3大匙，先炒香葱、薑末再入木耳、小黃瓜拌炒約30秒後，下酒及②料和明蝦拌勻盛盤。

■ 除明蝦外，可用其他蝦類，將蝦去殼後由背部順直剖切，使腹部連着成一大片，大的再橫切一刀成兩段，小的勿切，其他調味及做法同上。

蝴蝶明蝦

明蝦(6條)12兩
　葱…………1枝
① 薑…………2片
　鹽…………¼小匙
② 冬菇(切末)2大匙
　洋葱末……2大匙
　酒…………½大匙
　高湯………½杯
　鹽…………¼小匙
③ 味精………¼小匙
　番茄醬……1大匙
　太白粉……1小匙

① 明蝦處理法，參照本頁「炒蝦球」做法①，所不同者為每條蝦由背處順直剖切一刀，使腹部連着成一大片即可，調①料拌勻醃約20分鐘。

② 將明蝦片翻轉蝦身，切面朝下，由前端向尾包捲成筒狀，把帶殼之蝦尾向上翹起，以牙籤由圓筒中心插入固定，使呈蝶狀放在預先抹油之蒸盤內，水燒開大火蒸5分鐘至熟取出，另置盤。

③ 鍋熱，加油2大匙將②料炒香，入③料燒沸澆淋其上。

蛋白質···············４８克
脂質················５３克
醣質················７３克
熱量···········７９８仟卡
Protein 48g
Fat 53g
Carbohydrate. 73g
798 Kcal

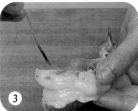

Deep-Fried prawn Balls Chekiang-Kiangsu 6 servings

8 prawns or scampi (about 1 lb.)

① ½ T. rice wine
¼ t. salt
½ egg white
1 T. cornstarch

1 T. minced green onion
1 T. minced ginger
1 C. oil for frying
6 dried wood ears
1 gherkin cucumber or small gourmet
seedless cucumber
1 T. rice wine

② ½ t. salt
¼ t. MSG
1 t. sesame oil
1 t. cornstarch
4 T. water

❶ Remove the heads (if necessary) and shells from the prawns, leave a portion of shell at the tail (fig. 1). Rinse lightly and pat dry. Score the prawns in 1 or 2 cuts along the back, slice halfway through the thickness (fig. 2). Devein (fig. 3). Cut the prawns lengthwise in half (fig. 4). Toss with mixture ① and marinate for 20 minutes.

❷ Soak the wood ears in warm water, to cover, until soft. Cut away any hard sections. Divide each large wood ear in half. Cut the cucumber in half; remove seeds and cut each half diagonally into thin slices.

❸ Heat pan and add oil, heat to about 250°F. Add the prawns and deep-fry for about 10 seconds, or until they change color. Remove and drain. The prawns should curl as soon as they are exposed to the hot oil. Remove all but 3 Tbsp. of oil from the pan and reheat. Add the minced green onion, ginger and stir-fry until fragrant. Add the wood ears and cucumber slices. Stir-fry for about 30 seconds and add 1 Tbsp. of rice wine and mixture ② . Add the prawns and toss lightly to combine the ingredients. Remove and serve.

■ Raw, shelled shrimp may be substituted for the prawns. Slice each shrimp along the back, stop just short of the opposite edge. Open the shrimp to lie flat on the counter. Cut any large shrimp crosswise diagonally in half, small shrimp should be left whole. Prepare the remaining steps as directed above.

Butterfly Prawns

❶ Prepare the prawns or scampi as directed in Step ❶ of the recipe shown above, make only one cut along the back. Spread the prawns flat out on the counter and place in a mixing bowl with mixture ①. Marinate for 20 minutes.

❷ Spread the prawns open on the counter with the cut-side down. Start at the head and roll up shrimp to the tail end to resemble a butterfly. Secure each roll with a toothpick. Arrange the rolled shrimp on a lightly-oiled heat-proof plate. Place in steamer, cover and steam for 5 minutes over high heat. Remove and place on a serving plate.

❸ Heat pan and add 2 Tbsp. of oil. Add mixture ② and stir-fry until fragrant. Add ③ and heat until boiling. Pour this mixture over the prawns and serve.

6-8 prawns or scampi (about 1 lb.)

① 1 stalk green onion mashed
2 slices ginger, mashed
¼ t. salt

② 2 T. minced, pre-softened Chinese
black mushrooms
2 T. minced onion

③ ½ T. rice wine
½ C. chicken broth
¼ t. salt
¼ t. MSG
1 T. catsup
1 t. cornstarch

6-8 wooden toothpicks

炸蝦捲
Fried Shrimp Rolls

百角蝦球
"One-Hundred Corner"
Deep-Fried Shrimp Balls

百角蝦球　　　　　　江浙菜　　6 人份

蝦仁…………6 兩
麵包（土司）…2 片
荸薺（去皮）…1 兩
肥肉（剁碎）…1 兩
① 料
　薑酒汁……½ 小匙
　鹽…………¼ 小匙
　味精………⅛ 小匙
　胡椒粉……⅛ 小匙
　蛋白………½ 個
　太白粉……½ 大匙
「炸油」………4 杯

❶ 麵包切除四邊硬皮，先切 0.5 公分長條，再切成 0.5 公分的小丁，成「麵包粒」。荸薺剁碎備用。

❷ 蝦仁加少許鹽拌一下，用水洗盡黏液，拭乾水份，加鹽¼小匙拌勻，用刀面壓碎再剁成蝦泥（圖 1），裝在大碗內，加①料順同一方向仔細攪拌至膠黏狀約 3 分鐘，再加荸薺及肥肉拌妥成「蝦絨」備用。

❸「蝦絨」用手擠成 12 個蝦丸，沾滾麵包粒（圖 2），再用手輕輕握緊，使麵包粒黏牢蝦丸。

❹ 鍋熱，加入「炸油」4 杯燒熱（275℉），將已沾滾麵包粒之蝦丸放入，用小火炸至蝦球浮出油面時，用鍋鏟在蝦球面上慢慢推動，使蝦球轉動炸約 2 分鐘呈金黃色，改大火炸 30 秒，肉熟皮脆撈出，趁熱供食。

■ 荸薺、肥肉可免用。薑酒汁：薑片拍碎加酒擠出的汁。

吉利蝦球

將麵包粒改用麵包粉，其他調味、做法同上。

炸蝦捲

麵包（土司）…1 節
蝦仁…………4 兩
① 料
蔥末………1 大匙
「炸油」………4 杯
番茄醬……1 大匙

❶ 麵包切 0.3 公分薄片後，切除硬邊，約 10 片。

❷ 參照本頁「百角蝦球」做法❷，加蔥末 1 大匙，不加荸薺及肥肉。

❸ 將每片麵包，用刀面薄薄塗滿蝦絨（圖 3），由邊捲起成筒狀，中間切一刀分成二段（圖 4），切口處沾麵粉待炸。

❹ 鍋熱，入「炸油」4 杯燒熱（325℉）放入蝦捲炸約 2 分鐘呈金黃色，改大火炸 30 秒撈起盛盤，食時沾番茄醬。

蛋白質 ·············· ４３克
脂質 ··············· ５０克
醣質 ··············· ４５克
熱量 ·········· ８３０仟卡
Protein 43g
Fat 50g
Carbohydrate 45g
830 Kcal

"One-Hundred Corner" Deep-Fried Shrimp Balls

Chekiang-Kiangsu 6 servings

½ lb. raw, shelled shrimp
2 slices white bread
6 water chestnuts, minced finely*
¾ oz. pork fat, minced finely*
① { ½ t. ginger-wine*¹
¼ t. salt
⅛ t. MSG
⅛ t. black pepper
½ egg white
½ T. cornstarch
4 C. oil for frying

❶ Trim the crusts from the bread, and dice into ¼-inch cubes.*² Mince the water chestnuts and squeeze to remove any excess water.

❷ Add ¼ tsp. of salt to the shrimp and mix. Devein and rinse the shrimp lightly with water and pat dry. Add another ¼ t. of salt and mash the shrimp with the flat side of the cleaver (fig. 1). Chop the shrimp to a smooth paste. Place the shrimp paste in a bowl and add mixture ① . Mix in a single, continuous direction for about 3 minutes until the consistency is sticky. Add the water chestnuts and minced pork fat.

❸ Separate the shrimp paste into 12 portions and roll into balls. Roll the balls in the bread crumbs (fig. 2) and press lightly to insure that the breadcrumbs will adhere to the surface.

❹ Heat pan and add oil, heat to 275°F. Add the shrimp balls and deep-fry until they float to the surface of the oil. Stir the balls with a spatula to insure their cooking evenly. Cook 2 minutes, or until golden. Turn the heat to high and fry for 30 seconds (to make the outside crisp). Remove, drain, and serve.

* The water chestnuts and pork fat may be omitted.

*¹ To prepare ginger-wine, mash 1 slice ginger root and mix with 1 Tbsp. rice wine. Remove the ginger slice and use the liquid as directed.

*² One cup bread crumbs may be substituted for the bread cubes.

Lucky Shrimp Balls

Substitute toasted bread crumbs for the plain bread crumbs and prepare as directed in the remaining steps of the recipe above.

Fried Shrimp Rolls

¼ loaf unsliced, white sandwich bread
½ lb. raw. shelled shrimp
① same as above
1 T. minced green onion
1 T. flour
4 C. oil for frying
1 T. catsup

❶ Trim the crust from the bread and cut into 10 slices about ⅛-inch thick.

❷ Follow Step ❷ as directed in "One Hundred Corner Deep-Fried Shrimp Balls," omit the water chestnuts and pork fat, but add the minced green onion.

❸ Spread the surface of each bread slice with the shrimp paste (fig. 3) and roll up jelly-roll style, start at the longest edge. Cut each roll into two (fig. 4) and dust the edges of the rolls with flour.

❹ Heat pan and add oil, heat to 325°F. Add the shrimp rolls and deep-dry about 2 minutes, or until golden. Turn the heat to high and cook for 30 seconds longer. Remove, drain, and arrange on a serving platter. Serve with catsup as a dipping sauce.

如意蝦捲

四川菜　　6人份

蝦仁…………6兩
肥肉…………1兩
薑酒汁………½大匙

①
鹽……………¼小匙
味精…………¼小匙
胡椒粉………少許
蛋白…………½個
（蛋黃留用）

太白粉………1大匙
雞蛋…………1個

②
鹽……………少許
太白粉1小匙 ⎫先
水……½大匙 ⎭攪勻

紫菜…………1張
（或青菜葉數張）
紅蘿蔔………½條

❶ 蝦仁挑出沙腸，加鹽半小匙拌一下，用水洗淨黏液，拭乾水份，置菜板上用刀面壓爛再剁成蝦泥，盛碗調①料順同一方向仔細攪拌成膠黏狀約3分鐘，再加肥肉（預先剁碎）拌妥成「蝦絨」。

❷ 雞蛋1個加拌蝦仁所剩蛋黃一齊用筷子仔細拌勻至蛋白全部打散，加預先調勻之②料，（以防煎蛋皮易破）。

❸ 鍋洗淨，均勻燒熱，用布或紙沾適量油塗擦鍋面，把調好蛋液倒入，手提鍋把順鍋滾圓攤成直徑約30公分之蛋皮，以小火烙至凝固，見蛋皮邊烙乾，用手輕輕提起翻面略烙即成蛋皮。

❹ 蛋皮攤開光滑面朝下置菜板略修齊，上撒少許太白粉，將½之蝦絨用刀（刀面先沾水）抹平（圖1），舖上紫菜（圖2），再把剩餘蝦絨以同樣方法抹平，兩端擺上紅蘿蔔條（紅蘿蔔煮至半熟切約0.8公分四方長條），由兩端捲起（圖3）至中央呈 ◎◎ 即爲如意型，接合處以蝦絨或麵糊沾黏（麵粉或太白粉1大匙加水1小匙調勻即爲麵糊），放在已預先抹油之蒸盤，接合處朝下使之定型，水燒開大火蒸約8分鐘至熟取出，接合處朝下置菜板，切約1公分厚片（圖4），盛盤即可沾椒鹽食之。

或將蒸好蝦捲，撒麵粉或太白粉於四週，用油煎炸至酥即可切片，又稱「如意酥蝦捲」。

■ 除蝦仁外，可用豬絞肉，雞胸肉去皮後剁碎代之，其調味及做法同上。亦可買現成魚漿免用①料。

蛋白質‥‥‥‥‥‥‥５８克
脂質‥‥‥‥‥‥‥‥４８克
醣質‥‥‥‥‥‥‥‥１４克
熱量‥‥‥‥‥‥‥‥７３６仟卡
Protein. 58g
Fat 48g
Carbohydrate 14g
736 Kcal

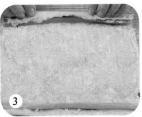

"Happy" Shrimp Rolls
Szechuan 6 servings

½ lb. raw, shelled shrimp
1 oz. pork fat, minced

①
½ T. ginger-wine*
¼ t. salt
¼ t. MSG
dash of black pepper
½ egg white (yolk set aside)
1 T. cornstarch

1 egg and retained egg yolk

②
dash of salt
1 t. cornstarch
½ T. water

1 sheet nori (purple laver) or a few green vegetable leaves
½ carrot, lightly parboiled and cut into ¼-inch-wide sticks

❶ Devein the shrimp and mix with ½ t. salt. Marinate for 30 minutes. Rinse the shrimp thoroughly and pat dry. Mash the shrimp with the flat side of the cleaver blade then mince thoroughly. Place in a bowl with mixture ①. Mix continuously for about 3 minutes until sticky. Add the minced pork fat and blend well to form a shrimp paste.

❷ Beat the whole egg and egg yolk thoroughly and add mixture ② (pre-mixed). Mixture ② will prevent the finished egg sheet from tearing easily.

❸ Heat a wok that has been washed clean, then heat it evenly. Wipe the surface of the wok with an oil-soaked paper towel. Pour in the pre-mixed egg mixture. Rotate the pan so that the egg spreads evenly to coat the pan and forms a thin 10-inch pancake. Cook over low heat until the egg is set and dry, then remove.

❹ Spread the egg sheet on the counter with the cooked surface up. Trim any rough edges to make a uniform square. Sprinkle the surface lightly with cornstarch. Dip a cleaver in water and use the cleaver blade to spread ½ of the shrimp paste over the egg sheet surface (fig. 1). Cover with the sheet of nori (fig. 2). Prepare remaining shrimp paste in the same manner, then place several carrot sticks at each end. Roll from both ends (fig. 3) toward the center to form a sceptre-of-happiness-shape. To secure the rolls, brush the roll edges with shrimp paste or flour paste (mix 1 Tbsp. flour or cornstarch with 1 tsp. water). Place in a lightly-greased, heatproof plate with the rolls facing downward to secure the shape. Place in steamer, cover, and steam over high heat for about 8 minutes, or until done. Remove and cut into ¾-inch thick slices with the rolls facing down (fig. 4). Remove to serving plate. Serve with pepper salt.

■ "Crispy Shrimp Rolls": Follow the directions, shown above, dust the steamed shrimp rolls with the cornstarch or flour. Then saute in oil until crisp. Cut into slices.

* To prepare ginger-wine, mash 1 slice ginger root and mix with 1 Tbsp. rice wine. Remove the ginger slice and use the liquid as directed.

■ Ground, ready-made fish paste, and minced skinless chicken breast can be used instead of the shrimp. Follow the procedure as directed above. If ready-made fish paste is available, mixture ① can be eliminated.

炸餛飩

北方菜　　12人份

蝦仁…………３兩
絞肉…………３兩
荸薺(切碎)…２兩
葱末………１大匙

① { 鹽…………⅓小匙
味精………¼小匙
麻油………１小匙
太白粉……１小匙 }

沙拉油……１大匙
餛飩皮……６０張
「炸油」………３杯

❶ 蝦仁洗淨切碎，加入絞肉（豬肉或雞肉均可）、荸薺、葱末及①料拌勻，最後再加入沙拉油攪拌作「餡」。

❷ 餛飩包法有三種：

1 餛飩皮一張，置少許「餡」於中央（圖１），然後對角摺合，捲半圈交叉扭合兩端（圖２），如粘不住可沾少許水。

2 餛飩皮一張，中央置「餡」對摺捲起，扭轉兩端，如糖果之包裝法（圖３）。

3 餛飩皮一張，中央置「餡」，用手在中腰捏緊使其粘合（圖４）。

❸ 鍋熱，入「炸油」３杯燒熱（３００℉），分兩次炸，每次放入餛飩炸約２分鐘至肉餡熟，皮呈金黃酥脆撈出，瀝淨油盛盤。

■盤飾：參照第１１頁辣椒類盤飾。

餛飩皮

60張

高筋麵粉……２杯

① { 鹽…………½小匙
雞蛋………１個
冷水………½杯
太白粉………⅓杯 }

❶ 將麵粉放在深盆內加入①料拌勻，用手揉搓至麵糰光滑而不黏手時，把麵糰留盆中，上覆蓋潔布（或塑膠袋）擱置約１０～１５分鐘，謂之「醒麵」。

❷ 麵板上灑少許麵粉，取出麵糰置板上，用桿麵杖桿製極薄之麵皮，邊桿邊灑麵粉，然後分切成７公分大小之四方塊即為餛飩皮。

蛋白質 ………… 1 3 4 克
脂質 ………………… 9 克
醣質 …………… 1 6 5 克
熱量 ……… 1 3 5 1 仟卡
Protein 134g
Fat 9g
Carbohydrate 165g
1,351 Kcal

Fried Won Ton

Peking 12 servings

¼ lb. ground pork or ground chicken meat

¼ lb. raw, shelled shrimp

½ C. minced water chestnuts

1 T. minced green onion

3 C. oil for frying

60 won ton skins

① ⅓ t. salt
¼ t. MSG
1 t. sesame oil
1 t. cornstarch

1 T. salad oil

❶ Devein the shrimp and rinse. Pat dry and mince. Mix with the ground pork, water chestnuts, green onion and mixture ① . Mix vigorously to a smooth paste. Add the salad oil, blend evenly (filling).

❷ There are 3 methods for wrapping the won tons:

A. Place a small amount of filling in the center of the won ton skin (fig. 1). Bring the 2 opposite corners together and seal. Gather the other opposite angle-edges together and press to seal (fig. 2). Add a little water, if necessary, to seal the corners together.

B. Place a small amount of filling in the center of the won ton skin. Twist the ends in opposite directions to seal--somewhat like a candy wrapper (fig. 3).

C. Place a small amount of filling in the center of the won ton skin. Place in the palm and gather squeeze the edges together. Press to seal (fig. 4).

❸ Heat pan and add 3 C. oil, heat to 300°F. Add half of the won tons and deep-fry for 2 minutes. When the outer skin is golden and the meat is cooked, remove and drain on an absorbent paper. Do the same with the second half of the won tons. Arrange on a platter and serve.

■ Garnish: See "Vegetable Garnish", P. 11.

Won Ton Skins

60 skins

2 C. high gluten flour or semolina
1 ½ t. salt
1 egg
½ C. cold water
⅓ C. cornstarch

❶ Place the flour in a deep bowl and add 1 , mix evenly. Knead the dough with both hands until it is smooth and doesn't stick to the hands. Cover the dough with a cloth or plastic and let dough rest for 10-15 minutes. (The covering will keep the surface of the dough from drying out.)

❷ Sprinkle cornstarch on a wooden board or counter surface. Place the dough on the board. Use a long rolling pin to roll out to a paper-thin skin*. While rolling, continue sprinkling with cornstarch. Finally, cut into 3-inch square pieces for won ton skins.

* A pasta machine may be used. Roll out the dough to the second thinnest setting on the machine.

海鮮粥

台灣菜　　6人份

①料
鮮蝦‥‥‥‥１２條
蛤蜊‥‥‥‥１２個
蟹‥‥‥‥‥‥１隻
生蠔(蚵)‥‥‥２兩
魚肉‥‥‥‥‥２兩
魷魚‥‥‥‥‥１條
米‥‥‥‥‥‥１杯
水‥‥‥‥‥１０杯

②料
酒‥‥‥‥‥‥½小匙
鹽‥‥‥‥１½小匙
味精‥‥‥‥‥½小匙
薑末‥‥‥‥‥１大匙

芹菜粒‥‥‥２大匙

❶ 把①料全部洗淨，蝦以牙籤挑出沙腸(圖１)。蟹去殼再切成八塊(圖２)。魚肉切片。魷魚斜切菱形花紋並切塊（圖３）。

❷ 米洗淨加水１０杯盛深鍋內，置爐上燒開改小火燜煮約４０分鐘成濃稠狀時，先入蛤蜊、蟹塊煮２分鐘(圖４)，再入魚肉、魷魚、蝦及生蠔續煮１分鐘，加②料並灑芹菜粒，便成營養可口的「海鮮粥」。

■ 蟹的處理法參照第１７８頁「醬爆青蟹」。

■ 除以上材料外可選用其他海產如干貝、鮑魚、墨魚、貝類‥‥‥等。

■ 蛤蜊吐沙法：請參照第２０４頁「蛤蜊蒸蛋」。

蛋白質⋯⋯⋯⋯⋯⋯71克
脂質⋯⋯⋯⋯⋯⋯⋯95克
醣質⋯⋯⋯⋯⋯⋯178克
熱量⋯⋯⋯⋯1850仟卡
Protein 71g
Fat 95g
Carbohydrate 178g
1,850 Kcal

Seafood Congee

Taiwanese 6 servings

① {
12 raw shrimp in shell
12 steamer clams
1 crab or 4 oz. crab meat *
3 oz.shucked oysters
3 oz.fish fillet
1 squid, cleaned
}

1 C. short-grain rice

10 C. water

② {
1½t. salt
½ t. rice wine
½ t. MSG
1 T. minced ginger
}

2 T. chopped celery

❶ Rinse each ingredient of ① thoroughly. Remove the upper shell of the body of the crab, rinse the inside parts, being careful not to dislodge the roe. Remove any dirty, extraneous matter. Cut the crab into 8 sections (fig. 2). Devein the shrimp with a toothpick (fig. 1). Diagonally cut the fish into thin slices. Score the squid lengthwise then crosswise and pieces (fig. 3). Place clams in 2 C. water and 1 Tbsp. salt. Let stand for at least 1 hour to allow sand to settle, remove the sand.

❷ Rinse the rice until the water runs clear. Place in a pot with 10C. water. Heat until boiling, then reduce the heat and simmer for about 40 minutes until thick. Add the clams, crab and cook for 2 minutes (fig.4). Add the fish, squid, shrimp and oysters; simmer for 1 more minute. Season with ② and sprinkle with chopped celery. This tasty and nutritious dish is now ready to serve.

* If using crab meat, add to the rice with the fish, squid and shrimp. In addition to the ingredients listed above, other varieties of seafood may be substituted according to individual preference.

排骨滷飯

台灣菜　　6 人份

大排骨（6 片）1 斤
蛋⋯⋯⋯⋯6 個
紅葱頭（切碎）¼ 杯

① 酒⋯⋯⋯⋯2 大匙
醬油⋯⋯⋯⋯半杯
糖⋯⋯⋯⋯1 大匙
八角⋯⋯⋯⋯1 顆
桂皮⋯⋯⋯1 小片
水⋯⋯⋯⋯2 杯

雪裡紅或酸菜 6 兩
紅辣椒（切碎）1 條

② 醬油⋯⋯⋯1 小匙
糖⋯⋯⋯⋯¼ 小匙
麻油⋯⋯⋯半小匙

飯⋯⋯⋯⋯6 碗

❶ 紅葱頭去蒂及外膜切薄片（圖 1），油 3 大匙燒熱，以小火將紅葱頭炒至呈金黃色並發出香味（圖 2），與①料同入滷鍋內，以小火慢慢熬煮成滷汁。

❷ 大排骨用刀背或搥肉器拍鬆，有筋部位斬斷數刀（圖 3）。蛋加水需淹蓋蛋面，以中火煮熟撈出，泡冷水待涼剝殼，同肉片放入滷汁內（圖 4），以小火滷至肉熟即可熄火。

❸ 雪裡紅或鹹酸菜洗淨，擠乾切碎，加油 2 大匙燒熱，先炒紅辣椒隨入雪裡紅及②料拌炒盛盤。

❹ 每碗飯上加滷好的排骨 1 塊、蛋 1 個及少許雪裡紅，再澆上 1 大匙滷汁即成經濟實惠的排骨滷飯。

■ 若無紅葱頭，以洋葱代替。

蛋白質··········１２５克
脂質···········２３４克
醣質···········２４１克
熱量·······３４４７仟卡
Protein. 125g
Fat 234g
Carbohydrate 241g
3447 Kcal

Braised Pork Chops over Rice Taiwanese 6 servings

6 center-cut pork chops
(about 1 ⅓ lbs.)

6 eggs

¼ C. shallots*（紅葱頭）

① {
2 T. rice wine
½ C. soy sauce
1 T. sugar
1 star anise
1 stick cinnamon peel
2 C. water
}

½ lb. salted cabbage or red-
in-snow

1 hot red pepper, minced

② {
1 t. soy sauce
¼ t. sugar
½ t. sesame oil
}

6 portions of cooked rice

❶ Peel the shallots and mince (fig. 1). Put 3 Tbsp. oil in pan, over low heat saute the shallots until golden and fragrant (fig. 2). Place in a pot with ① . Cook for about 30 minutes over low heat until slightly thick and very fragrant.

❷ Pound the pork chops with the blunt edge of the cleaver or with a meat mallet to tenderize (fig. 3). Cook the eggs for about 10 minutes in water to cover. Remove and place in cold water to cool. Peel off the shell. Place the eggs and pork chops in the pot containing mixture ① (fig. 4). Cover and cook over low heat until the meat is tender.

❸ Rinse the salted cabbage or red-in-snow (about ½ hour). Squeeze out the water and chop finely. Heat pan and add 2 Tbsp. oil, heat until very hot. Add the red pepper, salted cabbage, and mixture ② . Stir-fry briefly over high heat and remove.

❹ Place 1 pork chop, 1 egg, and a small amount of the salted cabbage mixture on top of each portion of rice. Pour 1 Tbsp. cooking liquid over all and serve.

* If shallots are unavailable, substitute ¼ C. minced onions.

三鮮豆腐燉　　　　北方菜　　12人份

干貝…………半兩
豆腐…………3塊
①{ 高湯…………3杯
　 鹽…………1小匙
②{ 冬菇絲………⅓杯
　 熟火腿絲……⅓杯
　 熟筍絲………⅓杯
　 熟紅蘿蔔絲…⅓杯
③{ 湯…………2杯
　 鹽…………半小匙
　 太白粉……2小匙
青菜…………半斤
雞油…………1大匙

❶ 干貝洗淨加水半杯，水開後蒸１５分鐘，趁熱以刀面壓成絲，或用手撕成細絲，湯汁留用。

❷ 青菜去老葉及尾部，修成１０公分長段，放入沸水中，用大火燙煮２分鐘，撈出用冷水漂涼，瀝乾備用。

❸ 豆腐(可預先泡鹽水，切時不易破)切成１.５公分之四方塊，加①料及干貝湯汁，用小火燜煮約３０分鐘至汁剩半杯。

❹ 備蒸碗一個，碗內先抹勻油，再將干貝絲置於碗底中央，然後把②料整齊的排在碗邊(圖１)，中間填滿煮好之豆腐連汁(圖２)，移入蒸鍋，水開中火蒸１小時以上。

❺ 蒸好的豆腐燉上覆蓋盤子傾斜倒出湯汁(圖３)，再將大盤蓋在蒸碗上，兩手上下墊布壓緊蒸碗及盤後，反轉倒扣(圖４)，並掀去蒸碗。

❻ 鍋熱加油２大匙，入青菜並加鹽、味精，各¼小匙炒熟圍邊。

❼ 把③料及倒出的湯汁燒開，淋在豆腐燉上，最後澆淋雞油趁熱端出。

■ 火腿處理法：參照第２４４頁「三鮮干絲湯」。

三鮮白菜燉

將豆腐改用大白菜１斤，其他調味及做法同上。

蛋白質‥‥‥‥‥‥６１克
脂質‥‥‥‥‥‥‥５９克
醣質‥‥‥‥‥‥‥３１克
熱量‥‥‥‥‥８２５仟卡
Protein. 61g
Fat 59g
Carbohydrate 31g
825 Kcal

Three-Flavor Stewed Bean Curd Peking 12 servings

3 dried scallops （干貝）
3 squares bean curd*
①{ 3 C. stock
 1 t. salt
②{ ⅓ C. shredded pre-softened
 Chinese black mushrooms
 ⅓ C. shredded, boiled ham
 ⅓ C. shredded, cooked
 bamboo shoots
 ⅓ C. shredded, precooked carrot
③{ 2 C. stock
 ½ t. salt
 2 t. cornstarch
 ¾ lb. heart of green vegetable*¹
 （青江菜）
1 T. rendered chicken fat

❶ Rinse the dried scallops and steam in ½ C. water for 15 minutes. Remove and tear into shreds while hot. Reserve the scallop liquid.

❷ Cut the bean curd into ½-inch squares. Add ① and the reserved scallop broth from step❶. Place in a pot and simmer uncovered for 30 minutes over low heat until the liquid is reduced to ½ cup.

❸ Set the shredded scallops in the center of a heatproof bowl. Arrange each ingredient of ② in descending order, around the scallops (fig. 1). Place the bean curd on top and pour its liquid in the bowl (fig. 2). Place the bowl in a steamer and cover. Steam (begin timing when the water boils) for at least 1 hour over medium heat. Remove and drain off the liquid into a separate bowl by covering with a plate and turning the bowl over (fig. 3). Set the liquid aside to be used later. Invert the bean curd and vegetables onto the serving platter (fig. 4).

❹ Add ③ and the retained cooking liquid together and place in a pot. Heat until boiling and pour over the bean curd mixture. Drizzle the chicken fat over all.

❺ Remove any old leaves and ends from the green vegetable. Cut into 4-inch lengths. Cook for 2 minutes in boiling water. Remove, rinse with cold water and drain. Heat pan and add 2 Tbsp. oil. Add the green vegetable, with ¼ tsp. salt and ¼ tsp. MSG. Remove and arrange the vegetables around the serving platter. Serve immediately.

* To make the bean curd more firm, soak in salt water to cover.

*¹ If unavailable, substitute bok choy.

Three-Flavor Stewed Chinese Cabbage

Substitute 1⅓ lbs. Chinese cabbage for the bean curd. Prepare the recipe as directed above.

蛤蜊蒸蛋

台灣菜　　4人份

蛤蜊…………半斤
水……………2杯
① ⎰ 雞蛋…………2個
　│ 鹽……………¼小匙
　│ 味精…………¼小匙
　⎱ 薑酒汁………½大匙
② ⎰ 高湯…………1杯
　│ 鹽……………¼小匙
　⎱ 味精…………¼小匙
嫩薑絲………½大匙

蛤蜊吐沙法： 按水2杯加鹽1大匙的比例，將鹽溶化後，擺進蛤蜊，此鹽水需淹過蛤蜊面，靜置半天使其吐沙，煮前再將蛤蜊洗淨。

❶ 水2杯燒開放入蛤蜊，用小火燒至蜊殼微開即熄火，用手將蜊殼打開，盛蒸碗內（圖1），湯汁待涼輕輕倒入（沙及沉澱物倒棄）預先打散之①料內拌勻（圖2），經過濾後倒進蛤蜊碗內（圖3），水燒開以小火蒸10分鐘，用牙籤試插蛋液不會流出即熟（圖4）。

❷ ②料燒開輕輕順碗邊倒進蒸好的蛋內，上擺薑絲趁熱分食。

■薑酒汁：薑片拍碎加酒擠出的汁。

蝦仁蒸蛋

蝦仁…………2兩
①料（鹽改½小匙）
② ⎰ 醬油…………1小匙
　│ 黑醋…………½小匙
　⎱ 麻油…………1小匙

❶ ①料盛湯碗，將蛋打散後加水2杯拌勻，置蒸鍋，水燒開以小火蒸約5分鐘至蛋稍凝固時，輕置蝦仁於其上，續蒸5分鐘至蝦仁熟，上淋②料便可。

生蠔蒸蛋

將蝦仁改生蠔，調味與做法與本頁「蝦仁蒸蛋」同。

蛋白質‧‧‧‧‧‧‧‧‧‧‧‧‧‧２６克
脂質‧‧‧‧‧‧‧‧‧‧‧‧‧‧‧‧‧‧‧‧１４克
醣質‧‧‧‧‧‧‧‧‧‧‧‧‧‧‧‧‧‧‧‧１０克
熱量‧‧‧‧‧‧‧‧‧‧‧‧‧‧‧２５７仟卡
Protein 26g
Fat 14g
Carbohydrate 10g
257 Kcal

Steamed Eggs with Clams　　Taiwanese 4 servings

⅔ lb. steamer clams
2 C. water

① {
2 eggs
¼ t. salt
¼ t. MSG
½ T. ginger-wine*
}

② {
1 C. stock
¼ t. salt
¼ t. MSG
}
½ T. shredded ginger root

❶ Heat 2 C. water until boiling. Add the clams and cook over low heat until the shells begin to open. Turn off the heat. Continue to open the clams by hand. Place the clams in a heatproof bowl. (fig. 1). Retain the clam liquid and let rest to allow the sand to settle. Beat mixture ① lightly and pour the clam liquid into ① , leave the sand behind (fig. 2). Strain this egg liquid into the bowl containing the clams (fig. 3). Place in a steamer and cover. Steam over low heat for 10 minutes. Test with a toothpick, if the eggs are set and the toothpick comes out clean, the dish is done. Remove.

❷ Heat mixture ② until boiling and pour over the steamed eggs along the edge of the bowl. Sprinkle the shredded ginger on top and serve.

* To prepare ginger-wine: mash a slice of ginger and add to ½ Tbsp. rice wine. Pinch the ginger to imbibe the wine with the flower. Remove the ginger slice and use the liquid as directed.

Steamed Eggs with Shrimps

3 oz. raw, shelled shrimp,
　　deveined, rinsed and dried
　　increase salt to ½ t. and
　　prepare ① as above

② {
1 t. soy sauce
½ t. black vinegar or
　　Worcestershire sauce
1 t. sesame oil
}

❶ Beat mixture ① lightly and 2 C. water. Pour into a heatproof bowl and place in steamer. Steam for 5 minutes over low heat until the top is just set. Place the shrimp on top. Steam for another 5 minutes until the shrimp are cooked. Sprinkle mixture ② on top and serve.

Steamed Eggs with Oysters

Substitute 3 oz. of shucked oysters for the shrimp. Prepare as directed in "Steamed Eggs with Shrimps."

205

紫菜蛋捲　　　　　　　　　台灣菜　　4人份

里肌肉………4兩
酒…………1小匙
① 鹽…………⅛小匙
　 味精………⅛小匙
　 糖…………½小匙
　 胡椒粉……⅛小匙
　 太白粉……½大匙
紫菜…………2張
鹹蛋黃(生)…4個
青菜葉………8片
麵 ┌麵粉…3大匙
糊 └水……3大匙
「炸油」………3杯
椒鹽…………½大匙

❶ 里肌肉切０．５公分厚大薄片共切8片，用刀背拍鬆，調①
　料拌勻醃１０分鐘。鹹蛋黃切半。麵糊拌勻待用。

❷ 紫菜１張先鋪上４片肉(圖１)，再塗麵糊(圖２)，並鋪上
　生菜，靠邊排鹹蛋黃(圖３)，捲成圓筒狀(圖４)，封口處
　及兩端均沾黏麵糊，以防炸時爆開。

❸ 鍋熱入「炸油」３杯燒熱(２７５℉)，將紫菜捲下鍋，以中
　火炸約６分鐘後，先夾出一條切開，若蛋黃熟時即可撈出
　，切２公分小塊排盤，如不夠鹹可沾椒鹽。

腐皮蛋捲

將紫菜改用腐皮，其它調味及做法同上。

■ 如無紫菜或腐皮亦可做蛋皮代之。蛋皮的做法：雞蛋３個
　加太白粉、水各１大匙拌勻，以小火煎成蛋皮２張使用。

■ 蛋捲內材料除鹹蛋黃外，改用蝦仁、墨魚、筍、紅蘿蔔、
　洋火腿、冬菇……等，單獨或數種合用均可。

蛋白質 · · · · · · · · · · · · ·４０克
脂質 · · · · · · · · · · · ·１０２克
醣質 · · · · · · · · · · · · · ·２７克
熱量 · · · · · · · ·１１７８仟卡
Protein 40g
Fat 102g
Carbohydrate. 27g
1,178 Kcal

Nori Egg Rolls
Taiwanese 4 servings

6 oz.boneless pork loin

① {
1 t. rice wine
⅛ t. salt
⅛ t. MSG
½ t. sugar
⅛ t. black pepper
½ T. cornstarch
}

2 sheets nori or purple laver
4 raw, salted duck egg yolks
8 leaves leafy or Boston
lettuce, flattened
paste { 3 T. flour
3 T. water }
6 C. oil for frying
½ T. Szechuan peppercorn salt

❶ Remove any fat or muscle from the pork loin and cut into 8 slices about ¼-inch thick. Pound each slice with the blunt edge of the cleaver to tenderize. Mix the slices with ① and marinate for 10 minutes. Cut each salty duck egg yolk in half. Mix the flour and water to a smooth paste.

❷ Spread out 4 pork slices to cover the surface of each purple laver sheet. Spread the surface with a layer of the flour paste (fig. 2). Arrange the lettuce leaves on top. Arrange the salty duck egg yolks along the nearest edge (fig. 3). Starting at the edge containing the duck yolks, roll up lightly to form a thin cylinder-shape (fig. 4). Dot the end seam with some of the flour paste to seal. Dip both edges of the rolls in the flour paste to seal any openings.

❸ Heat pan and add 6 C. oil for frying, heat to 300°F. Add the rolls and deep-fry for about 6 minutes. Test for doneness by cutting open a roll and checking the duck egg yolk;when the yolk is opaque, the rolls are cooked. Remove the rolls and drain. Cut the rolls into slices ¾-inch thick. Arrange the slices on a serving platter. Serve with the Szechuan peppercorn salt, for dipping.

Bean Curd Skin Egg Rolls

Substitute bean curd skins for the laver sheets. Soften in warm water for 30 minutes until soft. Drain and prepare the recipe as directed above.
If nori or purple laver sheets are unavailable, use egg sheets.
To prepare egg sheets: Mix 3 eggs with 1 Tbsp. cornstarch and 1 Tbsp. water. Fry over low heat into 2 thin crepes. Remove and prepare the recipe as directed above.
In addition to salted duck egg yolks, shrimp, squid, bamboo shoots, carrots, ham, pre-softened Chinese black mushrooms may be included. Use either one of the listed ingredients or mix several together.

豆豉小魚
Preserved Fingerlings

皮蛋豆腐
Cold Bean Curd Appetizer

皮蛋豆腐

家常菜　　4人份

嫩豆腐⋯⋯⋯1塊
雪裡紅⋯⋯⋯3大匙
（或鹹酸菜）
蝦米⋯⋯⋯⋯1大匙
葱花⋯⋯⋯⋯$\frac{1}{2}$大匙
皮蛋⋯⋯⋯⋯1個
① 醬油⋯⋯⋯⋯$\frac{1}{2}$大匙
鹽⋯⋯⋯⋯⋯$\frac{1}{8}$小匙
味精⋯⋯⋯⋯$\frac{1}{8}$小匙
麻油⋯⋯⋯⋯$\frac{1}{2}$大匙

❶ 嫩豆腐置盤，用滾開水冲燙後倒淨水備用。
❷ 雪裡紅（或鹹酸菜）漂洗淨，擠乾水份切碎，蝦米泡軟剁碎，皮蛋去殼切片（圖1）。
❸ 鍋熱，將雪裡紅（或鹹酸菜）以中火乾炒20秒，加油、糖各1小匙拌妥取出。蝦米同樣以中火乾炒至香約20秒取出。
❹ 將皮蛋排於豆腐四周，雪裡紅（或鹹酸菜）、蝦米，擺在豆腐上（圖2）淋上①料食時拌勻，即成可口的小菜。
■ 如喜食辣味，可加辣椒或辣油。

豆豉小魚

小魚干⋯⋯⋯3兩
（或熟小魚6兩）
① 豆豉⋯⋯⋯⋯2大匙
紅辣椒⋯⋯⋯2條
大蒜⋯⋯⋯⋯6粒
「炸油」⋯⋯⋯3杯
② 酒⋯⋯⋯⋯⋯1小匙
味精⋯⋯⋯⋯$\frac{1}{4}$小匙
糖⋯⋯⋯⋯⋯1小匙

❶ 小魚干洗淨，用溫水泡軟約20分鐘後，瀝乾。熟小魚（丁香魚）免泡水，紅辣椒切圓薄片，大蒜剁碎（圖3）。
❷ 做法有炒、炸兩種方法：
　炒法：油2大匙燒熱，將小魚干放入，以中火炒約3分鐘後，隨入①料及②料拌炒約1分鐘，即可鏟出置盤。
　炸法：鍋熱，入「炸油」3杯燒熱（350℉），將小魚干放入，以中火泡炸約3分鐘撈出（圖4）；鍋內留油1大匙炒香①料，隨入炸好的小魚干及②料拌炒約1分鐘即可置盤。
■ 烹調好小魚干亦可灑上少許麻油，冷吃熱食均適宜。

蛋白質‥‥‥‥‥‥１６克
脂質‥‥‥‥‥‥‥１６克
醣質‥‥‥‥‥‥‥‥‥３克
熱量‥‥‥‥‥‥２２２仟卡
Protein. 16g
Fat 16g
Carbohydrate 3g
222 Kcal

Cold Bean Curd Appetizer Family-Style 4 servings

1 square fresh bean curd
3 T. salted cabbage or red-in-snow
1 T. dried shrimp
½ T. minced green onion
1 thousand-year-old egg

① ½ T. soy sauce
⅛ t. salt
⅛ t. MSG
½ T. sesame oil

❶ Blanch the bean curd for 10 seconds. Remove and drain. Place on a plate.
❷ Wash the cabbage. Squeeze out the excess water. Mince finely. Soak the dried shrimp until softened (about 30 minutes). Drain and mince. Remove the shell from the thousand-year-old egg and cut into thin slices (fig. 1).
❸ Heat pan and stir-fry the cabbage for 20 seconds over medium heat. Add 1 tsp. oil and 1 tsp. sugar. Toss lightly and remove. Reheat pan and add the dried shrimp and stir-fry for 20 seconds over medium heat.
❹ Place the bean curd in the center of the serving plate. Sprinkle the stir-fried cabbage and shrimp on top of the bean curd (fig. 2). Arrange the thousand-year-old egg slices around the bean curd. Pour mixture ① on top. Before serving, mix the ingredients together.
For added spiciness, sprinkle minced red pepper on top of dried shrimp and vegetable.

Preserved Fingerlings

⅓ lb. salted, dried fingerlings*
(or 8 oz. cooked fingerlings)

1 { 2 T. fermented black beans (豆豉)
2 hot red peppers
6 cloves garlic
2 T. oil for frying

2 { 1 t. rice wine
¼ t. MSG
1 t. sugar

❶ Rinse the fingerlings and soak them in warm water for 20 minutes. (If using cooked fingerlings, omit soaking.)
Remove and drain. Cut hot red peppers into thin slices. Remove the seeds. Mince garlic (fig. 1).
❷ **To stir-fry:** Heat pan and add 2 Tbsp. oil. Add the fingerlings and stir-fry over medium heat for about 3 minutes. Add 1 and 2 . Continue stir-frying for 1 minute. Remove and arrange on serving plate. Serve.
To deep-fry: Heat pan and add 3 C. oil, heat to 350°F. Add the fingerlings. Deep-fry for 3 minutes. Remove and drain (fig. 2). Remove all but 1 Tbsp. oil from pan and reheat. Add 1 and stir-fry until fragrant. Add the fingerlings and 2 . Stir-fry for 1 minute and remove to serving plate. Serve.
* A few drops of sesame oil may be sprinkled over the fingerlings. Serve hot or cold. Fingerlings are tiny fish which have been dried and salted. They are available in packages at oriental grocery stores.

素三鮮　　　　北方菜　　6人份

青江菜……12兩
① 鹽…………½小匙
　味精…………¼小匙
　水…………2大匙
鮮金菇………½杯
（或罐頭）
② 酒…………1小匙
　鹽…………¼小匙
　味精…………¼小匙
　胡椒粉………⅛小匙
　太白粉……1小匙
　水…………½小匙
草菇…………1杯
葱段（2公分）6枝
③ 酒…………½大匙
　蠔油………2大匙
　（或醬油）
　味精…………¼小匙
　麻油…………½小匙
　太白粉……1小匙
　水…………½小匙

❶ 草菇去蒂（圖1），小的不切，大的切半。
❷ 青江菜去除老葉，取10～12公分長段，洗淨，在滾水內燙煮2分鐘，撈出用冷水沖涼後瀝乾；熱鍋加油2大匙燒熱，入青江菜及①料，大火爆炒至熟，即可盛盤圍邊（圖2）。
❸ 鍋熱，加油2大匙入金菇及②料，以大火爆炒15秒鏟出置盤的一邊（圖3）。
❹ 熱鍋，加油2大匙炒香葱段後鏟出丟棄，入草菇及③料大火爆炒30秒，即可盛於盤之另一邊（圖4）。

冬菇菜心

青江菜………1斤
冬菇…………6朵
① 鹽…………¾小匙
　味精…………¼小匙
　糖…………½小匙
　水…………½杯

❶ 青江菜去老葉取約10公分長之嫩菜薹，洗淨備用。冬菇泡軟去蒂切半。
❷ 熱鍋加油3大匙，炒冬菇及青江菜再倒入①料以大火炒約2分鐘至汁將收乾時盛盤。或參照上圖將青江菜圍邊，多餘青江菜置中央上擺冬菇便可。

蛋白質⋯⋯⋯⋯⋯⋯１４克
脂質⋯⋯⋯⋯⋯⋯⋯３１克
醣質⋯⋯⋯⋯⋯⋯⋯１８克
熱量⋯⋯⋯⋯⋯４０７仟卡
Protein 14g
Fat 31g
Carbohydrate 18g
407 Kcal

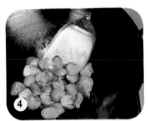

Three-Flavor Vegetarian Plate Peking 6 servings

1 lb. heart of green vegetable*
½ C. golden needle mushrooms, canned of fresh*
1 C. fresh or canned straw mushrooms*

① {
½ t. salt
¼ t. MSG
2 T. water
}

② {
1 t. rice wine
¼ t. salt
¼ t. MSG
⅛ t. pepper
1 t. cornstarch
½ t. water
}

6 1-inch sections green onion

③ {
½ T. rice wine
2 T. oyster sauce or soy sauce
¼ t. MSG
½ t. sesame oil
1 t. cornstarch
½ t. water
}

❶ Rinse the straw mushrooms and drain. Remove the stem (fig. 1) and cut the large ones in half; leave the smaller ones whole.

❷ Trim any old leaves from the green vegetable and remove any tough, outer skin. Cut the vegetable into 4-inch lengths and rinse well. Blanch to cover for 2 minutes. Remove and refresh in cold water. Drain. Heat pan and add 2 Tbsp. oil, heat until very hot. Add the green vegetable and mixture ① . Stir-fry for 1 minute over high heat and remove. (The vegetable should be cooked quickly so that it will retain its fresh green color and crisp texture.) Remove and arrange the vegetable around the edge of the serving platter (fig. 2).

❸ Heat pan and add 2 Tbsp. oil, heat until very hot. Add the golden needle mushrooms, stir-fry briefly, then add ② . Cook for about 15 seconds and remove. Arrange on one half of the serving platter (fig. 3).

❹ Heat pan and add 2 Tbsp. oil, heat until very hot. Add the green onion sections and stir-fry until fragrant. Add the straw mushrooms and stir-fry for 30 seconds. Add ③ and cook until the liquid has nearly evaporated. Remove and arrange on the remaining half of the serving plate (fig. 4). Serve.

* If unavailable, substitute Swiss chard, broccoli or spinach and revise cooking time accordingly.

* If using canned, first blanch briefly.

Chinese Black Mushrooms with Broccoli

1 lb. heart of green vegetable
6 Chinese dried black mushrooms

1 {
¾ t. salt
¼ t. MSG
½ t. sugar
½ T. water
}

❶ Trim any old leaves and tough skin from the broccoli. Cut the broccoli into 4-inch spears. If the stems are thick, cut in half lengthwise. Rinse thoroughly. Soften the black mushrooms in warm water to cover, remove and discard the stems. Cut the caps in half.

❷ Heat pan and add 3 Tbsp. oil, heat until very hot. Add the mushroom caps, broccoli and mixture 1 ; stir-fry briefly. Continue stir-frying over high heat for about 2 minutes or until the liquid has nearly evaporated. Remove the mixture; arrange most of the broccoli along the edge of the platter. Place the remaining broccoli spears on the bottom of the plate. Arrange the mushrooms on top of the broccoli in the center. Serve.

奶油蘿蔔球
Carrot and Radish Balls in Cream Sauce

蘆筍奶油白菜
Asparagus and Cabbage in Cream Sauce

奶油蘿蔔球　　　廣東菜　　6人份

紅蘿蔔１條…６兩
白蘿蔔１條…６兩
菜心１條……６兩
① 油…………３大匙
　洋蔥(切碎)…¼杯
　麵粉………３大匙
② 鹽…………１小匙
　味精………¼小匙
　高湯(或水)…１杯
　奶水…………¼杯

❶ 紅、白蘿蔔及菜心用挖球器挖成圓球狀（圖１），或用刀先切１寸見方小塊，再削修成圓球形。

❷ 把①料中的油３大匙先炒香洋蔥並鏟出，餘油入麵粉以小火炒約３０秒（圖２），重加入炒香之洋蔥拌炒後一齊盛碗備用。

❸ 將②料及蘿蔔球、菜心球，用中火燒煮５分鐘，倒進麵糊攪拌燒熱，最後淋入奶水拌勻（圖３）即可盛盤。

■ 如有烤箱，把烤箱先燒３５０°F，再將煮好的蘿蔔球盛烤盤(或烤盅)，擺進中層烤１５～２０分鐘，呈金黃色，味道更香醇。

蘆筍奶油白菜

大白菜………１個
①料
②料
奶水…………¼杯
蘆筍…………½罐
火腿末……½大匙

❶ 大白菜順直剖開成兩半洗淨，莖部切６公分長段，再順紋切２公分寬之長方塊（圖４），葉部可切大塊，用滾水燙軟（莖先放入）撈起，瀝乾。

❷ 參照本頁「奶油蘿蔔球」做法❷，做好麵糊。

❸ 鍋熱加油４大匙燒熱，白菜略炒加②料，以中火煮約１０分鐘，倒進麵糊攪拌至燒沸，後加奶水拌勻，並加蘆筍煮約１分鐘盛盤，上灑火腿末以增美觀。

■ 白菜內可加其他材料如蟹肉、蝦米……等。

■ 有烤箱，就把煮好的白菜置盤，再放進烤箱以３５０°F烤１５分鐘。

蛋白質‥‥‥‥‥‥‥２１克
脂質‥‥‥‥‥‥‥‥５５克
醣質‥‥‥‥‥‥‥‥５３克
熱量‥‥‥‥‥‥７５６仟卡

Protein. 21g
Fat 55g
Carbohydrate. 53g
756 Kcal

1

2

3

4

Carrot and Radish Balls in Cream Sauce

Cantonese 6 servings

9 oz. carrot or radishes
9 oz. Chinese radishes*
9 oz. stalk of green vegetable*[1]

① { 3 T. oil
¼ C. minced onion
3 T. flour

② { 1 t. salt
¼ t. MSG
1 C. stock or water

¼ C. evaporated milk

❶ Peel the vegetables and using a melon baller, shape into balls (fig. 1); or cut the vegetables into 1-inch squares and make into balls.

❷ Heat pan and add 3 Tbsp. oil from mixture ① . Add the onion and stir-fry until fragrant. Remove and set aside. Reheat the oil remaining in the pan and add the flour. Saute for 30 seconds over low heat (fig. 2) and add the cooked onion. Continue to saute briefly and remove the mixture. Set aside. (roux)

❸ Heat mixture ② until boiling and add the carrot, green vegetable and radish balls. Cook for 5 minutes over medium heat. Add the roux mixture and heat until boiling; add the milk (fig. 3) and remove. Serve.

* If unavailable, substitute icycle radishes.

*[1] If unavailable, substitute cucumber and reduce the cooking time to 3 minutes in Step ❷ .

■ For extra flavor, bake the vegetable mixture in a preheated 350°F oven for 15-20 minutes or until golden.

Asparagus and Cabbage in Cream Sauce

1⅓ lbs. Chinese cabbage
① same as above
② same as above
¼ C. evaporated milk
½ (1 lb. 3 oz.) can asparagus, drained and blanched
T. minced ham

❶ Cut the Chinese cabbage in half lengthwise and rinse well. Cut the stem portion into 2½-inch lengths, then cut lengthwise into strips three-quarters of an inch wide (fig. 4). Cut the leafy portions into large pieces. Blanch the cabbage sections until soft, cook the stem sections first. Remove and drain.

❷ To prepare mixture ① , follow Step ❷ of the recipe shown above. (roux)

❸ Heat pan and add 4 Tbsp. oil, heat until very hot. Add the cabbage sections and stir-fry briefly. Add ② and cook for about 10 minutes over medium heat. Add the roux mixture and heat until boiling. Add the milk and asparagus, cook for an additional minute. Remove and arrange on the serving platter. Sprinkle the ham on top to garnish and serve.

■ Crab and shrimp may also be added to the cabbage.

■ If desired, place the cooked dish in a casserole and bake at 350°F for 15 minutes.

鮑菇菜心
Stir-Fried Mushrooms
with Green Vegetable

雞油金菇
Stir-Fried Golden Needle
Mushrooms with Peas

鮑菇菜心

江浙菜　　6 人份

青江菜……１２兩
鮑菇…………４兩
高湯(或水)…３杯
酒…………１大匙
① ｛ 鹽…………１小匙
味精………¼小匙
水…………１大匙

❶ 青江菜去老葉，切取１０公分長段之嫩菜薹，小的不剖，大的切半或四開（圖１）。

❷ 高湯（或水）３杯燒沸，入鮑菇川燙１５秒，撈出去蒂切片（圖２、３）。

❸ 鍋熱，加油３大匙，青江菜放入並灑上水２大匙，用大火炒軟（不加水菜葉容易炒焦），續加鮑菇並下酒及①料，以大火爆炒２０秒即可盛盤。

雞油金菇

金菇………１２兩
毛豆…………２兩
高湯(或水)…１杯
蔥段(２公分)６枝
酒…………１大匙
① ｛ 鹽…………½小匙
糖…………¼小匙
味精………¼小匙

❶ 金菇切除根部１.５～２公分（圖４），（因根部有沙粒），撥開洗淨瀝乾。

❷ 高湯（或水）１杯燒沸，入毛豆煮約１分鐘至熟撈出。

❸ 鍋熱，加油５大匙燒熱，入蔥段炒香至金黃色撈出棄置，再把金菇、毛豆及①料用大火爆炒約１５秒至金菇熟即可盛盤。

蛋白質‥‥‥‥‥‥‥‥１４克
脂質‥‥‥‥‥‥‥‥‥４６克
醣質‥‥‥‥‥‥‥‥‥１５克
熱量‥‥‥‥‥‥‥５１０仟卡
Protein. 14g
Fat 46g
Carbohydrate 15g
510 Kcal

Stir-Fried Mushrooms with Green Vegetable
Chekiang-Kiangsu 6 servings

1 lb. heart of green vegetable *
（青江菜）

6 oz. fresh cepes *¹ （鮑菇）

3 C. stock or water

1 T. rice wine

①{
1 t. salt
¼ t. MSG
1 T. water

❶ Remove old leaves from the green vegetable and the tough, outer skin, if any. Cut the stem into 4-inch lengths. Cut the larger stalks in half or quarters (fig. 1), leaved the smaller ones whole.

❷ Heat 3 C. stock until boiling, blanch the mushrooms in the stock for 15 seconds. Remove and cut into bite-size sections (fig. 2,3). Discard the stock.

❸ Heat pan and add 3 Tbsp. oil and heat until very hot. Add the green vegetable and stir-fry briefly. Add 2 Tbsp. water and cook over high heat until tender. Add the mushrooms, rice wine, and mixture ① . Cook for 20 seconds and remove to the serving plate. Serve.

* If unavailable, substitute Swiss chard or bok choy.

*¹ If cepes are unavailable, substitute straw mushrooms.

Stir-Fried Golden Needle Mushrooms with Peas

1 lb. fresh golden needle mushrooms *

3 oz. peas

1 C. stock or water

6 1-inch sections green onion

1 T. rice wine

1{
½ t. salt
¼ t. sugar
¼ t. MSG

❶ Cut three-quarters to one inch off the ends of the golden mushrooms (fig. 4)*. Rinse lightly and drain.

❷ Heat stock or water until boiling and add the peas. Cook for 1 minute; remove and drain.

❸ Heat pan and add 5 Tbsp. oil, heat until very hot. Add the green onion sections and stir-fry until fragrant. Remove the onions and discard. Add the peas, mushrooms, and 1 over high heat for about 15 seconds. Remove to a serving platter and serve.

* If unavailable, use canned mushrooms and blanch briefly before using. Omit trimming the ends.

綠蘆筍炒肉片
Stirf Fried Pork with Asparagus

雞絲豌豆
Stir-Fried Chicken with Peas

綠蘆筍炒肉片　　　　　　家常菜　　6人份

綠蘆筍………4兩
里肌肉………3兩
① | 鹽…………⅛小匙
　| 水…………1大匙
　| 太白粉……1小匙
② | 葱段（2公分）6枝
　| 薑片………6小片
　| 蒜末………1小匙
　| 酒…………1小匙
③ | 鹽…………⅓小匙
　| 糖…………½小匙
　| 味精………¼小匙
　| 太白粉……½小匙
　| 水…………2大匙

❶ 綠蘆筍削或撕去外皮（圖1），切4～5公分長段（圖2），在滾水內燙煮1分鐘撈出（圖3），放入冷水內漂涼備用。
❷ 里肌肉切薄片，調①料拌勻，下鍋前再加油半大匙攪拌，炒時肉片易於散開。
❸ 鍋熱，加「油」半杯燒熱（275℉），將肉片落鍋，迅速用鍋鏟拌開，以大火泡炒見肉色轉白，約30秒撈出，瀝淨油，鍋內留油2大匙將②料炒香再下蘆筍大火略炒，續入肉片，灑酒1小匙及③料拌勻盛盤（圖4）。
■ 綠蘆筍可改用蒜苔，調味及做法相同。

雞絲豌豆

雞胸肉（去皮）6兩
① | 鹽…………¼小匙
　| 蛋白………½個
　| （或水1大匙）
　| 太白粉……1小匙
　| 葱段………6枝
　| 嫩豌豆……2兩
　| （或蠶豆仁）

❶ 雞胸肉切成細絲調①料拌勻，醃30分鐘，下鍋前加油1大匙攪拌，炒時雞絲易於撥散。
❷ 鍋熱，加「油」半杯燒熱（275℉），入雞絲拌炒見雞絲色轉白且熟取出，餘油入葱段炒香（後葱段棄置不用），豌豆仁（洗淨）下鍋並加鹽、酒少許炒至剛熟，再倒進雞絲拌和起鍋。
■ 這是一道火侯菜，火旺速炒即刻上桌。

蛋白質 · · · · · · · · · · · · ２１克
脂質 · · · · · · · · · · · · · · · ７３克
醣質 · · · · · · · · · · · · · · · ９克
熱量 · · · · · · · · · · ７７２仟卡

Protein 21g
Fat 73g
Carbohydrate. 9g
772 Kcal

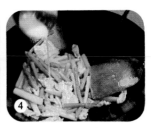

Stir-Fried Pork with Asparagus
Family-Style
6 servings

6 oz. fresh asparagus

4 oz. boneless pork loin

① { ⅛ t. salt
1 T. water
1 t. cornstarch }

② { 6 1-inch sections green onion
6 slices ginger root
1 t. minced garlic }

1 t. rice wine

③ { ⅓ t. salt
½ t. sugar
¼ t. MSG
½ t. cornstarch
2 T. water }

❶ Remove the tough skin from the asparagus (fig. 1) and cut into 2-inch sections (fig. 2). Blanch for 1 minute, then remove (fig. 3). Plunge into cold water to cool.

❷ Remove any fat or muscle from the pork and slice thinly. Mix with ① and marinate for 10 minutes. Add ½ Tbsp. oil before stir-frying to prevent the meat from sticking together.

❸ Heat pan and add 6 Tbsp. oil and heat to medium hot (275°F). Stir-fry the meat over medium heat for about 30 seconds or until the meat changes color. Remove and drain. Remove all but 2 Tbsp. oil from the pan and heat until very hot. Stir-fry ② until fragrant. Add the asparagus and stir-fry briefly. Add the pork slices, rice wine, and mixture ③. Toss lightly and remove to a serving platter. Serve (fig. 4).

Stir-Fried Chicken with Peas

½ lb. skinned, chicken breast meat

① { ¼ t. salt
½ egg white or 1 Tbsp. water
1 t. cornstarch }

6 stalks green onion

3 oz. peas (or lima-beans)

¼ t. salt

1 t. rice wine

❶ Shred the chicken breast meat. Mix with ① and marinate for 30 minutes. Before cooking, add 1 Tbsp. oil to prevent the meat from sticking together while stir-frying.

❷ Heat pan and add 5 Tbsp. oil, heat until medium hot (275°F). Stir-fry chicken until the meat changes color and is cooked. Remove and drain. Reheat pan and the remaining oil and stir-fry the green onion until fragrant, then remove and discard. Add the peas (rinsed lightly), salt, and rice wine. Cook until the peas are just tender. Add the shredded chicken and toss lightly. Remove to a serving platter and serve.

■ For optimum flavor, the oil should be very hot and all of the stir-frying done over very high heat. Serve immediately while still hot.

涼拌藕片

北方菜　　6人份

嫩蓮藕………半斤
① 青椒…………1個
　紅辣椒………1條

　鹽…………$\frac{1}{3}$小匙
② 糖………1$\frac{1}{2}$大匙
　白醋………1大匙
　麻油………$\frac{1}{2}$大匙

❶ 將藕削或刮去皮(圖1)，切薄片浸泡涼水中以防久擺藕片
　變紅（圖2），把①料之青椒除蒂並挖去籽切圓薄片，紅
　辣椒去籽切斜片（圖3）。

❷ 水3杯燒開，放進藕片燙煮2分鐘撈出，泡入冷開水漂涼
　後瀝乾，加①②料拌勻（圖4）醃30分鐘即可食用。

■涼拌的調味料除糖醋汁外，可依個人喜愛調製多種不同的
　口味。

素炒蓮根

嫩蓮藕………半斤
花椒粒………1小匙
蔥、薑末(各)$\frac{1}{2}$大匙
① 鹽…………1大匙
　黑醋………$\frac{1}{2}$小匙

❶ 蓮藕處理，參照本頁「涼拌藕片」做法❶。

❷ 鍋熱，加麻油(或油)2大匙燒熱，以小火炒香花椒粒後撈
　出丟棄，續加藕片翻炒，時時灑水炒至藕片有漿汁即加①
　料待藕片呈白色清脆時(約需10分鐘)，即可盛盤。

糖醋黃瓜

小黃瓜………半斤
紅辣椒………1條
醬油………1大匙
① 鹽…………$\frac{1}{4}$小匙
　糖…………2大匙
　醋………1$\frac{1}{2}$大匙

❶ 小黃瓜切除兩端洗淨，順直剖切成4～6開，用刀削去籽
　，加鹽半小匙醃拌使其變軟，用冷開水沖洗拭乾備用。紅
　辣椒直剖兩半去籽切細長絲。

❷ 鍋熱，加麻油3大匙燒熱，入黃瓜爆炒10秒，下紅辣椒
　絲及①料以大火拌炒盛起，使糖醋汁醃泡黃瓜。

■這是一道涼拌菜，爆炒黃瓜時間宜短，不然就不脆。

蛋白質···················4克
脂質····················8克
醣質···················４２克
熱量··········２４９仟卡

Protein . . . .　4g
Fat . . . .　8g
Carbohydrate. . . . . . .　42g
249 Kcal

 1    2    3   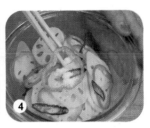 4

Lotus Root Salad   Peking 6 servings

¾ lb. fresh lotus root

① { 1   green pepper
    1   hot red pepper

② { ⅓ t. salt
    1½ T. sugar
    1   T. rice vinegar
    ½ T. sesame oil

❶ Rinse the lotus root and peel (fig. 1). Cut into thin slices. Place immediately cold water to prevent darkening (fig. 2). Remove the stem and seeds from the green pepper, then cut into thin slices. Cut the red pepper diagonally into thin slices (fig. 3) and remove the seeds.

❷ Heat 3 C. water until boiling. Parboil the lotus root for 2 minutes and remove. Refresh in cold water, then drain. Combine the lotus root with ① and ② . Mix evenly (fig. 4) and let stand 30 minutes before serving.

■ For cold salad dishes, other sauce flavorings may be created to suit individual taste.

Fried Lotus Root

¾ lb. lotus root
1   t. whole peppercorns

☐ { ½ T. minced green onion
    ½ T. minced ginger
    1   t. salt
    ½ t. black vinegar or
         Worcestershire sauce

❶ To prepare the lotus root, see Step ❶ in recipe shown above. "Lotus Root Salad."

❷ Heat pan and add 2 Tbsp. sesame oil or oil. Heat until very hot, then turn heat to low and stir-fry the peppercorns until fragrant. Remove and discard the peppercorns. Add the lotus root and stir-fry. Sprinkle a few drops of water on top while frying. When the lotus root begins to emit liquid, add mixture ☐ to thicken. Continue frying for about 10 minutes; remove and serve.

Sweet and Sour Cucumber Salad

¾ lb. gherkin cucumbers or
      gourmet, seedless cucumbers
1   hot red pepper

☐ { 1   T. soy sauce
    ¼ t. salt
    2   T. sugar
    1½ T. rice vinegar

❶ Cut off both ends of the cucumbers and rinse. Slice lengthwise into 4 to 6 sections. Remove the seeds and let macerate with ½tsp. salt. Rinse in cold water and pat dry. Set aside. Cut the red pepper half lengthwise. Remove the seeds, then cut into long shreds.

❷ Heat pan and add 3 Tbsp. sesame oil. Heat until very hot and stir-fry the cucumber over high heat for about 10 seconds. Add the shredded red pepper and ☐ . Stir-fry briefly, then remove. Marinate the cucumbers in the sauce until serving time.

■ To retain the crisp texture of the cucumber, stir-fry over high heat.

和菜戴帽　　　　　北方菜　　6人份

里肌肉………３兩
① 酒…………½小匙
　 醬油………½大匙
　 太白粉……１小匙
　 水…………１大匙
韮黃…………２兩
蔥末…………１大匙
② 醬油………１大匙
　 鹽…………½小匙
　 湯(或水)……１杯
粉絲…………１把
綠豆芽………３兩
菠菜…………３兩
雞蛋…………２個
鹽…………⅙小匙
③ 太白粉１小匙 ｝先
　 水……½大匙 ｝調匀

❶ 里肌肉去除白筋後切片再切細絲，調入①料拌匀，下鍋前加油１大匙拌開，炒時肉絲易於撥散。

❷ 韮黃、菠菜洗淨後，切成３公分長段（圖１）。粉絲用溫水泡軟，切(或剪)斷。

❸ 鍋熱，加油５大匙燒溫，放進肉絲用鍋鏟拌開，見肉色轉白且熟，加韮黃用大火略炒僅熟的程度盛盤（圖２）。

❹ 油３大匙燒熱，將蔥末炒香加②料及粉絲燒煮至汁將收乾時，放進綠豆芽炒至剛熟起鍋（圖３）。

❺ 油３大匙燒熱，用大火爆炒菠菜，加鹽⅓小匙翻炒數下，隨加以上各料拌妥混合盛盤。

❻ 雞蛋加③料拌匀。備乾淨鍋燒熱，用刷子或布沾少許油抹匀鍋邊，倒進蛋汁即將鍋提起傾斜順鍋圓方向轉動，攤成圓薄皮，等凝固時輕輕由邊掀起整片取出（圖４）覆蓋和菜上，如戴一頂帽子，由此而取名「和菜戴帽」。

北方簡單的和菜，則只用豆芽菜、菠菜及粉絲三樣來炒。

■和菜戴帽通常用荷葉餅(參照第１１６頁做法)或春捲皮（參照中國餐點內之做法），以蔥段蘸沾料連同和菜包捲而食。

■沾料做法：甜麵醬、糖、水各１大匙，麻油半大匙燒熱使用。

蛋白質‥‥‥‥‥‥‥３５克
脂質‥‥‥‥‥‥‥‥‥９４克
醣質‥‥‥‥‥‥‥‥‥４９克
熱量‥‥‥‥‥１１８６仟卡
Protein. 35g
Fat 94g
Carbohydrate. 49g
1,186 Kcal

Stir-Fried Vegetables Topped with Egg Pancake

Peking 6 servings

4 oz.	boneless pork loin	
①	½ t.	rice wine
	½ T.	soy sauce
	1 t.	cornstarch
	1 T.	water
	3 oz.	Chinese leeks
	1 T.	minced green onion
②	1 T.	soy sauce
	½ t.	salt
	1 C.	stock or water
	1	2-oz. package bean threads (cellophane noodles)

¼ 1b.	bean sprouts	
¼ 1b.	spinach, trimmed and cleaned	
2	eggs	
③	⅙ t. salt	mixed thoroughly
	1 t. cornstarch	
	½ T. water	

❶ Remove any fat or muscle from the pork, then shred finely. Mix with mixture ① and marinate for 20 minutes. Before stir-frying, add 1 Tbsp. oil so that the shreds will separate while frying.

❷ Rinse the Chinese leeks. Cut into 1-inch lengths (fig. 1). Soak the bean threads in warm water to soften, then cut them into shorter lengths (scissors may be used).

❸ Heat pan and add 5 Tbsp. oil, heat until medium hot. Stir-fry the shredded pork until the color changes. Add the Chinese leeks and stir-fry over high heat several seconds. Remove and set aside (fig. 2).

❹ Heat pan and add 3 Tbsp. oil, heat until very hot. Stir-fry the minced green onions until fragrant. Add ② and the bean threads. Cook until the liquid is nearly absorbed. Add the bean sprouts and stir-fry briefly. Remove to a serving plate (fig. 3).

❺ Heat pan and add 3 Tbsp. oil, heat until very hot. Briefly stir-fry the spinach with ⅓ tsp. salt over high heat. Add the other cooked ingredients from above and toss together to mix. Remove to serving a plate.

❻ Beat the eggs lightly with ③ . Rub the surface of the pan with an oil-soaked paper towel. Add the egg mixture, rotate the pan slowly to spread the egg evenly into a thin, round pancake. When the egg has set, gently remove the egg in one piece (fig. 4) and place over the stir-fried ingredients like a hat.

For a simple method: Omit the egg hat, pork, and only stir-fry the bean sprouts, spinach, and bean threads.

■ This dish is usually served with Mandarin pancakes (refer to P.116) or Spring Roll Skins (refer to "Chinese Snacks" for preparation). Green onion sections and sweet bean paste are usually placed inside the pancakes along with some of the stir-fried mixture.

■ To prepare the dip: Blend 1 Tbsp. sweet bean paste (甜麵醬), 1 Tbsp. sugar, 1 Tbsp. water; and ½ Tbsp. sesame oil together; place in a pan and heat until boiling. Remove to a small bowl and serve.

醬汁茄子
Saucy Eggplant

油爆冬筍
Fried Bamboo Shoots

醬汁茄子　　　　　北方菜　　6人份

茄子………１２兩
「炸油」………３杯
蒜末………１大匙

① {
醬油………２大匙
糖………２大匙
味精………¼小匙
鹽………¼小匙
黑醋………１大匙
水………¼杯
}

❶ 茄子洗淨去除頭尾，切約１０公分長段，再直剖成兩半（圖１），在表皮切菱形交叉花紋，切至一半深度（圖２）。
❷ 「炸油」３杯燒熱（３００°F），將茄子落炸約１分半鐘，撈出瀝淨油（圖３），留油２大匙，以小火炒香蒜末，加茄子及①料（圖４），用中火燒煮３分鐘至汁將收乾時盛盤。

蒸茄泥

茄子………１２兩

① {
芝麻醬………½大匙
醬油………２大匙
醋………½大匙
麻油………１大匙
蒜末………１大匙
}

❶ 茄子切法參照本頁「醬汁茄子」做法❶。
❷ 烹調法有兩種：
　　１蒸法：將茄子置盤，移入蒸鍋內水開大火蒸２０分鐘，或擺放在飯上一齊蒸爛。
　　２煮法：水６杯燒開，入茄子煮熟透而軟，撈出盛盤。
❸ 將１料拌勻，澆淋在茄泥上，冷吃熱食均適宜。
■ 如喜食辣味，可酌加辣椒油或辣椒末。

油爆冬筍

冬筍………１斤半
榨菜………少許
高湯………３杯
「炸油」………３杯
葱、薑末(各)１大匙

① {
酒………１大匙
醬油……１½大匙
味精………¼小匙
}
豆苗………半斤

❶ 冬筍去殼，在高湯內煮熟撈出，切成桔瓣狀；或剖四開，再切滾刀塊。榨菜切碎備用。
❷ 鍋熱，加「炸油」３杯燒熱（３７５°F），放入筍片炸約２分鐘，呈淡黃色撈出，瀝乾油，留油１大匙炒香葱薑末，再入冬筍、１料及榨菜末以中火拌炒１分鐘，淋油１大匙拌勻即可盛盤。
❸ 鍋熱加油３大匙，下豆苗加鹽¼小匙、糖¼小匙，用大火爆炒５秒，即取出置盤邊即成。

222

蛋白質 · · · · · · · · · · · · · · · 4克
脂質 · · · · · · · · · · · · · · · 13克
醣質 · · · · · · · · · · · · · · · 20克
熱量 · · · · · · · · · · · · · 367仟卡

Protein 4g
Fat 13g
Carbohydrate 20g
367 Kcal

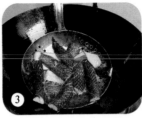

Saucy Eggplant — Peking 6 servings

1	1b.	eggplants
3	C.	oil for frying
1	T.	garlic, minced

① {
- 2 T. soy sauce
- 2 T. sugar
- ¼ t. salt
- ¼ t. MSG
- 1 T. black vinegar or Worcestershire sauce
- ¼ C. water

1	1b.	eggplants

1 {
- ½ T. sesame sauce (芝麻醬)
- 2 T. soy sauce
- ½ T. rice vinegar
- 1 T. sesame oil
- 1 T. garlic, minced

❶ Rinse the eggplants. Cut off both ends and cut the remaining section into 3-inch lengths. Halve lengthwise (fig. 1). Score section on skin-side diagonally in both directions about halfway through thickness (fig. 2).

❷ Heat pan and add oil, heat to 300°F. Add the eggplants and deep-fry for 1½ minutes. Remove and drain (fig. 3) all but 2 Tbsp. of oil from the pan and reheat. Add the garlic and stir-fry over low heat, until fragrant. Add the eggplant sections and ① (fig. 4). Cook over medium heat for about 3 minutes or until the liquid is nearly evaporated. Remove to a serving platter and serve.

Steamed Eggplant

❶ To prepare the eggplants, see Step ❶ of the recipe shown above.

❷ To cook eggplant one of the two methods shown below may be used.

To steam: Place the eggplant sections on a heatproof plate and place in steamer. Cover and steam for 20 minutes over high heat. If the eggplant is tender when prodded with a chopstick, the eggplant is cooked. Remove and place on a serving plate.

To boil: Heat 6 C. of water until boiling. Add the eggplant sections and cook until tender. Arrange the sections on a serving plate.

❸ Mix the ingredients of 1 to a smooth paste and pour over the eggplant sections. Serve hot or cold.

■ For more spiciness, add hot pepper oil or chopped red hot pepper according to individual taste.

Fried Bamboo Shoots

2	1bs.	bamboo shoots*

Szechuan pickled mustard green . .
. . . . a little bit

3	C.	stock or water
3	C.	oil for frying
1	T.	minced ginger
1	T.	minced green onion

1 {
- 1 T. rice wine
- 1½ T. soy sauce
- ¼ t. MSG

1	1b.	spinach, trimmed and cleaned
¼	t.	salt
¼	t.	sugar

❶ Peel the tough, outer skin from the bamboo shoots and cook in the boiling stock or water for 30 minutes. Remove and roll-cut into bite-size sections. Set aside. Mince the Szechuan pickled mustard green.

❷ Heat pan and add oil for trying, heat to about 375°F. Add the bamboo pieces and deep-fry for about 2 minutes or until lightly browned. Remove and drain. Remove all but 1 Tbsp. oil from pan and reheat. Add the minced ginger and green union, stir-fry until fragrant. Add the bamboo pieces and mixture 1, and Szechuan pickled mustard green minced Stir-fry for about 1 minute. Sprinkle 1 Tbsp. oil over ingredients toss lightly and remove to a serving platter.

❸ Heat pan and add 3 Tbsp. oil, heat until very hot. Add the spinach, salt, sugar and stir-fry for 5 seconds over high heat. Remove and arrange around the edge of the serving platter. Serve.

* If fresh bamboo shoots are unavailable, use canned bamboo shoots and blanch for a minute. Remove; refresh in cold water and use as directed.

鑲節瓜

廣東菜　　　6人份

節瓜２條……１斤
絞肉…………４兩
雞肝…………１付
雞油…………½兩
①{
鹽…………½小匙
味精………¼小匙
胡椒粉……⅛小匙
麻油………¼小匙
太白粉……½大匙
「炸油」……３杯
②{
高湯…………２杯
鹽…………⅓小匙
味精………¼小匙
③{
蠔油………１大匙
（或醬油）
麻油………½小匙
太白粉…１½小匙
水…………１大匙

❶節瓜用金屬匙柄或筷子柄爲四方形者，輕輕刮除表皮（圖１），但仍保有綠色爲佳，切開兩端把籽挖除（圖２），中心挖空內灑太白粉。

❷雞肝、雞油剁碎與絞肉調入①料仔細攪拌成「肉餡」，塞入瓜內（圖３），再把兩端合上，插上牙籤固定備炸（圖４）。

❸「炸油」３杯燒熱（３７５℉），順鍋邊入節瓜，用中火炸約３分鐘至瓜肉稍軟撈出。

❹把②料燒開放入炸過之節瓜，蓋上鍋蓋用小火燜煮至節瓜熟透湯汁剩一半（約１０分鐘），撈出節瓜拿掉牙籤並切塊置盤，餘汁續入③料燒沸淋在節瓜上便可。

■除節瓜外，大黃瓜、苦瓜亦可。無雞肝、雞油可免用。

鑲大黃瓜

大黃瓜２條…１斤
絞肉…………４兩
蝦米………２大匙
冬菇…………３朶
①料
②料（高湯改３杯）

❶將大黃瓜去皮洗淨，切開兩端，把瓜子瓜囊刮出，中心挖空內灑太白粉。

❷蝦米、冬菇洗淨分別加水泡軟後剁碎與絞肉調入①料攪拌成「肉餡」，塞入瓜內，再把切開之兩端合上用牙籤固定。

❸把鑲好大黃瓜置砂鍋內加②料及泡蝦米、冬菇的水，用小火煨燉約１小時至瓜軟湯汁剩一半即可。

■此菜清爽味鮮，夏日至爲適口。

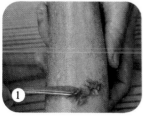

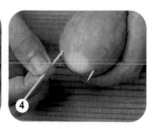

蛋白質‥‥‥‥‥‥３３克
脂質‥‥‥‥‥‥‥‥７０克
醣質‥‥‥‥‥‥‥‥３克
熱量‥‥‥‥１１１１仟卡
Protein. 33g
Fat 70g
Carbohydrate. 3g
1,111 Kcal

Stuffed Zucchini

Cantonese 6 servings

2 zucchini *(about 1⅓ lbs.)
6 oz. ground pork
1 pair chicken livers
¾ oz. chicken fat (optional)

①
- ½ t. salt
- ¼ t. MSG
- ⅛ t. black pepper
- ¼ t. sesame oil
- ½ T. cornstarch

3 C. oil for frying

②
- 2 C. stock
- ⅓ t. salt
- ¼ t. MSG

③
- 1 T. oyster sauce or soy sauce
- ½ t. sesame oil
- 1½ t. cornstarch
- 1 T. water

2 large cucumbers (about 1⅓ lbs.)
6 oz. ground pork
2 T. dried shrimp
3 Chinese dried black mushrooms
① same as above
② same as above, except increase the stock to 3 cups

❶ Lightly pare the Zucchini leave some of the green skin for color (fig. 1). Slice off both ends and retain. Scoop out the meat from the middle (fig. 2). Dust the cavity of each zucchini with cornstarch.

❷ Chop the chicken liver and chicken fat (if using). Thoroughly mix into the ground pork and ① . Stuff the ground meat mixture into each zucchini (fig. 3). Cover the ends with the two retained ends of the zucchini and secure with toothpicks (fig. 4).

❸ Heat pan and add 3 C. oil, heat to 375°F. Add the stuffed zucchini, and deep-fry over medium heat about 3 minutes or until the zucchini is slightly tender. Remove and drain.

❹ Heat ② until boiling. Add the stuffed zucchini; cover and simmer for about 10 minutes over low heat. The zucchini should be very tender and the liquid reduced to half. Remove the zucchini; remove the toothpicks; cut into slices and arrange the slices on a serving platter. Continue to cook the liquid and add ③ to thicken. Heat until boiling and pour over the zucchini slices. Serve.

* If zucchini is unavailable, large cucumbers or bitter squash may be used.

Stuffed Cucumbers

❶ Pare the cucumbers and rinse. Slice off both ends and retain. Remove the seeds from each end piece. Scoop out the seeds from the center of each cucumber and dust the cavity with cornstarch.

❷ Rinse the dried shrimp and black mushrooms. Soak each separately in hot water until softened. Retain the soaking liquid; mince shrimp and mushrooms. Mix thoroughly with the ground pork and mixture ① to make filling. Stuff each cucumber cavity with filling. Cover the ends with the two retained ends of the cucumbers and secure with toothpicks.

❸ Place the stuffed cucumbers in a casserole. Add ② and the soaking liquids from step ❷ cover; simmer over low heat for about one hour or until the cucumbers are tender and the liquid is reduced to half. Remove and arrange the cucumbers on a serving plate. Pour the reduced sauce over the top and serve.

■ This dish is an excellent summer entree because of its lightness and freshness.

225

蟹黃菜心

廣東菜　　6 人份

蟹‧‧‧‧‧‧‧‧‧‧‧‧‧1 隻
①
　酒‧‧‧‧‧‧‧‧‧‧‧½ 大匙
　葱‧‧‧‧‧‧‧‧‧‧‧2 枝
　薑‧‧‧‧‧‧‧‧‧‧‧2 片
小青江菜‧‧‧12 棵
②
　鹽‧‧‧‧‧‧‧‧‧‧‧½ 小匙
　味精‧‧‧‧‧‧‧‧‧¼ 小匙
　高湯‧‧‧‧‧‧‧‧‧2 杯
葱、薑末(各)½ 大匙
酒‧‧‧‧‧‧‧‧‧‧‧½ 小匙
③
　鹽‧‧‧‧‧‧‧‧‧‧‧½ 小匙
　味精‧‧‧‧‧‧‧‧‧¼ 小匙
　高湯‧‧‧‧‧‧‧‧‧1 杯
④
　太白粉‧‧‧‧‧‧2 小匙
　水‧‧‧‧‧‧‧‧‧‧‧1 大匙
蛋白‧‧‧‧‧‧‧‧‧1 個

❶ 揭開蟹蓋，挖除內臟，刷洗乾淨，置盤加①料擺進蒸籠或蒸鍋內（圖1），水開大火蒸約１０分鐘，取出切開（圖2），用叉子剔出蟹肉（圖3），蟹殼敲破取肉（圖4）蟹黃切小粒。

❷ 青江菜去除老葉及根部，取長１０公分之嫩菜薳，整棵沖洗淨。鍋熱，入②料燒沸，將青江菜落鍋燙煮１分鐘，撈出整齊排盤（湯汁不用）。

❸ 鍋熱，加油３大匙燒熱，將葱、薑末爆香，蟹肉、蟹黃略炒，並下酒及③料燒開，以④料勾芡，再徐徐淋下蛋白（預先打散），邊淋邊用鍋鏟攪勻，最後加油１大匙（以增光澤），再澆淋在青江菜上便成。

■ 如用蟹罐，可省略做法❶。

蟹黃芥菜

將青江菜改用芥菜心１２兩，芥菜心處理參照第２２８頁「干貝芥菜」做法❷，其他調味及做法同上。

蟹黃花菜

青花菜(玉蘭菜)‧‧‧半斤
②料
葱、薑末(各)‧‧‧½ 大匙
酒‧‧‧‧‧‧‧‧‧‧‧‧½ 大匙
③料
④料
蛋白‧‧‧‧‧‧‧‧‧‧‧1 個

❶ 青花菜一朵朵切開，並削除硬皮，沖洗淨，把②料燒沸放入青花菜，大火煮約２分鐘至莖熟便可撈出，湯汁不要。

❷ 參照本頁「蟹黃菜心」做法❸，最後將已煮過的青花菜倒入再拌和即可全部盛盤。

■ 除青江菜、芥菜心、青花菜外，白花菜、綠蘆筍、大白菜均可代替。

| 蛋白質⋯⋯⋯⋯⋯５２克 |
| 脂質⋯⋯⋯⋯⋯⋯⋯４９克 |
| 醣質⋯⋯⋯⋯⋯⋯⋯１０克 |
| 熱量⋯⋯⋯⋯⋯６９５仟卡 |

Protein 52g
Fat 49g
Carbohydrate 10g
695 Kcal

Stir-Fried Crab Meat and Vegetables

Cantonese 6 servings

1 fresh crab or 1 C. frozen crab meat* (about 4 oz. meat)

① { ½ T. rice wine
2 stalks green onion mashed
2 slices ginger root, mashed

½ lb. heart of green vegetable*¹

② { ½ t. salt
¼ t. MSG
2 C. stock or water
½ T. minced green onion
½ T. minced ginger root
½ T. rice wine

③ { ½ t. salt
¼ t. MSG
1 C. stock or water

④ { 2 t. cornstarch
1 T. water

1 egg white

❶ Remove the upper shell of the body of the crab and rinse the inside parts, being careful not to dislodge the roe. Remove any dirty, extraneous matter and combine with mixture ① . Place in a pan to steam (fig. 1). Cover and steam for 10 minutes in steamer over high heat. Remove and cut the crab in half (fig. 2). Use a fork to remove the central body meat (fig. 3). Crack open the claws and remove the meat (fig. 4). Chop the roe lightly and shred the meat.

❷ Remove any old leaves and tough skin from the green vegetable. Cut into 4-inch lengths. Heat pan and mixture ② until boiling. Add the green vegetable and cook for 1 minute. Remove and arrange on a serving platter.

❸ Heat pan and add 3 Tbsp. oil, heat until very hot. Add the minced green onion and ginger; stir-fry until fragrant. Add the crab meat and roe; stir-fry gently. Add the rice wine and mixture ③ . Heat until boiling then add mixture ④ to thicken. Beat the egg white until frothy; add gradually to the crab meat mixture while mixing constantly. Add 1 T. oil for sheen and toss lightly. Remove and pour mixture over the vegetable. Serve.

* If frozen crab is used, step ❶ should be omitted.

*¹ Any green vegetable may be used, such as spinach, broccoli, bok choy, asparagus, cabbage, etc.

Stir-Fried Crab with Mustard Cabbage

Substitute about 1 lb. mustard cabbage for the green vegetable. Prepare recipe as directed above. To prepare the mustard cabbage, see Step ❷ "Scallops with Mustard Cabbage", P. 228.

Stir-Fried Crab with Mustard Cabbage

¾ lb. cauliflower
② same as above
½ T. minced green onion
½ T. minced ginger
½ T. rice wine
③ same as above
④ same as above
1 egg white

❶ Cut the cauliflower into flowerets, remove the stem. Rinse and drain. Heat ② until boiling. Add the cauliflower and cook for 2 minutes over high heat. Remove and drain.

❷ To prepare ③ , ④ , and egg white, see Step ❸ "Stir-fried Crab Meat and Vegetables ". Add the cauliflower to the crab meat mixture; remove to a serving plate and serve.

干貝芥菜 廣東菜 12人份

干貝…………½兩
芥菜心……1斤半
① {
酒…………½大匙
高湯………½杯
鹽…………½小匙
味精………¼小匙
}
② {
太白粉……1小匙
水…………1大匙
}

❶干貝洗淨加水半杯（圖1），水開後蒸15分鐘，趁熱以刀面壓成絲，或用手撕成細絲（圖2），湯汁留用。
❷芥菜心去老葉後，取10～12公分長段（圖3），水6杯燒滾，將芥菜心放入燙煮2分鐘後撈出，用冷水沖涼，瀝乾，再對開或切成4份（圖4）。
❸油1大匙，燒熱，倒入①料及干貝絲連汁燒開後放進芥菜，以小火煮5分鐘，用②料勾芡即可盛盤。

干貝京白

干貝…………½兩
大白菜1顆1斤半
酒…………1大匙
鹽…………2小匙
②料

❶干貝處理參照本頁「干貝芥菜」做法❶。
❷大白菜由中間順直剖成兩半，剝除外葉，約手掌大之嫩菜心，沖洗淨（沖洗時不使菜瓣散開）。
❸備蒸盤，白菜心切口朝上，灑酒1大匙，水燒開以中火蒸約30分鐘。另備蒸碗底放干貝絲連汁，上置已蒸過之白菜心，上灑鹽2小匙續蒸30分鐘至白菜變黃色且軟（以筷子試夾易爛程度），取出上蓋菜盤傾斜倒出汁。將大湯盤覆蓋在蒸碗上兩手壓緊碗盤反轉倒扣，並掀起碗蓋，湯汁以②料勾芡淋其上即可。
■家常可用蝦米代干貝，蝦米約2大匙洗淨使用。
簡易方法：將大白菜置淺湯碗，把蝦米、酒、鹽撒在白菜上置蒸鍋，以大火蒸約1小時，即可原碗趁熱上桌。

干貝銀芽

干貝…………½兩
綠豆芽………半斤
① {
鹽…………½小匙
糖、醋(各)½小匙
麻油………½小匙
太白粉……½小匙
}

❶干貝處理參照本頁「干貝芥菜」做法❶
❷綠豆芽摘除兩端即為銀芽，洗淨瀝乾。油2大匙燒熱，先放入銀芽用大火爆炒數下，入蒸軟之干貝絲連汁及①料以大火爆炒約30秒剛熟即可盛盤。

蛋白質 ············ 18克
脂質 ············· 16克
醣質 ············· 10克
熱量 ··········· 243仟卡

Protein 18g
Fat 16g
Carbohydrate. 10g
243 Kcal

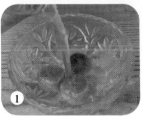

Scallops with Mustard Cabbage
Cantonese 12 servings

3 dried scallops (干貝)
2 1bs. mustard cabbage*
① ½ T. rice wine
½ C. stock
½ t. salt
¼ t. MSG
② 1 t. cornstarch
1 T. water

❶ Rinse the dried scallops. Place them in ½ C. water (fig. 1) and steam for 15 minutes. Remove and mash with flat of a cleaver or shred them by hand (fig. 2).

❷ Remove any old leaves from the mustard cabbage and cut into 3-inch sections (fig. 3). Add to 6 C. boiling water and cook for 2 minutes; remove. Refresh immediately in cold water and drain. Halve or quarter each vegetable section lengthwise (fig. 4).

❸ Heat pan and add 1 Tbsp. oil until very hot. Add ① followed by the scallops and the retained scallop liquid. Heat until boiling. Add the mustard cabbage sections. Simmer for 5 minutes over low heat. Add ② to thicken and remove to a serving platter. Serve.

* If unavailable, substitute bok choy.

Scallops with Chinese Cabbage   12 servings

3 dried scallops (干貝)
2 1bs. Chinese cabbage
1 T. rice wine
2 t. salt
② same as above

❶ To prepare the scallops, see step ❶ of the recipe shown above.

❷ Cut the Chinese cabbage in half lengthwise and remove any tough outer leaves. Use only the center leaves (about the size of the palm of the hand). Rinse and try to keep whole stalks intact.

❸ Arrange the cabbage in a heatproof pan cut-side up and add the rice wine. Cover and steam for 30 minutes over medium heat. Put the steamed scallops with liquid in a large heatproof bowl; arrange the cooked cabbage on top. Sprinkle with salt and steam for another 30 minutes or until the cabbage becomes transparent and very tender. Drain the liquid into a separate bowl by covering the bowl with a plate and turning the bowl over. Invert the bowl with the cabbage and scallops onto a serving platter. Add the liquid to a pan and heat until boiling; add ② to thicken and pour over the scallops and cabbage. Serve.

■ For family cooking: Substitute 2 Tbsp. dried shrimp for scallops.
For a simple method: Put the cabbage in a shallow heatproof pot and sprinkle the dried shrimp, wine, and salt on top. Simmer for 1 hour over high heat. Serve directly from the pot.

Scallops with Silver Sprouts

3 dried scallops (干貝)
⅔ 1b. bean sprouts
½ t. salt
½ t. sugar
① ½ t. rice vinegar
½ t. sesame oil
½ t. cornstarch

❶ To prepare the scallops, see Step ❶ of the recipe shown above.

❷ Trim the end tips from the bean sprouts. (They are now called silver sprouts because of their lovely color.) Rinse thoroughly and drain. Heat pan and add 2 Tbsp. oil; add the bean sprouts and stir-fry briefly over high heat. Add the shredded scallops, liquid, and ① . Stir-fry for about 30 seconds and remove to a serving plate. Serve.

草菇扒菜胆　　　廣東菜　6人份

生菜…………1斤
① 鹽…………⅓小匙
味精………¼小匙
鮮草菇………4兩
（或草菇罐頭1罐）
② 蠔油………2大匙
（或醬油）
味精………¼小匙
高湯………½杯
太白粉……1小匙
麻油……半小匙

❶ 生菜去老葉，取10～12公分長段之嫩菜薹（圖1）。鮮草菇去蒂（圖2），小的不切，大的切半在沸水內燙煮1分鐘撈出，泡入冷水內漂涼，瀝乾。
❷ 鍋熱加油2大匙，加入生菜及①料用大火爆炒約1分鐘至熟，再淋油1大匙以增光澤，盛出排列盤內（圖3）。
❸ 鍋熱，加油2大匙，草菇落鍋大火爆炒30秒入②料，燒至湯汁剩一半，再淋麻油半小匙（以增色香）盛於盤中央（圖4）。

冬菇鍋粑

冬菇…………6朵
冬筍…………1個
紅蘿蔔………1條
① 高湯………3杯
醬油………2大匙
鹽…………1小匙
糖…………1大匙
黑醋………½大匙
② 太白粉……2大匙
水…………2大匙
鍋粑…………4兩
「炸油」………3杯

❶ 冬菇洗淨加水泡軟後去蒂切片。冬筍去殼切片。紅蘿蔔亦切片。
❷ 鍋熱，加麻油2大匙將冬菇、冬筍炒香，入①料及紅蘿蔔片燒沸，以②料勾芡成略稠之湯汁盛碗。
❸「炸油」3杯燒熱，將鍋粑落鍋炸至泡鬆發大時撈起瀝淨油置盤，趁熱上桌將湯汁澆在鍋粑上即發出爆響聲，趁熱供食香脆有趣。
■ 鍋粑自製法：糯米或米1滿杯洗淨，加水¾杯，鹽¼小匙、油1大匙蒸熟，趁熱鋪在已抹油之盤上，厚約0.5公分壓平晾半乾先切6公分見方塊，再晾乾，或置爐上以小火烤乾，亦可置烤箱內以低溫烤乾，冷後密封置冰箱內冷藏。

蛋白質 ·············· 10克
脂質 ··············· 48克
醣質 ··············· 16克
熱量 ·········· 525仟卡

Protein 10g
Fat 48g
Carbohydrate 16g
525 Kcal

Stir-Fried Lettuce with Straw Mushrooms

Cantonese 6 servings

1 ⅓ 1bs. leafy lettuce

①
- ⅓ t. salt
- ¼ t. MSG

6 oz. fresh straw mushrooms
or 1 (15-oz) can

②
- 2 T. oyster sauce or soy sauce
- ¼ t. MSG
- ½ C. stock
- 1 t. cornstarch
- ½ t. sesame oil

❶ Remove any wilted leaves from the lettuce use only the young leaves. Cut the leaves into strips 4 to 5-inch long (fig. 1). Remove the stems from the fresh straw mushrooms (fig. 2). Leave small ones whole and cut the large caps half. Blanch for 1 minute then remove. Refresh the mushrooms immediately in cold water. Drain and set aside.

❷ Heat pan and add 2 Tbsp. oil until very hot. Stir-fry the lettuce with ① over high heat for about 1 minute. Add 1 Tbsp. oil for a sheen. Toss lightly and arrange around the edge of the serving platter (fig. 3).

❸ Heat pan and add 2 Tbsp. oil until very hot. Stir-fry the straw mushrooms for about 30 seconds. Add ② and continue to cook over high heat until liquid is reduced to half. Sprinkle with sesame oil for a sheen. Toss lightly and place in the center of the lettuce (fig. 4). Serve.

Chinese Black Mushrooms with Puffed Rice

6 Chinese dried black mushrooms

1 bamboo shoot

1 carrot

2 T. sesame oil

[1]
- 3 C. stock
- 2 T. soy sauce
- 1 t. salt
- 1 T. sugar
- ½ T. black vinegar or Worcestershire sauce

[2]
- 2 T. cornstarch
- 2 T. water

6 oz. rice cakes*

3 C. oil for frying

❶ Soak the mushrooms in water until soft; cut off the stems and discard. Slice the caps. Remove the tough skin of the bamboo shoot and slice. Slice the carrot.

❷ Heat pan and add 2 Tbsp. sesame oil. Add the mushrooms and bamboo shoot. Stir-fry until fragrant. Add [1], the carrots, and heat boiling. Add mixture [2] to thicken and remove to a soup bowl.

❸ Heat pan and add 3 C. oil until very hot. Fry the rice cakes until puffed and light golden. Remove to a serving plate and pour the soup mixture over the cakes while still hot. It should make a crackling sound. Serve while hot to enjoy the taste and sound.

* Method for Preparing Rice Cakes:
Rinse 1 C. long-grain rice until the water runs clear. Add ¾ C. water, ¼ tsp. salts, and 1 Tbsp. oil. Place in a heatproof bowl and steam until the grains are tender and cooked. While still hot, spread the rice on a pre-greased plate about $\frac{1}{12}$ of an inch thick. Allow to dry or bake over low heat or in a warm oven. (When half dry, cut into 2-inch squares.) Wrap the dried pieces tightly in plastic bags. If baking, wait until cool off before wrapping. Store in the refrigerator.

小冬菇……12朵
①{
醬油………1大匙
糖…………¼小匙
豬油………½大匙
}
小青江菜…12棵
洋菇(或草菇)1罐
蘆筍…………1罐
②{
高湯…………2杯
鹽…………¾小匙
味精………¼小匙
}
③{
高湯…………1杯
鹽…………½小匙
味精………¼小匙
太白粉……½大匙
}

紅蘿蔔………1條
①{
鹽…………½小匙
糖…………1小匙
番茄醬……1大匙
高湯…………1杯
太白粉……½小匙
}
玉米筍………1罐
②料
③{
奶水………1大匙
太白粉……1小匙
水…………2大匙
}
草菇…………1罐
④{
蠔油………1大匙
(或醬油)
糖…………1小匙
高湯…………1杯
太白粉……½小匙
}

❶ 冬菇加水泡軟去蒂,加①料水開大火蒸１０分鐘備用。
❷ 青江菜去老葉,取１０～１２公分長段之嫩菜薹(圖１),在開水內燙煮２分鐘撈出,泡入冷水內漂涼後瀝乾。
❸ 把②料燒沸,分別將青江菜、洋菇燒煮１分鐘取出。將青江菜、蘆筍整齊排於盤底(圖２),再把冬菇排成環形(圖３),上置洋菇(圖４),把③料燒沸澆淋其上便可。

素排三樣

❶ 紅蘿蔔入高湯內煮熟取出切直花條,放入1料以小火燒沸取出,相對排盤,餘汁淋其上。
❷ 玉米筍入②料內燒煮,使其入味撈出,相對排盤,湯汁以3料勾成濃稠狀淋在玉米筍上。
❸ 草菇入4料燒沸,置盤中央,湯汁淋其上。此盤菜紅、白、黑三色色澤鮮明。

蛋白質‥‥‥‥‥２０克
脂質‥‥‥‥‥‥‥‥‥９克
醣質‥‥‥‥‥‥‥‥２７克
熱量‥‥‥‥‥２２１仟卡

Protein. 20g
Fat 9g
Carbohydrate. 27g
221 Kcal

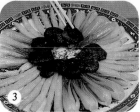

Buddha's Delight   Family-Style 12 servings

12 small Chinese dried black
   mushrooms
①{
1 T. soy sauce
¼ t. sugar
½ T. lard

12 stalks green vegetable heart*
1 (15 oz.) can button mushrooms or
   straw mushrooms
1 (1 lb. 3 oz.) can asparagus

②{
2 C. stock
¾ t. salt
¼ t. MSG

③{
1 C. stock
½ t. salt
¼ t. MSG
½ T. cornstarch

❶ Soak the black mushrooms in warm water until soft; cut away stems and discard. Mix the caps with ① . Steam over high heat for 10 minutes. Set aside.

❷ Remove the tough, outer leaves from the green vegetable. Cut the tender leaves into 4-to 5-inch lengths (fig. 1). Blanch for 2 minutes. Refresh in cold water immediately, then drain.

❸ Heat ② until boiling. Cook each of the following ingredients separately in ② for 1 minute, then remove: green vegetable, asparagus and button mushrooms. After cooking, arrange the vegetables on a serving platter (fig. 2). Place the black mushrooms (fig. 3) and button mushrooms on top (fig. 4). Heat ③ until boiling. Pour over the vegetables and serve.

* If unavailable, substitute spinach, Swiss chard, or broccoli.

Three-Vegetables in Cream Sauce

1 carrot
2 C. stock or water

1{
½ t. salt
1 t. sugar
1 T. catsup
1 C. stock
½ t. cornstarch

1 (15 oz.) can baby corn shoots,
   blanched
② same as above

3{
1 T. evaporated milk
1 t. cornstarch
2 T. water

1 (15 oz.) can straw mushroom,
   blanched

4{
1 T. soy sauce or oyster sauce
1 t. sugar
1 C. stock
½ t. cornstarch

❶ Peel the carrot and cook in the stock until tender. Remove and cut into long strips. Mix with ① and place in a pan. Heat until boiling over low heat. Arrange the carrots on each end of the serving platter. Pour the remaining sauce on top.

❷ Cook the baby corn shoots in ② for 1 minute. Arrange the baby corn shoots on the platter in two different piles, opposite each other. Thicken the cooking liquid with ③ and pour over the corn shoots.

❸ Place the mushrooms in ④ and heat until boiling. Remove and arrange in the middle of the platter. Pour the remaining sauce on top. The contrasting colors of the various vegetables makes this dish exceptionally attractive.

雞湯蛤蜊　　　　　　台灣菜　　6人份

雞(半隻)……1斤
蛤蜊…………半斤
① 水……………4杯
酒…………1大匙
鹽…………½小匙
薑絲………1大匙

❶ **蛤蜊吐沙法**：參照第２０４頁「蛤蜊蒸蛋」做法❶。

❷ 此湯有燉、煮兩種做法：

　雞剁塊，在燉(煮)前，應先在滾水內燙煮２分鐘撈出（圖
　１），洗淨再燉(煮)出之湯汁較清。

燉法：雞塊盛入燉盅或其他容器內，加①料（圖２）蓋妥
　　　　鍋蓋或用玻璃紙沾濕密封(圖３)，放進蒸鍋內，水
　　　　燒開中火燉３０分鐘後，再加蛤蜊(圖４)續燉１０
　　　　分鐘，即可連燉盅一起上桌分食。

煮法：將①料之水改為６杯盛鍋內，大火燒開再入雞塊，
　　　　蓋上鍋蓋，改小火燒煮３０分鐘（如用土雞燒煮約
　　　　５０分鐘），最後加蛤蜊再煮１０分鐘便可盛大湯
　　　　碗，以供食用。

■ ①料之薑絲，如使用嫩薑絲時宜在湯燉(煮)好後，再予擺
　　進較為理想。

蛋白質‥‥‥‥‥‥81克
脂質‥‥‥‥‥‥‥14克
醣質‥‥‥‥‥‥‥4克
熱量‥‥‥‥‥486仟卡
Protein. 81g
Fat 14g
Carbohydrate 4g
486 Kcal

Steamed Chicken With Clams in Broth

Taiwanese 6 servings

½ whole chicken (about 1⅓ 1bs.)

¾ 1b. steamer clams

① { 4 C. water
1 T. rice wine
1 t. salt
1 T. shredded ginger* }

❶ Cut the chicken, through bones, into bite-size serving pieces. Blanch the chicken for 2 minutes, remove and rinse with water (fig. 1). Drain. (Blanching the chicken pieces will result in a very clear broth).

Clean the clams as directed in Step ❶ , "Steamed Eggs with Clams", P. 204.

❷ The soup may be prepared by either of the following methods:

To steam: Place the chicken pieces in a heatproof soup bowl or casserole. Add mixture ① (fig. 2) and cover. (Aluminum foil or heavy-duty cellophane may be used, fig. 3). Place in a steamer, cover and steam for 30 minutes over medium heat. Add the steamer clams (fig. 4) and continue to steam for an additional 10 minutes. Remove and serve the soup from the casserole.

To boil: Reduce the amount of water in mixture ① from 4 C. to 6 C. Place mixture ① in a pot and heat until boiling. Add the chicken pieces, cover, reduce the heat to low and cook for 30 minutes. Add the clams and cook for an additional 10 minutes. Pour the soup into a serving bowl and serve.

* If young, spring ginger (a tender variety available in the spring) is available, add the shredded ginger just before serving.

雞粒玉米湯　　　　　　廣東菜　　6人份

雞肉…………3兩
①　酒…………1小匙
　　鹽…………⅛小匙
　　太白粉……1小匙
　　玉米醬………半罐
②　高湯…………3杯
　　鹽…………1小匙
　　味精…………¼小匙
③　太白粉……2大匙
　　水…………2大匙
④　蛋白…………1個
　　水…………1大匙
　　熟火腿末…½大匙

❶ 雞肉切成小粒狀（圖1），調入①料拌勻備用。將④料用筷子打勻成蛋白水。

❷ 把②料燒沸，加入玉米醬（圖2），雞粒（圖3），立刻用鍋鏟將雞粒拌開，續燒滾後改小火，徐徐倒入③料並迅速用鍋鏟攪拌，勾芡成適當濃度時，再慢慢淋下已拌勻的④料（圖4），即可盛大湯碗，上灑火腿末以增美觀。

雞絨玉米湯

❶ 雞絨做法，參照第254頁「雞絨鮑魚羹」做法❷，將雞絨拌妥，其他調味及做法同上。

■ 簡易雞絨做法：把④料改為3倍，雞肉及①料免用，其他調味及做法同上。

蟹肉玉米湯

將雞肉改用蟹肉，①料免用，其他調味及做法同上。

豬腦玉米湯

把雞肉改用豬腦2付，用牙籤挑除紅薄膜，加少許葱、薑、酒預先蒸熟切塊．①料免用，其他調味及做法同上。

蛋白質	⋯⋯⋯⋯ ３７克
脂質	⋯⋯⋯⋯⋯ ９克
醣質	⋯⋯⋯⋯⋯ ５９克
熱量	⋯⋯⋯⋯ ４６６仟卡

Protein 37g
Fat 9g
Carbohydrate 59g
466 Kcal

Diced Chicken with Corn Soup
Cantonese
6 servings

¼ 1b.　boned chicken meat
①{ 1 t.　rice wine
 ⅛ t.　salt
 1 t.　cornstarch
½ (17 oz.) can creamed corn
②{ 3 C.　stock
 1 t.　salt
 ¼ t.　MSG
③{ 2 T.　cornstarch
 2 T.　water
④{ 1　egg white
 1 T.　water
½ T.　cooked ham, chopped

❶ Cut the chicken into cubes about ¼-inch square (fig. 1). Add ① and marinate for 20 minutes. Beat mixture ④ until frothy.
❷ Place mixture ② in a pot and heat until boiling. Add the creamed corn (fig. 2) and chicken (fig. 3). Mix immediately to separate the chicken. Cook for about 30 seconds, reduce heat to low and slowly add ③ , mix constantly. When the liquid has thickened, add mixture ④ in a thin stream (fig. 4). Transfer the soup to a serving bowl and sprinkle the ham on top.

Chicken and Corn Soup

❶ To prepare the chicken, see Step ❷ , P.254. "Abalone with Chicken Soup." Prepare the remaining ingredients as directed in the recipe shown above.
■ Simple variation: Increase the ingredients of mixture ④ three times and substitute for the chicken paste in the mixture above. Prepare the remaining ingredients as directed in the recipe show above.

Crab Meat and Corn Soup

Substitute 3 oz. crab meat for the chicken and omit ① in the recipe above. Prepare the remaining ingredients as directed in the recipe shown above.

Pork Brain with Corn Soup

Substitute 2 pork brains for the chicken in the recipe above and omit ① . Use a toothpick to remove the thin membrane from the pork brain. Marinate with 2 stalks green onion, 2 slices ginger and 1 Tbsp. rice wine. Place in a steamer and steam for 10 minutes over high heat. Prepare the remaining ingredients as directed above.

酸菜雞絲湯　　　　四川菜　　6人份

①
雞胸肉………3兩
酒…………1小匙
鹽…………⅙小匙
太白粉……1小匙
筍…………1枝
酸菜…………2兩
粉絲…………1把

②
高湯(或水)…4杯
鹽…………½小匙
味精………½小匙
麻油………1小匙

❶ 雞胸肉去皮切片再切成細絲(圖1)，調①料拌勻。酸菜洗
　淨，用手握乾水份，在莖較厚處先片薄成兩片再切絲（圖
　2），粉絲泡軟剪或切成１０公分長段（圖3）。筍剝殼（
　圖4）切筍片後切絲。

❷ 把②料燒開，放入筍絲、酸菜絲及粉絲煮開後，改小火並
　將雞絲下鍋，立刻用筷子或鍋鏟撥散，見雞絲色轉白且熟
　，即可盛於湯碗內，上淋麻油即成。

■ 除雞肉外可用鴨肉、豬里肌。肉宜先放在冰箱冷凍稍硬約
　３０分鐘，比較好切。

榨菜肉絲湯

將雞肉改用豬里肌，酸菜改用榨菜，粉絲可免用，其他做法
及調味同上。

蛋白質⋯⋯⋯⋯⋯３２克
脂質⋯⋯⋯⋯⋯⋯⋯⋯⋯８克
醣質⋯⋯⋯⋯⋯⋯⋯⋯６０克
熱量⋯⋯⋯⋯⋯４２７仟卡

Protein 32g
Fat 8g
Carbohydrate 60g
427 Kcal

Shredded Chicken with Pickled Mustard Green Soup

Szechuan
6 servings

¼ 1b. boned chicken breast
    meat

① { 1 t.   rice wine
    ⅙ t.   salt
    1 t.   cornstarch

1 fresh bamboo shoot*

2 oz. pickled mustard greens

1 (2 oz.) pkg. bean threads

② { 4 C.   stock or water
    ½ t.   salt
    ½ t.   MSG

1 t.   sesame oil

❶ Remove the skin from the chicken (discard) and shred the meat (fig. 1). Mix with ① and marinate for 20 minutes. Rinse the pickled mustard greens, squeeze out any water and shred (fig. 2). Soak the bean threads in warm water until soft, cut into 4-inch lengths (fig. 3). Remove the tough outer skin from the bamboo shoot and shred (fig. 4).

❷ Heat mixture ② until boiling. Add the bamboo shoot, pickled mustard green and bean threads. Heat until boiling and reduce the heat to low. Add the shredded chicken shreds and stir with a spatula or chopsticks to separate. When the chicken changes color, remove and pour into the serving bowl. Sprinkle the sesame oil on top and serve.

* If unavailable, substitute 1 canned bamboo shoot, blanch briefly and shred.

■ Duck or boneless pork loin may be substituted for the chicken. Partially freeze the meat for 30 minutes to facilitate cutting.

Shredded Pork and Szechuan Pickled Mustard Green Soup

Substitute ¼ 1b. boneless pork for the chicken and Szechuan pickled mustard green for the pickled mustard green in the recipe above. The bean threads may be omitted. Prepare the remaining ingredients as directed in the recipe shown above.

汽鍋蒸雞

四川菜　　6 人份

雞半隻⋯⋯⋯1 斤
（或雞腿）
冬菇⋯⋯⋯⋯6 朵
火腿⋯⋯⋯⋯2 兩
魚肉乾⋯⋯⋯2 兩

① ⎰滾水⋯⋯⋯⋯5 杯
⎱酒⋯⋯⋯⋯⋯1 大匙
⎰葱⋯⋯⋯⋯⋯4 枝
⎱薑⋯⋯⋯⋯⋯2 片
⎰鹽⋯⋯⋯⋯⋯$\frac{1}{2}$ 小匙
⎱味精⋯⋯⋯⋯$\frac{1}{4}$ 小匙

❶ 雞剁塊（圖１），在滾水內川燙１分鐘撈出，用水洗淨瀝乾，再燉出的湯較清。

❷ 火腿去皮切片（圖２）。冬菇泡軟去蒂切半，魚肉乾洗淨泡軟約３０分鐘以去鹹味，再切３公分長段（圖３）。

❸ 雞塊、冬菇、火腿片、魚肉乾及①料全部放進汽鍋內（圖４），蓋妥鍋蓋入蒸鍋內，水燒開大火蒸４０分鐘，即可連汽鍋一齊端出分食。

■ 除雞肉外，鴨、排骨、牛肉等均可取代。雞以土雞為佳，但蒸的時間稍長約需１小時，無火腿或魚肉乾均可免用，唯酌加鹽。

蛋白質 ············· １１０克
脂質 ················ ６９克
醣質 ················ １８克
熱量 ········· １１５４仟卡
Protein 110g
Fat 69g
Carbohydrate 18g
1,154 Kcal

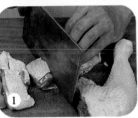

Steamed Chicken in Yunnan Pot

Szechuan
6 servings

1. whole chicken (1 ⅓ lbs.) or
   1⅓ lbs. chicken legs
6 Chinese black mushrooms
2 oz. Chinese ham*
2 oz. dried fish*¹

① {
5 C. boiling water
1 T. rice wine
4 stalks green onions
2 slices ginger
½ t. salt
¼ t. MSG
}

❶ Cut the chicken, through bones, into bite-size rectangular or square pieces (fig. 1). Blanch for 1 minute then remove. Rinse with cold water and drain. (Blanching the chicken will result in a very clear broth.)

❷ Remove any skin from the ham and cut into pieces (fig. 2). Soften the black mushrooms in warm water until soft, remove the stems, discard and cut the caps in half. Rinse the dried fish, and soak for 30 minutes in water to remove the excess salt. Cut the dried fish into 1¼-inch lengths (fig. 3).

❸ Place the chicken, mushrooms, ham and dried fish with ① in a Yunnan pot*² (fig. 4). Cover and place in a steamer. Steam for 40 minutes over high heat. Remove and serve the soup form the Yunnan pot.

* If unavailable, substitute proscuitto.

*¹ If the dried fish is unavailable, omit.

*² The pictured casserole is called a Yunnan Pot. It is unique in that it has a central chimney which allows the food inside to be sprayed with a mist from the steam. It is available at any large oriental grocery store. If unavailable, use a heatproof dutch oven or casserole.

菊花鱈魚羹

廣東菜　　6人份

鱈魚…………半斤

① 酒…………1小匙
　 鹽…………½小匙
　 葱…………1枝
　 薑…………1片

筍…………1枝
冬菇…………3朵
干貝…………3粒
豆腐…………1塊
大白菊花……2朵
餛飩皮………5張
「炸油」………1杯

② 高湯…………6杯
　 鹽………1¼小匙
　 味精………¼小匙

③ 太白粉……3大匙
　 水…………3大匙

④ 蛋白………1個
　 水…………1大匙

❶ 鱈魚洗淨，調①料拌醃後，水燒開大火蒸１０分鐘至熟，用筷子或叉子把魚肉拆出，魚皮及骨均不要（圖１）。

❷ 筍、冬菇（泡軟）切小薄片（圖２）。干貝加水¼杯蒸約１５分鐘，趁熱以刀面壓成絲或用手撕成細絲，湯汁留用。豆腐切小丁，菊花取花瓣（圖３），用蔬果清潔劑洗淨後，泡水１０分鐘。把④料打勻成蛋白水。

❸ 餛飩皮切０.５公分之小菱型片。「炸油」1杯燒熱（４００℉），放入餛飩皮炸約１０秒呈金黃色撈出（圖４）。

❹ 油1大匙燒熱，將冬菇炒香下酒半大匙及②料，隨入筍片，干貝絲連汁及豆腐丁燒沸，傾下魚肉連蒸魚汁，再以③料勾成薄糊狀，改小火徐徐倒入④料邊攪拌，並淋少許麻油及胡椒粉即可盛大湯碗，上灑炸好餛飩皮及菊花瓣，趁熱分食。

■鱈魚可改用黃魚，蒸熟取肉所做出的湯菜叫「黃魚羹」。

■除筍、冬菇、干貝外可用洋菇、草菇、火腿、蹄筋等配料。

■如無餛飩皮、菊花可免用。

蛋白質‥‥‥‥‥‥‥88克
脂質‥‥‥‥‥‥‥‥27克
醣質‥‥‥‥‥‥‥‥43克
熱量‥‥‥‥‥‥764仟卡
Protein 88g
Fat 27g
Carbohydrate 43g
764 Kcal

Chrysanthemum Fish Soup   Cantonese 6 servings

¾ 1b. fish fillets*
① {
1 t. rice wine
½ t. salt
1 stalk green onion, smashed
1 slice ginger, smashed
1 bamboo shoot, blanched
3 Chinese black mushrooms
3 dried scallops
1 square bean curd
2 large chrysanthemums*¹
5 won ton skins*¹
1 C. oil for frying
½ T. rice wine
② {
6 C. stock
1¼ t. salt
¼ t. MSG
③ {
3 T. cornstarch
3 T. water
④ {
1 egg white
1 T. water
½ t. sesame oil
¼ t. black pepper

❶ Rinse the fish fillets, drain and add mixture ① . Marinate for 10 minutes. Place in a steamer and cover. Steam for 10 minutes over high heat. Use a fork or chopsticks to remove the meat. Discard the skin and bones (fig. 1). Retain the liquid in the pan from steaming.

❷ Soak the black mushrooms in warm water until soft. Remove the stems, discard and dice the caps and the bamboo shoot (fig. 2). Add ¼ cup of water to the dried scallops and steam for 15 minutes over high heat and remove. Drain the scallops, retain the liquid from steaming and tear the scallops into shreds. (See step ❶ P. 228. "Stir-Fried Scallops with Pickled Mustard Cabbage"). Dice the bean curd and cut or tear the chrysanthemum petals from their stems (fig. 3). Rinse lightly and soak in cold water for 10 minutes. Whisk mixture ④ unitl forthy.

❸ Cut the won ton skins into diamond-shaped squares about the size of a fingernail. Heat pan and oil to about 400°F. Add the won ton pieces and deep-fry about for 10 seconds until golden. Remove, drain and set aside (fig. 4).

❹ Remove all but 1 Tbsp. oil from the pan and heat until very hot. Add the black mushroom and stir-fry until fragrant. Add the rice wine, mixture ② , the bamboo shoot, shredded scallops, retained steaming liquid and bean curd. Heat the mixture until boiling, add the fish and retained steaming liquid. Add mixture ③ to thicken. Turn off the heat and gradually add ④ in a thin stream. Add the sesame oil, black pepper and pour into a serving bowl. Sprinkle the fried won ton pieces and chrysanthemum petals over the top and serve.

* Fillets of sole, pickerel, and flounder may be used.

*¹ If won ton skins or chrysanthemum petals are unavailable, omit.

■ Button mushrooms, straw mushrooms and ham may be used instead of Chinese mushrooms, bamboo shoot and scallops.

243

三鮮干絲湯　　　北方菜　　6人份

①料

白豆腐干…1½塊

①
- 高湯…………3杯
- 鹽…………½小匙
- 味精………¼小匙

②
- 熟雞絲………⅓杯
  （圖2）
- 熟火腿絲…2大匙
  （圖3）
- 冬菇絲……2大匙

❶ 白豆腐干先切薄片再切絲，狀如火柴棒粗（圖1），在滾水內燙煮３０秒撈出瀝乾，放入①料內，以小火燜煮１０分鐘，再加②料續以小火煨煮５分鐘盛湯碗便可。
　講究的將豆干絲煨好後撈出盛碗，入②料續煮後撈出整齊排列（圖4），再徐徐倒進湯汁即成。

■ 如無白豆腐干，可用干絲３兩代替，但須預先泡軟使用。

■ **干絲泡軟法**：水４杯加鹼塊½個（或鹼粉１大匙）燒開，待鹼溶化時熄火，泡入干絲用筷子攪拌泡約１０分鐘，見干絲呈白色發軟易於捏斷時撈出，用冷水漂洗數次以去鹼味。

■ **火腿處理法**：火腿去皮並削除表面污垢，再刷洗乾淨，盛碗加酒、葱、薑預先蒸熟，或另加適量水煮熟。
　例：火腿３兩、酒、糖各１大匙、葱２枝、薑２片。

■ 三鮮材料除②料外，可用肉絲、蝦仁、魷魚、海參、鮑魚……等。

三絲湯

②料

- 熟火腿絲……⅓杯
②
- 筍絲…………½杯
- 雞肉絲………４兩

❶ 把①料、②料燒滾，再入雞肉絲（雞絲要預先拌入太白粉），速以鍋鏟或大湯勺拌開，以防雞絲沾黏，續燒沸盛出。

蛋白質 ················· ３６克
脂質 ················· １９克
醣質 ················· ８克
熱量 ··········· ３３１仟卡

Protein 36g
Fat 19g
Carbohydrate 8g
331 Kcal

① ② ③ ④

Three-Flavor Bean Curd Soup Peking 6 servings

1½ squares firm bean curd*

① ⎰ 3 C. stock
⎱ ½ t. salt
  ¼ t. MSG

② ⎰ ⅓ C. shredded, cooked chicken (fig. 2)
⎱ 2 T. shredded, cooked ham*¹ (fig. 3)
  2 T. shredded, pre-softened Chinese black mushrooms

2 slices ginger
Adjust the ingredient quantities in proportion to the size of the ham
¼ 1b. lean ham
1 T. sugar
1 T. rice wine
2 stalks green onion

② ⎰ ① same as above
⎱ ⅓ C. shredded, cooked ham
  ½ C. shredded, bamboo shoots
  1 C. shredded, cooked chicken
  ½ T. cornstarch

❶ Cut the bean curd into thin slices and shred into julienne strips (fig. 1). Blanch for about 30 seconds, remove and drain. Place in a pan and add mixture ① . Simmer over low heat for about 10 minutes. Add mixture ② and continue to simmer for another 5 minutes. Remove to a soup bowl and serve.

■ For a lovely design, cook the bean curd as directed in mixture ① and remove. Cook mixture ② in ① as directed and remove. Arrange the bean curd and ingredients of ② in a bowl as illustrated (fig. 4). Slowly ladle into the soup.

* If firm bean curd is unavailable, you may press the bean curd between two paper towels (place a weight on top) for 2 hours.

*¹ To prepare Chinese ham:
Remove the skin from the ham. Rinse and drain. Marinate with the rice wine, green onion, sugar and ginger. Place in steamer or boil in a pot with water to cover for 10 minutes. Remove, drain and use as directed.

■ Shredded pork loin, shrimp, squid or abalone may be used for the ingredients in mixture ②

Shredded Meat Soup

❶ Heat ① and ② until boiling. Mix the chicken with the cornstarch and add to the boiling liquid. Stir to separate the chicken shreds. When the soup boils again, remove to a serving bowl and serve.

火鍋

12人份

①	猪里肌肉……4兩 雞肉…………4兩 嫩牛肉………4兩 魚肉…………4兩 明蝦肉………4兩 （或蝦仁）

荷蒿菜或菠菜4兩
大白菜………半斤
乾粉絲（1把）2兩
「炸油」………5杯

②	高湯…………6杯 鹽…………2小匙 味精………1小匙

雞蛋………12個

❶ 將①料先置冰箱內，冰至肉略硬（約30分鐘，較好切），取出切大薄片。
　　魚肉取法：由脊背剖開，順大骨邊切取魚肉成兩大片（圖1），再去皮並切薄片（圖2）。
　　明蝦：去頭由背剖切開使腹部連成一大片，用刀面輕輕拍扁（圖3）。把上述材料整齊排列盤內。

❷「炸油」5杯燒熱（400℉），放入乾粉絲炸約5秒，成泡鬆狀，撈出盛盤。或不炸祇加溫水泡軟。

❸ 把②料盛入火鍋內燒滾，先下白菜煮軟，續入所有材料，俟全部放進，蓋上火鍋蓋燒沸，見肉色轉白剛熟，肉滑嫩可口，速分盛小碗內供食。或依個人喜愛，將肉類分別夾進燙熟，夾出沾佐料吃。

■宜備小碗，先加雞蛋（黃）或其他沾料拌勻，作為蘸食用。

■除上述材料外，可用墨魚、魷魚切花，魚丸、猪肝、猪腰、羊肉、鴨肉、肝、肫。
　　肫的處理法：將肫由一個筋處切開，洗淨穢物並剝除內面之黃色綯皮，從肫白色筋處縱切一刀，順筋皮橫刀推出肫肉，在肫肉上交叉切菱形花紋，深約⅗處（圖4）。

■無火鍋用普通鍋或砂鍋代替。

蛋白質‥‥‥‥‥‥２２０克
脂質‥‥‥‥‥‥‥１４６克
醣質‥‥‥‥‥‥‥‥８３克
熱量‥‥‥‥‥２５８９仟卡

Protein 220g
Fat 146g
Carbohydrate 83g
2,589 Kcal

①

②

③

④

Eight-Flavor Firepot   12 servings

6 oz. boneless pork loin
① 6 oz. chicken meat
6 oz. sirloin roast
6 oz. fish fillets
6 oz. raw, shelled prawns
(or shrimp)
6 oz. spinach, trimmed and
cleaned
⅔ lb. Chinese cabbage, cut
into 2-inch squares
1 (2 oz.) pkg. bean threads
5 C. oil for frying
6 C. stock
② 2 t. salt
1 t. MSG
12 eggs

❶ Partially freeze the pork loin, chicken and sirloin (for about 30 minutes) to facilitate slicing and cutting into paper-thin slices.
To bone the fish fillets: Cut open the fish section along the back and cut the fillets away from the central bone (fig. 1). Remove the skin and cut the fish into paper-thin slices (fig. 2). Cut each prawn open (Do not cut through to the opposite edge.) and spread out each one flat on the counter. Pound lightly with the blunt edge of the cleaver (fig. 3). Arrange the meat, prawn and fish slices in a decorative pattern around a serving platter.

❷ Heat pan and add oil, heat to 400°F. Add the bean threads and deep-fry for about 5 seconds until they puff up. Remove and drain; or soften them in warm water to cover for about 5 minutes. Remove and arrange on the serving platter.

❸ Place mixture ② in a firepot* and heat until boiling. Add the cabbage sections and cook until tender. Add the remaining ingredients, cover and heat until boiling or the meat changes color. If the meat is over-cooked, it will be tough. Portion into serving bowls. Each portion should contain a lightly beaten egg and served immediately.

* If a firepot is unavailable, use any deep pot or casserole.

■ Other seasonings may be added to the egg to serve as a dip.

■ Chicken meat, duck meat, liver, gizzard and lamb may be substituted for the sliced ingredients, according to personal taste. To cut the gizzard, refer to fig. 4.

東江牛肉丸

瘦牛肉‥‥‥‥‥6兩	
鹽‥‥‥‥‥‥½小匙	
① 薑酒汁‥‥‥1小匙	
糖‥‥‥‥‥‥¼小匙	
蛋白‥‥‥‥‥1個	
太白粉‥‥‥‥1大匙	
香菜(切碎)2大匙	
(或芹菜)	
② 高湯‥‥‥‥‥3杯	
鹽‥‥‥‥‥‥1小匙	
味精‥‥‥‥‥½小匙	
胡椒粉‥‥‥⅛小匙	
麻油‥‥‥‥‥½小匙	

❶ 牛肉順紋切1公分厚片(圖1),上灑鹽½小匙,再用搥肉器(以平面)搥至有黏性之肉泥(圖2),如無黏性做出之肉丸不脆,盛入容器內調①料(圖3),順同方向用力攪拌並甩打約3分鐘成「肉漿」。

❷ 把②料盛鍋燒開,用手抓起「肉漿」,擠成丸子用湯匙挖起(圖4),放入鍋內,每做一肉丸前應先將湯匙沾水或油,以防粘匙,用中火煮約3分鐘至肉丸浮出湯面即熟,倒入大湯碗內,上灑香菜或芹菜。

貢 丸 湯

將瘦牛肉改用新鮮豬後腿瘦肉,其他調味、做法同上。

蛋白質‥‥‥‥‥‥‥３０克
脂質‥‥‥‥‥‥‥‥‥１１克
醣質‥‥‥‥‥‥‥‥‥５克
熱量‥‥‥‥‥‥２４３仟卡
Protein 30g
Fat 11g
Carbohydrate 5g
243 Kcal

Meatball Soup

Cantonese 6 servings

8 oz.	flank steak
①	½ t.	salt
1 t.	ginger-wine*
¼ t.	sugar
1	egg white
1 T.	cornstarch
2 T.	minced coriander, parsley or celery

	3 C.	stock
	1 t.	salt
②	½ t.	MSG
	⅛ t.	black pepper
	½ t.	sesame oil

❶ Remove any muscle from the beef and cut ¼-inch thick slices along the grain (fig. 1). Add salt and pound or chop to a smooth paste (fig. 2). (If the meat is not pounded or chopped adequately, it will be tough). Place the chopped meat in a bowl and add mixture ①. Stir vigorously in one direction to blend the ingredients to a smooth paste (fig. 3). Throw the mixture lightly against the inside of a mixing bowl for about 3 minutes to thoroughly combine the ingredients.

❷ Place mixture ② in a pot and heat until boiling. Take a handful of the meat paste and make a fist, squeeze the mixture out of the space between the index finger and thumb. Use a spoon dipped in water or oil to scoop the meat ball off of the thumb and index finger. (fig. 4). Add the balls to the boiling liquid and cook for 3 minutes over medium heat, until the meatballs float to the surface. Pour the mixture into a serving bowl, sprinkle the top with the chopped coriander, parsley or celery and serve.

* To prepare ginger-wine: Place 1 slice mashed ginger in 1 tsp. rice wine. Pinch the ginger to imbibe the wine with the ginger flavor. Remove the ginger slice and use the liquid as directed above.

Pork Ball Soup

Substitute 8 oz. lean pork (preferably tender cuts) for the beef. Prepare the recipe as directed above.

枸杞當歸鰻

台灣菜　　12人份

活河鰻（1條）1斤

① {
葱…………… 2 枝
薑…………… 2 片
當歸………… 2 片
枸杞……… 1 大匙
}

② {
水…………… 6 杯
酒………… 6 大匙
鹽……… 1 $\frac{1}{2}$ 小匙
味精……… $\frac{1}{4}$ 小匙
}

❶ 河鰻先剁斷頭，擱置片刻，至河鰻不滾動時，再去除內臟（圖1）。

❷ 半鍋水燒滾後熄火，再將鰻魚下鍋燙約１０秒，至鰻魚表皮之黏液呈白濁狀，撈出浸泡冷水，不燙時再用刷子輕輕刷除鰻魚皮上之白濁物(圖2)，或用乾毛巾包裹鰻魚由上而下搓淨亦可，再洗淨，每隔３公分切一長塊(圖3)。

❸ 把①料置燉盅底，上擺鰻魚塊(圖4)，再倒入②料，蓋上燉盅蓋，移入蒸鍋，水燒開中火燉約４０分鐘，即可與燉盅一齊端出，趁熱分食。

蛋白質‥‥‥‥‥‥‥７６克
脂質‥‥‥‥‥‥‥‥‥４６克
醣質‥‥‥‥‥‥‥‥‥‥１克
熱量‥‥‥‥‥‥‥７６２仟卡
Protein. 76g
Fat 46g
Carbohydrate. 1g
762 Kcal

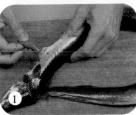
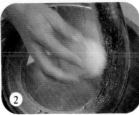

Stewed Eel   Taiwanese 12 servings

1   live fresh water eel
  (about 1 ⅓ 1bs.)

① {
2   stalks green onion
2   slices ginger
2   pieces levisticum*
1 T.   medlar*
}

② {
6 C.   water
6 T.   rice wine
1½t.   salt
¼ t.   MSG
}

❶ Cut off the head of the eel. Let it rest for about 20 minutes until all movement stops. Remove the entrails (fig. 1).

❷ Fill a wok halfway with water, heat until boiling and turn off the heat. Add the eel to the water and blanch for 10 seconds, until the membrance on the skin turns white. Remove and refresh in cold water. With a coarse brush, lightly brush off the white membrane (fig. 2) or wrap a dry towel around the eel and rub off the membrane. Rinse well and drain. Cut the eel into 1-inch sections (fig. 3).

❸ Add mixture ① to a casserole. Add the eel sections (fig. 4) and mixture ②. Cover and place in a steamer. Steam over medium heat for 40 minutes. Remove and serve the eel directly from the casserole.

* These two ingredients are Chinese herbs which are nutritionally beneficial. They may be purchased at a Chinese pharmacy.

竹節鴿盅

湖南菜　　6人份

嫩鴿…………1隻
（或雞胸肉）
荸薺（去皮）…3個

① 酒…………1小匙
鹽…………½小匙
醬油………½大匙
味精………⅛小匙
水…………1½杯
竹節盅………6個

❶ **鴿肉取法：** 從鴿胸劃一刀，深觸及大骨（圖1），並將翅膀關節切斷，拉開取肉（圖2），淨重約4兩。

❷ 鴿肉（或雞胸肉去皮），與荸薺一齊剁成泥狀（圖3），盛大碗內，加①料拌勻，再徐徐加水並速以攪拌成濃稠狀，即分盛在6個竹節盅內（圖4），擺進蒸籠（鍋）內，水燒開以中火蒸約1小時，趁熱與竹節盅一齊端出。此道湯菜肉質鬆軟，湯汁鮮美，真不愧為湖南名菜。

■ 鴿子不易採購，且價格昂貴，一般均改用雞肉（去皮、筋）豬里肌（去筋）或腿肉，均需剁成泥狀，亦可兩種混合使用。

■ 容器除用竹節盅外，亦可分盛小湯碗或大湯碗蒸，蒸好端出分食。

■ 此菜肴所蒸時間越久，湯汁越多，肉更鬆嫩可口。

蛋白質 · · · · · · · · · · · · · ３３克
脂質 · · · · · · · · · · · · · · · · · １克
醣質 · · · · · · · · · · · · · · · · · ７克
熱量 · · · · · · · · · · ３３２仟卡
Protein 33g
Fat 1g
Carbohydrate 7g
332 Kcal

Minced Squab in Bamboo Cups Hunan 6 servings

6 oz. squab meat or 1 boned
    chicken breast*

3 water chestnuts

①
1 t.   rice wine
½ t.   salt
½ T.   soy sauce
⅛ t.   MSG

1½ C. water

6 bamboo cups*¹

❶ To bone the squab: Make a cut in the center of the breast, cut down to the bone (fig. 1). Make 2 cuts at the shoulder joints next to the wings. Remove the breast section and wing from each side (fig. 2).

❷ Remove the skin from the squab or chicken breast and mince with the water chestnuts to form a smooth paste (fig. 3). Place the paste in a bowl with mixture ①. Gradually add the water and mix constantly. Stuff the bamboo cups with a portion of the squab paste (fig. 4). Place the cups in a steamer, cover and steam for 1 hour over medium heat. Remove and serve directly from the cups. The meat should be very tender and the broth, rice and flavorful.

* Pork loin may also be substituted for the squab meat or a combination of pork and chicken. Remove any fat or muscle from the pork and mince finely.

*¹ If bamboo cups are unavailable, finger bowls or rice bowls may be used; or the minced mixture may be steamed in one large soup bowl and may be sprinkled with chopped coriander which may be used as a garnish.

■ The longer this dish is steamed the more tender it will be and it will also have more broth.

雞絨鮑魚羹

廣東菜　　12人份

鮑魚…………半罐
雞柳肉………２兩
① 酒…………１小匙
鮑魚汁……４大匙
（或水）
蛋白…………２個
② 油…………６大匙
麵粉………５大匙
③ 高湯…………６杯
鹽…………１小匙
味精………$\frac{1}{4}$小匙
熟火腿末…１大匙

❶ 鮑魚切成薄片，湯汁留用。

❷ 雞柳肉去除白筋(圖１)，用刀面壓成絨狀（圖２），或剁成泥狀盛大碗，調入①料拌勻，再加蛋白（預先打散），邊加邊攪拌(圖３)，蛋白加完並攪勻即為「雞絨」。

❸ 把②料中的油先燒溫再加麵粉，以小火炒拌約３０秒，加入③料迅速攪勻，改大火燒滾變稠，再放進鮑魚片燒沸，即改小火並徐徐倒入「雞絨」，邊加邊攪拌（圖４用打蛋器或鍋鏟均可攪拌），全部拌合後立即熄火，以防「雞絨」老硬，盛大湯碗，上灑火腿末即成。

蛋白質‥‥‥‥‥‥‥３９克
脂質‥‥‥‥‥‥‥‥９９克
醣質‥‥‥‥‥‥‥‥５１克
熱量‥‥‥‥‥１２５７仟卡

Protein. 39g
Fat 99g
Carbohydrate 51g
1,257 Kcal

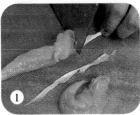

Abalone with Chicken Soup Cantonese 12 servings

½ (10 oz.) can abalone

3 oz. fillet mignon of
chicken or chicken
breast

① { 1 t.   rice wine
4 T.   abalone liquid or
water

2 egg whites, beaten lightly

6 T.   oil for frying

5 T.   flour

② { 6 C.   stock
1 t.   salt
¼ t.   MSG

1 T.   minced, boiled ham

❶ Drain the abalone (retain the liquid) and cut into thin slices.

❷ Remove the tendons from the fillet mignon sections. Use the blunt edge of the cleaver to mince the chicken to a smooth paste (fig. 1). Add ① and mix thoroughly. Add the egg whites, one at a time, mix well after each addition (fig. 3) (chicken paste).

❸ Heat pan and add 6 Tbsp. oil, heat until hot. Add the flour and mix for 30 seconds over low heat. Add ② and continue mixing. Turn the heat to high. When the liquid boils, add the sliced abalone and heat until boiling. Reduce the heat to low and slowly add the chicken paste. Mix continuously with chopsticks, a spatula, or a wire whisk (fig. 4).

東江豆腐湯

廣東菜　　12人份

豆腐…………3塊
絞肉…………2兩
蝦仁（或魚肉）1兩
蝦米（泡軟）…½兩
① ⎰薑酒汁……1小匙
⎱鹽…………¼小匙
⎰味精………¼小匙
⎱胡椒粉……¼小匙
水………1½大匙
太白粉……½大匙
青菜…………6兩
香菜…………2兩
② ⎰高湯（或水）…6杯
⎱鹽………1½小匙
⎱味精………½小匙

❶ 蝦仁（或魚肉）、蝦米先剁碎，同絞肉一齊盛碗內，調①料攪拌至有黏性，加太白粉調勻成「肉餡」備用。

❷ 每塊豆腐先切除硬邊，再切成4小塊，共計12小塊（圖1），在每小塊中間用小匙挖出部份豆腐成凹狀（圖2），內灑太白粉（圖3）再塞入「肉餡」抹平（圖4），照此法把所有豆腐塊鑲好待用。

❸ 將②料燒開，放入鑲好豆腐，用小火燜煮約6分鐘，再加青菜、香菜燒沸盛大湯碗，趁熱分食。
　或用蒸的方法：鑲好豆腐塊，預先蒸熟（水燒開用中火蒸5分鐘），再放入已燒滾的②料內即成。

■ 如無蝦米、蝦仁、魚肉可免用，但絞肉需增至3兩，加蔥末1大匙或荸薺末。

蛋白質‥‥‥‥‥‥‥‥３８克
脂質‥‥‥‥‥‥‥‥‥３３克
醣質‥‥‥‥‥‥‥‥‥‥‥８克
熱量‥‥‥‥‥‥‥‥４７９仟卡
Protein. 38g
Fat 33g
Carbohydrate 8g
479 Kcal

Stuffed Bean Curd Soup   Cantonese 12 servings

3 squares bean curd
3 oz. ground pork
1½ oz. raw, shelled shrimp or
    fish fillet
¾ oz. dried shrimp, pre-softened

① {
1 t. ginger-wine
¼ t. salt
¼ t. MSG
¼ t. black pepper
1½ T. water
½ T. cornstarch
}

½ 1b. spinach, trimmed and
    cleaned
1 bunch coriander or parsley

② {
6 C. stock or water
1½ t. salt
½ t. MSG
}

❶ Mince the dried shrimp finely. Devein, rinse and drain the fresh shrimp. Mince finely and place in a bowl with the ground pork. Add ① and mix continuously in one direction to a smooth paste. Add the cornstarch and throw the meat lightly against the inside of the mixing bowl to blend. Roughly chop the coriander or parsley.

❷ Cut each square of bean curd into 4 sections for a total of 12 squares (fig. 1). Use a knife to outline a square in the center of each piece and scoop out the bean curd (fig. 2). Sprinkle the center with cornstarch (fig. 3) and stuff each section with some of the minced meat mixture (fig. 4). Use a teaspoon dipped in water to smooth the surface of the meat.

❸ Place mixture ② in a pot and heat until boiling. Add the stuffed bean curd and cook until the liquid is boiling. Turn heat to low and simmer for about 6 minutes. Add the spinach coriander and heat until boiling. Pour into a large soup bowl and serve; or the stuffed bean curd may be steamed over medium heat for 5 minutes, then added to boiling mixture ②.

* To prepare ginger-wine: Place the 1 slice smashed ginger in 1 tsp. rice wine. Pinch the ginger to imbibe the wine with the ginger flavor. Remove the ginger slice and use the liquid as directed above.

■ The dried or fresh shrimp or fish may be omitted and the pork loin increased to ¼ lb. Add 1 Tbsp. minced green onions or water chestnuts for extra flavor.

味全

令您賞心悅目的叢書

中國菜
- 180道菜
- 204頁
- 精裝本及平裝本
- 中文版、中英對照版及英文版

中國菜實用專輯
- 89道菜附10道點心
- 104頁
- 平裝本
- 中文版、英文版及法文版

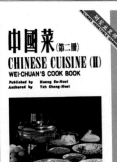

中國菜第二冊
- 187道菜附50種盤飾
- 280頁
- 精裝本
- 中英對照版

拼盤與盤飾
- 拼盤78道，蔬果盤飾86種
- 164頁
- 精裝本及平裝本
- 中英對照版

點心專輯
- 98道點心
- 100頁
- 平裝本
- 中英對照版

海鮮專輯
- 161道菜
- 120頁
- 平裝本
- 中文版及英文版

愛與美插花
- 90種花藝
- 184頁
- 精裝本
- 中英對照版

家常菜
- 226道菜
- 200頁
- 精裝本及平裝本
- 中文版

A Series of Books
for Your Pleasure and Enjoyment

CHINESE CUISINE

- 180 recipes
- 204 pages
- Paperbound edition
- Chinese, Chinese/English (bilingual), English editions

CHINESE COOKING FOR BEGINNERS

- 89 recipes and 10 snacks
- 104 pages
- Paperbound edition
- Chinese, English and French editions

CHINESE CUISINE II

- 187 recipes and 50 garnishes
- 280 pages
- Hardbound edition
- Chinese/English (bilingual) edition

CHINESE APPETIZERS AND GARNISHES

- 78 appetizers and 86 garnishes
- 164 pages
- Paperbound edition
- Chinese/English (bilingual) edition

CHINESE SNACKS

- 98 snacks
- 100 pages
- Paperbound edition
- Chinese/English (bilingual) edition

CHINESE SEAFOOD

- 127 recipes
- 108 pages
- Paperbound edition
- Chinese and English editions

MEDITATIONS ON NATURE

- 90 flower arrangement methods
- 184 pages
- Hardbound edition
- Chinese/English (bilingual) edition

These books are all 7¼"x10¼" and include full-color photographs. Each paperbound book is encased in a clear plastic cover.

WEI-CHUAN'S COOK BOOKS

中國菜 第二冊

味全食譜

版權所有	著作權執照號碼 臺內著字第15051號

出版者　　黃　淑　惠

編著者　　葉　澄　惠

烹飪製作　葉　澄　惠
　　　　　李　木　村

發行者　　黃　淑　惠

味全出版社有限公司
台北市仁愛路四段28號二樓
電話／702-1148・702-1149
　　　　704-2729
郵政劃撥0018203-8號

Wei-Chuan's Cooking
(Publisher and Bookseller)
1455 Monterey Pass Rd. #110 B
Monterey Park, Ca., 91754
U. S. A.
Tel: (213) 261-3880, 261-3878

中華民國69年7月初版發行
中華民國76年元月A2版發行

中華民國臺灣省	中華彩色印刷公司　承印

美術設計　董明輝　汪金光　攝影指導　王鐵石